Praise for *Wise Women*

"Wondrously wise, clever, and insightful *Women* maps a new path made of old stori women in the second half of life — a refr experience rather than a dying off."

T0286635

— Dr. Angela (A.G.) Slatter, award-winning author of
The Briar Book of the Dead

"The book I've been longing for. I immediately want to give it to all my woman friends. It is so important, and Sharon Blackie is exactly the right inspirational person to bring this topic and these new stories of old women to the culture."

— Jill Dawson, author of *The Bewitching*

"A fascinating collection of female myths and legends that read like both dreams and nightmares."

— Sara Sheridan, author of *The Fair Botanists*

"This scrumptious new collection took me into much-loved tales from evergreen folklorists and story gatherers and gifted me the bonus of meeting marvelous new beings. Nestled in insightful notes, this collection turns the spotlight on older women, celebrating their perspicacity and clout with the flair of a seasoned Broadway performance. This will be a smash hit of a show starring mature and canny women in its second and third acts! Read it, absorb it, treasure it!"

— Shahrukh Husain, author of *The Virago Book of Witches*

"This rich curation reiterates the truth that women in midlife — and beyond — are a vital source of wisdom. Reading them ignited a fire in my belly!"

— Julia Bueno, author of *Everyone's a Critic*

"The glorious possibility that we might age and ripen, age and grow greater, age and be-come, while also accepting that we will age and die — this is what I have come to expect from Sharon Blackie's expansive work, and why I am especially excited by this collection with Angharad Wynne that revisits our old stories, making them thrilling for us now, as the midlife and older wise women we are be-coming."

— Stella Duffy, OBE

"I adored *Wise Women* — this is the missing piece of the jigsaw puzzle when it comes to reframing the narrative in our culture about the role of older females. Sharon Blackie has unearthed the tales we Queen-agers need to see what we can be and become as we age. Essential reading. So important to reclaim these inspirational tales of what older women are for and the crucial roles that they play."

— **Eleanor Mills**, founder of Noon.org.uk, home of the Queenager, and author of *Much More to Come: Lessons on the Mayhem and Magnificence of Midlife*

Praise for Sharon Blackie's Work

"Mind-blowing in the most profound and exhilarating sense. [*If Women Rose Rooted*] is an anthem for all we could be, an essential book for this, the most critical of recent times."

— **Manda Scott**, author of *Boudica* and *A Treachery of Spies*

"*Hagitude* is already becoming a beloved cult classic, as a myth-infused manifesto for the possibilities for life from middle age onward."

— **Katherine May**, *New York Times* bestselling author of *Enchantment* and *Wintering*

"Fascinating, packed with stories, and bursting with lovely descriptions of the natural world. There's plenty in *Hagitude* to inspire women of every age."

— **Christina Patterson**, *Sunday Times*

WISE WOMEN

Also by Sharon Blackie

The Long Delirious Burning Blue

If Women Rose Rooted:
A Life-Changing Journey to Authenticity and Belonging

The Enchanted Life:
Reclaiming the Magic and Wisdom of the Natural World

Foxfire, Wolfskin and Other Stories of Shapeshifting Women

Hagitude: Reimagining the Second Half of Life

WISE WOMEN

Myths and Stories for Midlife and Beyond

SHARON BLACKIE

AND ANGHARAD WYNNE

New World Library
Novato, California

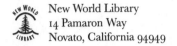

New World Library
14 Pamaron Way
Novato, California 94949

Illustrations by Joe McLaren
Type design by M Rules

Library of Congress Cataloging-in-Publication Data

Names: Blackie, Sharon, author. | Wynne, Angharad, author.
Title: Wise women : myths and stories for midlife and beyond / Sharon Blackie and Angharad Wynne.
Description: Novato, California : New World Library, [2024] | Includes bibliographical references. | Summary: "A collection of stories from European myth and folklore that celebrate older women. Each story is accompanied by commentary that offers historical background, highlights important themes, and inspires women readers to live with purpose in the second half of life" -- Provided by publisher.
Identifiers: LCCN 2024024787 (print) | LCCN 2024024788 (ebook) | ISBN 9781608689668 (paperback) | ISBN 9781608689675 (epub)
Subjects: LCSH: Older women. | Older women--Social conditions. | Mythology.
Classification: LCC HQ1063.7 .B54 2024 (print) | LCC HQ1063.7 (ebook) | DDC 398.22--dc23/eng/20240615
LC record available at https://lccn.loc.gov/2024024787
LC ebook record available at https://lccn.loc.gov/2024024788

First published in the United Kingdom by Virago, an imprint of Little, Brown Book Group

First New World Library printing, October 2024
ISBN 978-1-60868-966-8
Ebook ISBN 978-1-60868-967-5

10   9   8   7   6   5   4   3   2

New World Library is committed to protecting our natural environment. This book is made of material from well-managed FSC®-certified forests and other controlled sources.

Printed in Canada

Contents

Gifts for the Young

The Earth Itself

Don't Mess with Old Women

Seeing Deeply

Wisdom for the World

Death and Rebirth

Introduction

We are narrative creatures, hardwired for story. We make sense of the world, from childhood onward, through the stories we find — or the stories that find us. They are the stars we navigate by; they bring us the wisdom we need to thrive. Always share your porridge with the hungry mice who know how to sort the wheat from the chaff. Whenever you're invited, be sure to kiss the frog. Don't insist on being a princess if you're really a mermaid. Never slip out of your skin and leave it unattended.

An abundance of fairy tales shows us how beautiful goose girls and golden-haired princesses can find their way in the world — but what about older women? We too have a deep thirst for stories that illustrate ways in which we might live richly and meaningfully, but at first glance there would seem to be a dearth of inspiring characters to serve as role models for the second half of our lives. In the better-known stories — "Rapunzel," "Hansel and Gretel," "Snow White," and many more — we're presented with older women who are malevolent witches, who are jealous tyrants, or who are easily outwitted by any handsome young prince who happens along. Material across European folklore reflects a fundamental distrust of women as we age, and so a German proverb warns that *If the devil can't come himself, he sends an old woman*, and another that *He who walks between two old women early in the morning will have only bad luck for the rest of the day.*[*]

There's certainly no positive, coherent image of female elderhood in contemporary Western culture — or at least, not one that any of us might want to inhabit. Although, throughout ancient European mythology, women have always personified wisdom — think of Sophia, Athena, Minerva, Metis — older women today are often ignored, encouraged to stay out of the way, or held up as objects of ridicule. The Wise Woman, symbolizing the essence of mature female wisdom, is no longer a prominent archetype in our culture.

As I stood, hot-flushed and frantic, on the threshold of menopause just over a decade ago, all the cultural signposts seemed to be pointing in the direction of an end to my useful life. The good bits of my story were over, it seemed; now was the time to resign myself to its long, gray ending. I wasn't having any of that; I'm a psychologist who believes that the essence of life is transformation, and I'd long specialized in all the ways in which story can transform us and how we might find ourselves in fairy tales. The outward-focused narrative of the first half of my life might be drawing to a close, but I was looking for a new narrative to illuminate the second half. I was determined that this ending would be followed by a new beginning. And so, though no longer your typical fairy-tale heroine, I set out on a quest through the dark woods of European folklore to look for stories about women like me: older women who refused to be redundant and irrelevant, and who were searching for ways to reimagine the second half of their lives.

During years of obsessive excavation, ever-growing piles of musty, beautifully illustrated old fairy-tale collections and

---

[*]   J. Grimm and E. H. Meyer, *Deutsche Mythologie*, vol. 3. Nabu Press (2010).

folklore monographs tottered precariously on my desk while I searched through them for lost and hidden gems. Much to my delight, I unearthed a surprising number of stories populated by old women who hold the protagonist's fate in the palm of their gnarly old hands, who see the bigger picture (and probably were the ones who painted it in the first place), or who have the last laugh. My previous book *Hagitude** was focused on the distinctive archetypal characteristics of some of these women, but I didn't have room in it to tell their stories in full, or to write about the entire, lavish array of enchanting elder women I'd discovered, right here in my own European tradition. So the motivation for this book was, by gathering this folklore together for the first time, to bring back to life the funny and feisty aging women who have been so thoroughly forgotten. My hope is that this rich and diverse collection of characters will offer insight into the ways that each of us could uniquely embody a bold and purposeful elderhood.

Stories like this are important, because the way in which we think about who we are depends on the stories we tell about who we are. How we think about women in the second half of their lives depends on the images we hold of them — and if the stories we tell about older women and the images we hold of them are dysfunctional, then our elderhood will be dysfunctional too. If the contemporary cultural mythology suggests that older women serve no purpose then, quite simply, we need to change that mythology. It's long past time to take control of and tell our own stories — and, for that purpose, we need tales in which we can shine. The stories that are retold in this book, based on originals scattered throughout several European

---

* Sharon Blackie, *Hagitude: Reimagining the Second Half of Life*. New World Library (2022).

traditions, are stories in which older women positively dazzle. In bringing together these ungainly giantesses, glamorous fairy godmothers, misunderstood witches, fierce grandmothers, and perspicacious wise women, my aim was both to challenge and change the current cultural discourse around aging — to help older women to transform themselves, and to live and tell their own stories in their own unique way.

Throughout human history, we've sat around fires telling each other myths, folk tales, and fairy tales. Myths explain how things came to be and generally deal with substantial matters: deities, cultural heroes, the creation of the cosmos, the purpose and meaning of life. They provide the foundational narratives for entire civilizations: narratives that underpin their religions, values, and behaviors. Folk tales are rather different: they're secular narratives and the province, by definition, of "the folk." They reflect the concerns and aspirations of ordinary people, and they're often deeply rooted in the specific places in which those people live. Fairy tales, or "wonder tales," are included within the category of folk tales; they usually contain supernatural characters such as fairies and giants, and involve magic and enchantments. In the oral tradition, fairy tales are constantly shapeshifting to reflect and accommodate changing times.

At the heart of all fairy tales is transformation: they help us to believe in the possibility of change. We come to understand how we might escape an impossible situation and begin as a consequence to reimagine ourselves; we see that there are so many ways of living fully and authentically in a world that is filled with challenge and sorrow. These are the stories that offer us a more fertile and functional set of values to live by;

they remind us that, tucked up safe in the rambling, round-about lines between once upon a time and happily ever after, lie the secrets of a meaningful life.

These stories are so very compelling because of the archetypal characters, images, and motifs interwoven through them: they're like keys that unlock the imagination, opening the door to the shadowy, cobweb-covered rooms that shelter the mysteries of our inner lives. In the vehicle of a myth or a fairy tale, archetypal characters become energies, interlaced with instructions that guide us through the entanglements of life. In different periods of our lives, new archetypes can rise up inside us, demanding to be known, insisting on revealing new and more authentic ways of being in the world. This certainly happens as we journey through the last rich decades of life, and together, the archetypes that call to us can form a kind of "Council of Grandmothers" to watch over us and guide us.

My hope for this book was that the stories in it wouldn't just be read but would also be told, and it was with this aim in mind that I invited storyteller Angharad Wynne to contribute to *Wise Women*; I'm grateful for her input. It can be difficult to strike the right balance between the written and the oral, but I hope that these new versions of the old stories will work both for readers and for those who might like to share them by telling them or reading them aloud.

Folklore is made up of more than folk and fairy tales, though: it includes nursery rhymes and songs. Nursery rhymes are traditional poems or songs for children; their primary function is in the development of linguistic skills and, in particular, the rhymes and rhythms of language and the act of memorization. The content of nursery rhymes also informs us about the values and images held by the culture that produced them; in this context, the ways in which they depict older women can sometimes be enlightening. Just as there's a paucity of nursery rhymes that feature kind and interesting older women, there are very few narrative songs and ballads that tell us stories of benign and wise older women, and because of the difficulty of finding significant bodies of work in translation, those included here are predominantly British in origin.

Such a collection wouldn't be complete without reference to some other formidable older women who are scattered across the mythic map of Europe and whose penetration into our folklore is significant. Unlike the characters in the stories, who play a key role in a specific narrative, these women appear as characters in many different narratives, or are threaded throughout an entire mythological tradition, or are prominent archetypal figures in a particular strand of folk culture. They've come together here as the "Gaggle of Hags" who pepper the sections of this book.

It's worth noting that the traditional folklore of Europe is populated with characters who are pretty much always depicted as heterosexual and white, and the older women in these stories are no exception. Migration of course has been a key force throughout human history, but these old stories usually have their roots in poor, rural communities in which travel — either in or out — was much less available. They also arise from cultures in which there was more conformity to social norms and, as a consequence, much less visible diversity than we experience in our world today. But this doesn't mean that our folklore excludes others. These potent old stories offer up wisdom that is accessible and relevant to all women — whatever their skin color, sexual orientation, or ancestry. They're not in the business of excluding: the archetypal characters who inhabit them are universal and, as students of folklore know perfectly well, most of the themes and motifs in these stories are cross-cultural too. The simplicity of these stories, songs, and rhymes allows each of us to bring to them our own history, our own predilections, and our own interpretations. We draw from them what we need, and they give with equal generosity to all those who come looking for their wisdom.

The primary purpose of this collection is to reenchant a time of life that can seem dreary, and that most of us approach with trepidation. In spite of the evident challenges of midlife, menopause, and the decades that follow, more and more mature women today are looking for ways to reimagine and reclaim the power of the second half of life. We're all looking to become wise women, each in our own unique way. This book re-members the beautiful, lost fragments of our rich European traditions, and offers ideas for weaving them into the fabric of a more meaningful and exhilarating everyday.

Sharon Blackie
Cumbria, January 2024

Finding Ourselves Older

When we're young, few of us spend much time thinking about our elder decades. But as we hurtle through our thirties and approach the disquieting period we call midlife, many of us will begin to feel as if we're racing to the edge of a cliff. There are no brakes that can bring this journey to a halt, though: we'll already be experiencing profound physical changes, and soon enough we'll find ourselves beset by a bewildering assortment of alterations to our body's rhythm and response. We'll try — and often fail — to come to terms with wrinkles, sagging flesh, fatigue, and shifts in sexual desire. And then, as if all this wasn't unsettling enough, along comes menopause — disassembling our everyday, liberally dispensing mood swings and a supersized dose of existential angst.

We can believe that this radical transition will inaugurate a time of decline, or we can embrace the idea that it will offer us a life-changing opportunity to transform and grow. It might be *an* end, but menopause is not *the* end: it passes, and there's so much more life to come. Wisdom at this time of life, though it's far from easy to pull off, means letting the wave carry us: allowing the shriveled leaves of the old self to die back so that the seeds of a new consciousness can push their way out of the dark. This is work that most of us are ill-prepared for, because our youth- and beauty-obsessed culture offers us nothing remotely resembling an enlivening vision for the long journey ahead. It wants instead to carve us into a silent, biddable form, a sanitized version of acceptable elderhood that will cut the wild heart out of us — but if we assume that shape, few of us will thrive.

It would hardly be surprising, then, if we not only resisted the idea of growing old but also came to actively fear it. Happily, there are old folk and fairy tales that afford us glimpses of the gifted, creative selves we might grow into after midlife. They suggest that this is a time when we might become more ourselves, rather than less. The women in this part of the book, from midlife to the threshold of death, find themselves older — and embrace the idea that the second half of life is a whole new adventure. They decide to leave home, finally to get married, to lay down their burdens, make their gardens beautiful — or just to have a good laugh. They don't flinch from the change; rather, they find new and original ways of affirming it and fully accepting themselves in their new incarnation.

The Woman Who Became a Fox

Once, near the sharp, rocky shoreline of the White Sea, where islands float amid the ice like moon-drenched promises, there lived a woman and a man — a one-eyed man. They had been married a long, long time and had grown to middle age together. Each night he would stay at home with her, but each morning at dawn he would slip out of bed and leave the house. Winter and summer, from polar night to midnight sun. She had no idea where he went, or what he did during the long hours that he spent away from her, but she so very badly wished she understood.

An autumn day dawned, as Cholbon the morning star rose bright in the southern sky, when she found she could bear it no longer; she crept out of the house and followed him as he walked away. She followed him as he trudged along the main street of their small village; she followed him as he walked toward the vast coniferous forest beyond and crossed into its gloomy shadows. After a while, the man came to a clearing in the dark wood; he sat down on a fallen tree trunk. As he'd drawn closer to the place where he spent his days, she'd noticed him begin to change. His mood seemed to darken, his demeanor shifted, and his only eye disappeared. As she stood there for hours in the shelter of the tall, thin trees and watched

11

him, the woman realized that over their long years together she and her husband had become strangers. She was tired of all this secrecy, which seemed, now that she knew just what it was that he did all day — nothing — to have no purpose. He had become repugnant to her, and so she made up her mind to leave.

She melted away into the woods and returned home. She gathered together only those small things that she loved most and that would fit into the pockets of her shabby old coat, and she set off along the road that led out of the village to the sea. She had no idea where she was going: she knew only that she was going. But she hadn't walked very far before she ran into a giant who — without speaking a single word to her — snatched her up, slung her over his shoulder, and then bounded all the way to the top of a great, snowcapped mountain. The giant strode into an enormous cave and flung the woman down on its hard, rocky floor.

And then he left.

Her coat was torn, and the small treasures had fallen from her pockets along the way; she was sore and scared and chilled to the bone. She sobbed, mourning for her home, her husband, and a life that, although empty, had at least been safe and familiar. After a while, she heard a voice say, "Come on, dry your tears. Look up, and you'll find the skins of land birds hanging above you. Take them and put them on."

The woman looked up and, squinting into the gloom, made out a large, grass-plaited basket hanging on a wooden hook that was wedged into a crevice in the wall of the cave. She took it down, and inside she found a coat made of crow skins. She removed it from the basket, shook out the shiny feathers, and tried to put it on — but it was too small. Hard as she tried, she couldn't make the beautiful black coat fit her. Even more miserable now, she huddled up against the cold, hard rock and buried her tear-soaked face in her hands. And then, once again, she heard the voice whispering, "Come on now, don't despair. Look up again, and you'll find the skins of land animals above you. Take them and put them on."

So the woman looked up again, and this time she made out a little ledge, high in the wall above her. On it was a pile of fox skins. She reached up and brought them down, sank her fingers into the soft, rust-red pelts, and realized that they had been stitched together to make a coat. She tried it on — and it fitted her perfectly. Within minutes, she was warm and, feeling a little braver now, she decided it was time to escape.

She slipped out of the cave and stepped lightly across the packed snow, leaving a trail of delicate prints behind her. Down the mountainside she went, in search of the road home. Partway down she felt thirsty and stopped at a stream to drink — but when she caught a glimpse of her reflection in the clear water, she was shocked to see that she had grown long, russet ears. On she went again, and when she reached the bottom of the mountain, she had a strange feeling that there was something close behind her. Quickly, she twisted around — but what she saw was her own snow-tipped foxtail, and though she tried to shake it free, she could not. It was bound to her, flesh and fur and bone. A little later, she found herself at the seashore close to her village; her old father was there at the edge of the water, just setting out to hunt seals.

As the father loaded his canoe, a sudden blaze of red against the gray stone shore caught his eye. There, just a few yards away from him, was a vixen; her amber eyes watched him, and she seemed unafraid. He walked toward her, but she retreated, keeping well out of his reach. He threw her some of his meat bait before pushing his canoe into the waves. As he paddled along the shoreline, dodging vast translucent ice floes, the vixen devoured the food; she paused to gaze at him before running off into the trees.

When darkness fell, the vixen crept out of the forest and trotted toward the firelit glow of her father's cabin. Every time she approached the door flap and made to poke her head through it, her head turned away, and the rest of her body would follow. Time and time again she tried to go inside, but her animal body would not allow it.

Finally, she turned away, and headed out into the open fields and the life that lay beyond.

As we approach midlife, many of us will find that we've stumbled unwittingly into a story in which we seem to be playing the part of a heroine who has outgrown her life. Some new, unexpected (and often unwelcome) urge or longing will be leading us to question the way we've lived up till now. Because, just as our body is starting to change, our inner world is teetering on the brink of a major shift too — whether we're ready for it, or not. This might seem like the last thing we need, especially if we feel as if we're finally settling into some kind of stability after the growing and testing times of our youth. But midlife — as the woman in this story finds — is a powerfully metamorphic time and, whether or not we actively choose to surrender to its dark alchemy, change is inevitable. It's a time between stories, when we stand on a threshold. We see what's behind us very clearly, but the path ahead is shrouded in mist. This beautiful Siberian tale captures the essence of this tender but sometimes terrifying metamorphosis.

At the beginning of the twentieth century, ethnographer and folklorist Arnold van Gennep suggested that, in Indigenous cultures, rites of passage have three phases; they're usually called separation, initiation, and return. This story can be read as one such potent rite of passage. In the separation stage, the woman follows the instinct that urges her to leave her old life behind. She doesn't know who her husband is anymore, and perhaps she doesn't know who she is anymore, trapped in the staleness of her long marriage. So she walks away: a shocking severance from all that's safe and familiar. At midlife, we too might find ourselves strangely compelled to leave behind people or places, friendships, jobs, or situations that just don't seem to nourish us anymore. The textures and structures of our homelife can be sorely tested, and our partners might well feel threatened by the changes in us as we outgrow old roles, and as they perhaps fear that we might outgrow them too. But although we often know that something in our life needs to change, we don't always know what that change should look like. This is a journey, then, in which we might simply just leave. Step out of the door, put one foot in front of the other, grit our teeth, and walk. We trust in fate, or the gods — or a stony-faced giant — to point us in the right direction.

Then comes the phase of initiation: the testing time in the cave. We're taken apart there in the dark, as the dead parts of ourselves and our lives are slowly stripped away. The woman in this story discovers that inhabiting this inert in-between space can be uncomfortable. She weeps, fearful and grieving for what she has lost, but she stays there in the cave until, finally, she is presented with the fox coat — the agent of her ultimate transformation — and summons the strength to find the way out and onto her strange new path. Like her, we too might have to try on several possible skins before we find one that properly fits our changing self. Some of us are black-winged birds; some of us are fleet-footed foxes. But when you do find the skin that fits, you can't turn away from it: it simply won't be refused. So, off the fox-woman goes into the cold night — russet ears, snow-tipped fox tail, and all.

The vixen's head wants to return to her father's house, but the wisdom of her new, wild-hearted body tells her that she can't go back to the home that once sheltered her: she can't revert to what she once was. The "return" phase of this woman's journey, then, is a coming home to her own wild self. She turns inward to find her own embodied wisdom; to accomplish this, she has to turn away from the men who have defined — and confined — her life until now. She has to turn away from the masculine, from the patriarchy, and find her own way. And that is precisely what happens: first, she walks away from it (her husband), then she escapes from it (the giant), and finally, she refuses it (her father's house).

This powerful shapeshifting story, then, illuminates the Wild Woman archetype that comes knocking at the door of our psyche at midlife and forces us out and into the stormy seas of menopause, out and into the dawn of a new consciousness. While it's doing this necessary work of waking us up, it reminds us of the instinctual, intuitive, creative ways of knowing we need at this time of our lives. So many of us lose this wild, embodied knowing, and we lose it young. The consequences of the loss, of this disconnectedness, this separation from our true nature and what nourishes and empowers us, often become apparent only after many years. Midlife is the time to take it back, and the Wild Woman is an archetype that urges us, like this brave fox-woman, to follow our own twitching nose across the threshold of a new story.

Mother Mansrot

GERMANY

Long, long ago, a king lived in a land east of the West Wind and west of the East Wind; his only child was a daughter. When the princess was old enough to marry, the king brought together all the magicians in his kingdom and ordered them to create a great, gleaming glass mountain. He then declared that each of the young men who dreamed of having her for his wife must scale its polished slopes and cross its jagged peaks. If one of them should be clever and brave enough to make it across to the other side alive, then that man would be rewarded with his daughter's hand in marriage.

One of the gallants who flocked to the palace to attempt this fine adventure had been in love with the princess for a long time; as the noble and kind-looking young man presented himself to the king in the great golden throne room, she glanced at him shyly out of the corner of her dark eyes and decided that he would suit her very well. When he asked the king if he might try his luck with the glass mountain, the princess declared that she would accompany him on the treacherous journey. With her help, she imagined, he would be successful; then they would marry and live a long and happy life together.

So they set out to climb the gleaming glass mountain that now dominated the landscape around her father's palace.

Up its slippery sides they crawled, sliding downward again as often as they gained ground. They inched along sheer-sided ridges and picked their way carefully around jutting shards — but when they were halfway up the mountainside, the princess stumbled and fell down the slope. Before the young man could help, the mountain opened beneath her; she tumbled into the crevasse and disappeared. Distraught, he skidded down to where she had fallen, but the mountain had closed again, and there was no trace of her. He peered into the crystal walls of the mountain, but all he saw were a hundred thousand refracted reflections of himself. He had no choice but to give up his search, and he carefully picked his way down the mountain.

When the young man returned without the princess, the grief-stricken king sent men up the mountain to smash it open and bring her out, but they could find no hint of the place where she had disappeared. All that they saw were vast, glittering plains and inaccessible pinnacles of shining glass.

Meanwhile, when she came to her senses after the fall, the bruised princess found herself deep inside the mountain, lying on the floor of a tall, wide crystal cave. At the center of the cave was a funny little house, and as she squinted at it with aching eyes, the door opened and an old man with a very long gray beard emerged. He told the princess that if she would stay and become his servant, she might live. If not, he would kill her at once.

The princess saw no possibility of escape. Slowly and sadly, she followed the old man into the house and set to work. She did everything that he told her to — everything that was necessary to survive. She cooked and cleaned; she made his bed and mended his clothes; she kept his funny little house in perfect order. Each morning, he took a magic ladder out of his pocket and set it up against the great glass wall of the cave. He climbed all the way to the top of it, then vanished into a narrow cleft in the mountain; he drew the ladder up after him and put it back in his pocket. Each evening he came home again, laden with bags of gold and silver.

Days turned to weeks, weeks turned to months, months became years — but the cold, diffuse light in the glass-walled cave never changed. The princess grew stiffer and slower, and her raven-black hair began to turn silver. The old man taunted her and took to calling her Mother Mansrot; she should call him Old Rinkrank, he told her. She wondered still how she might escape, how she might get hold of the magic ladder — but Rinkrank was cunning and careful, and never let it out of his sight. And for the first time, she began to imagine that she might die here after all, trapped in the cave with this vile and cruel old man.

She could never afterward explain what changed; she could never quite put her finger on the trigger for her subsequent actions. Perhaps there wasn't one. Perhaps, as sometimes happens, she simply woke up that morning and decided that it was now or never. However it came to be, that day, after she had made his bed and washed his dishes, the princess closed the door, drew the curtains, and fastened the windows as tightly as she could — except for one small sash window in the larder, through which the house lights still shone. She hid in the kitchen and waited for him to come home.

That evening, Old Rinkrank knocked at the door and cried — as he always did — "Mother Mansrot, open the door for me."

"No!" she declared, very much to his surprise. "I will not open the door for you." So Old Rinkrank said:

"Here I stand, poor Rinkrank,
On my seventeen long shanks,
On my weary, worn-out foot,
Wash my dishes, Mother Mansrot."

"I have already washed your dishes," she said. He replied
to her:

"Here I stand, poor Rinkrank,
On my seventeen long shanks,
On my weary, worn-out foot,
Make me my bed, Mother Mansrot."

"I have already made your bed," she said. So, for a third
time, he spoke to her:

"Here I stand, poor Rinkrank,
On my seventeen long shanks,
On my weary, worn-out foot,
Open the door, Mother Mansrot!"

As soon as the last word was out of his mouth, Old Rinkrank ran around the house and checked all the windows to
see if he could find a way in. At the side of the house, he
found the little larder window open and tried to peep inside it
to discover what the princess was up to, but his whiskers were
so long and thick that he couldn't get his head through. So
he lifted his beard and pushed it through the open window.
BANG! — the princess, who earlier had tied a long cord to
the window latch, pulled it and slammed the window shut,
trapping Rinkrank's beard. He cried and wailed, because it
hurt him very much; he begged her to release him, but nothing he said could shake her resolve. She would not release

him, she declared, until he gave her the magic ladder. Eventually, Rinkrank relented, fumbled in his pocket, and threw it to the front of the house.

With the end of the cord that she had tied to the window still firmly in her hand, the princess ran out of the door to retrieve the magic ladder. Fearing all the while that Rinkrank might somehow find a way to free his beard, she quickly set the ladder against the far wall of the cave and — just as she'd seen him do day after day, month after month, and year after year — she climbed it. Up, up, up, with all her strength and courage, up toward the moonlight she went, up toward that tiny gap between the thick walls of glass — and out, finally, into the night and the clean, fresh air of freedom. The princess took a deep, fortifying gulp before pulling up the ladder behind her, then she tugged at the cord so that it raised the window and set Old Rinkrank free. She clung for a moment to a great glass pillar to steady herself, then carefully made her way down the other side of the moonlit glass mountain and on to her father's palace.

Though many long years had passed and the king had grown old and frail, his joy at this unexpected reunion with his daughter was boundless. And that young suitor? He was living there still, and had never married. He'd kept faith with his first great love, hoping beyond all reasonable hope that one day he would meet her again.

The king ordered that the glass mountain should be destroyed, and as the great glass peaks shattered and fell away, the strange little house in the cave was revealed. Inside it, the king's men discovered a vast hoard of gold and silver. Old Rinkrank was put to death for his crimes against the princess, and all his wealth was taken into the kingdom's treasury to be put to good use. Some of it surely paid for the lavish feast to which all in the land were invited — to celebrate the marriage of the silver-haired princess and her faithful love, who lived happily and joyfully ever after.

The glass mountain. Beautiful, but perilous in every possible way. Too large to walk around; seemingly impossible to scale. It's hard to get traction. There are no footholds, and as soon as you set your foot on the glistening slope of it, you slide back down again. And yet everything you need is on the other side of it. The glass mountain, then, is an exquisite image for the obstacles we might encounter during the course of our life. By the time we reach midlife, all of us will, in one way or another, have been frustrated by transparent but unbreachable barriers that stand in the way of whatever it is that we yearn for. The glass mountain in this story stands for all of that and more.

This curious Frisian tale found its way into the sixth of the seven editions of *Grimm's Fairy Tales*, in which it is titled "Old Rinkrank." It's one of many glass mountain stories threaded through European folklore (we'll meet another of them later in this book). But the mountain in this story isn't an original feature of the fairy-tale landscape, as it is in so many others: the king causes it to be built. He doesn't appear to do it with the intention of causing his daughter harm; he's presented as a loving father who just wants to test the worthiness of her suitors. This is a fairy tale, and fairy tales don't always have to make perfect real-world sense, but it would be reasonable to wonder how Old Rinkrank arrived in this newly constructed glass mountain created by the king. The story, unfortunately, doesn't tell us, and whatever the king's intentions, the princess is clearly taken with the young man who is prepared to risk everything for her, so they set out together to face the glass mountain.

Like Persephone in Greek myth, she then undertakes an archetypical Descent to the Underworld. The Descent always destroys old and outdated ways of being and prepares the ground for the wisdom we need to give birth to our most authentic self. It requires us to make a sacrifice before we continue on our path: the sacrifice of our old upper-world self. It's a hard process, but in that place of destruction, gestation, and rebirth, we begin to explore the biggest question of all: If we have to let go of everything that once we imagined defined us and mattered to us, what then might we become?

Just as the earth opens to swallow Persephone and transport her to the realm of Hades, then, the glass mountain opens up and swallows the princess, transporting her to the territory of Old Rinkrank, where the "happily ever after" she had planned for herself in the upper world is lost to her. The trick to navigating the Descent is not to despair, and not to push too hard — but to let the new story emerge in its own time. So our sad princess becomes mired in the dank marshes of simple survival, with Old Rinkrank symbolizing whatever it might be — "the system," our own conditioning, fate — that keeps so many of us trapped in a life we hadn't entirely planned to be living, and which offers us neither the time nor the opportunity to plan a great escape. Hers isn't a happy life, but it is a life — and, in all the best fairy tales, where there's life, there is hope. Through all the long years, this princess refuses to give up. She endures the stasis and apprentices herself to the hard lessons of the Underworld, playing the long game — until one day, finally, she is ready to act, to move on. She seizes her opportunity to escape and is ready to put all her effort into climbing out of her "stuckness."

One of the finest things about this story is that no one rescues this princess. After she's suffered her time in the Underworld and grown old enough, and wise, she discovers that now she has the resources, finally, to rescue herself. Is Rinkrank's naming of her the final straw? In most fairy tales, to name something is to have power over it; perhaps our aging heroine has had enough of being controlled and insists now on demonstrating the fact to her captor. The story then offers us a rare and beautiful ending: the marriage of a much older heroine to the suitor who, against all odds, has waited for her through their long years apart. They're no longer walking on the slippery glass slopes of hopes, expectations, and dreams, but on the solid ground of maturity and self-knowledge. We can celebrate this ending — their enduring love and the unlikeliness of their eventual marriage — as a much-deserved reward for the princess's survival, her commitment to the long view, and the steadfastness she displayed through the trials of her life.

Kate Dalrymple

SCOTLAND

Although the dialect will be difficult for those who don't speak Scots, it's hard not to love this ballad about a poor, lonely "old maid" whose face was "gruesome and grim" — as well as rather heavily spotted — and whose nose curved all the way down to her chin. Kate had been a hard worker all her life but couldn't find a man — until she inherited a good deal of money. After which, of course, lords and lawyers all came calling. Kate, though, wanted only her first love: Willie Speedyspool, a weaver with a lazy eye and a limp. Whether he took her for love or for "interest" — her money — isn't entirely clear, but Kate happily married her true love, nevertheless.

In a wee cot house far across the muir
Where pease-weeps, plovers, an' waups cry dreary,
There liv'd an' auld maid for mony lang years,
Wha ne'er a woo-er did e'er ca', dearie.
A lanely lass was Kate Dalrymple,
A thrifty quean was Kate Dalrymple;
Nae music, exceptin' the clear burnie's wimple,
Was heard round the dwellin' o' Kate Dalrymple.

Her face had a smack o' the gruesome an' grim,
That did frae the fash o' a' woo-ers defend her;
Her long Roman nose nearly met wi' her chin,

That brang folk in mind o' the auld witch o' Endor.
A wiggle in her walk had Kate Dalrymple,
A sniggle in her talk had Kate Dalrymple;
An' mony a cornelian an' cairngorm pimple,
Did blaze on the dun face o' Kate Dalrymple.

She span terry woo' the hale winter thro'
For Kate ne'er was lazy, but eident and thrifty;
She wrocht 'mang the peats, coil'd the hay, shor the corn,
An' supported hersel' by her ain hard shift aye.
But ne'er a lover came to Kate Dalrymple,
For beauty an' tocher wanted Kate Dalrymple;
Unheeded was the quean, baith by gentle and simple,
A blank in existence seem'd puir Kate Dalrymple.

But mony are the ups an' the downs in life,
When the dice-box o' fate's jumbled a' tapsal-teerie,
Sae Kate fell heiress to a rich frien's estate,
An' nae langer for woo-ers had she cause to weary.
The Laird came a-wooin' soon o' Kate Dalrymple,
The Lawyer, scrapin', bowin', fan oot Kate Dalrymple;
Owre ilk woo-ers face was seen love's smilin' dimple,
Sae noo she's nae mair, Kate, but Miss Dalrymple.

She often times thocht when she dwelt by hersel',
She could wed Willie Speedyspool, the sarkin' weaver;
An' noo unto Will she the secret did tell,
Wha for love or for interest did kindly receive her.
He flung by his beddles soon for Kate Dalrymple,
He brent a' his treddles doon for Kate Dalrymple;
Tho' his richt e'e doth skellie an' his left leg doth limp ill,
He's won the heart an' got the hand o' Kate Dalrymple.

The Magic Forest

Once, an old woman lived with her son on the threshold of a strange, enchanted forest. The magic threaded through the roots of that old forest was very potent and very particular: some of it was good and some of it was bad, and everyone who came there received exactly what they deserved. It was said that the forest would remain enchanted forever — unless someone should enter it who preferred the sorrows of their present life to all the joys of another world.

One warm and sunny day at the beginning of winter, the old woman's son decided to go for a stroll in the forest, but he hadn't been walking among the dense, bare beech trees for long before he happened upon a snake. Oh, and it was a beautiful snake, and such an unusual color: it was rich, iridescent, shimmering along the spectrum between black and blue, and so very lithe and sensuous. It slithered up to him and began to coil itself around his leg. The young man was utterly charmed by the snake, and declared out loud that he would love to take it home with him. He reached down to stroke its dry, warm skin — but as soon as he laid his fingers on it, the snake suddenly changed into a lovely young woman. Her hair was as dark as the heart of a midnight forest, and her lustrous black dress was embroidered with blue butterflies. Surprised, but delighted and thoroughly smitten, the young man brought the

27

woman home to his mother and declared that she would be his wife.

The son couldn't possibly have known that the forest had transformed his bride-to-be into a snake as a punishment for her evil deeds — and that she could be set free only if she found someone to marry her. His mother, though, was old and wise, and as she looked closely at the stranger, she saw that the flickering tongue in her mouth was that of a snake. She tried to talk to her son about her worries. "You've found a beautiful young woman to be your wife," she said, "but you really should be careful: I think she might be a snake." The young man was astonished: How could she possibly know that his new love had once been a snake? He grew angry with his mother, called her a witch, and from that moment on he took against her. All too soon, he married his betrothed.

The newly married couple had no house of their own and so they settled in the cottage at the edge of the forest with the old woman. It might have worked out, as it often does — if not for the fact that the daughter-in-law was ill-tempered and spiteful. She bullied the old woman into doing all the house-work, and every day she piled more tasks on her. One morning, she sent her to fetch fresh, pure snow from the top of the highest nearby mountain, so that she could wash in it.

"But there's no path up that mountain!" the mother said.

"Then take the goat and let her guide you. While she skips up the mountain, you can amuse yourself by tumbling down it."

Keen to please his new wife, the son laughed at her words. And so his mother, heartsick and tired of her life, set out to fetch the snow. As she scrambled wearily up the steep, rugged mountain after the goat, she thought of asking God to help her; but she changed her mind, because God would then know that her son had rejected her. But God, it seemed, was intent on helping her anyway, and she safely brought the snow from the cloud-capped peak back to her sullen daughter-in-law.

The next day, the snake-woman gave her a new order: "Go to the frozen lake outside the village; there's a hole in the middle of it. Catch me a carp from it for dinner."

"But the ice will give way under me, and I'll drown," the old mother replied.

"Well then, I'm sure the carp will be delighted if you go down there to play with him."

The son laughed again at his wife's words, and his mother was so distraught that she left the house and went straightaway to the vast, frigid lake. The ice cracked beneath her as she stepped onto it, and her tears froze on her face, but still she wouldn't pray for help: she was determined that God shouldn't find out that her son was sinful.

"It's very much better that I should perish than bring harm upon him," she said to herself as she carefully picked her way across the ice. But her time, it seemed, had not yet come: a gull flew over her head, carrying a carp in its beak. The fish wriggled out of the bird's grip and fell down at the old woman's feet; she picked it up and took it safely to her daughter-in-law.

Late one afternoon, the old woman picked up one of her son's torn shirts to mend it, but his new wife scolded her. "Put it down, you old fool," she shouted. "You'll only ruin it!" The mother turned to her son for support, but he simply said, "You have to obey my wife." Heartsick and weary to her bones, the old woman put the shirt away and went outside to sit on the freezing front porch, still holding her needle and thread. Shortly afterward, she saw a poor girl coming toward her. The girl's bodice was torn, and her shoulder was blue with cold where the sleeve had given way. She smiled at the old woman and asked her whether she would like to buy some of her kindling.

"I have no money, my dear; but if you like, I'll mend your sleeve for you." So that is what she did, and the girl gave her a bundle of kindling in return, thanked her kindly, and went happily on her way.

That night, the son and his wife went to the village to have supper with his godmother. Before they left, the snake-woman gave her mother-in-law a long list of tasks to complete by their return. As soon as they had gone, the old woman sighed and then set her old bones to work. She took the kindling that the poor girl had given her, lit the fire on the hearth, and went out to the shed for wood. As she approached the cottage with her arms full of logs, she heard a rustling in the kitchen.

"Whoever is that?" she called from the doorway.

"Brownies! Brownies!" came the reply, in voices that sounded for all the world like a family of sparrows chirping in a hedge.

As the old woman walked into the kitchen, the kindling flared up on the hearth, and a group of tiny men, dressed in dark fur coats, were dancing there; their caps and shoes were red as fire, their beards were gray as ashes, and their eyes sparkled like live coals. More and more of them came dancing out of the flames; they laughed and chattered and turned somersaults on the hearth. They danced among the ashes, under the cupboard, on the table, in the water jug, and on the chairs. They scattered the salt; they spilled the milk; they upset the flour — and all just for the fun of it. The fire on the hearth blazed and crackled, and the old woman looked on in delight, grateful for the comfort of their company. It seemed to her as if she were growing young again, and she laughed and clapped her hands. But in the end, she couldn't push aside the heaviness in her heart, and when the brownies noticed it too, the music stopped at once.

"What's the matter, old mother?" one of them asked.

The old woman sighed and told them everything that had happened. They sat round the edge of the hearth and listened to her, and as they wagged their heads in disbelief, their red caps caught the glow of the flames — and unless you looked very closely, you'd have thought there was nothing there but the fire burning on the hearth. "Can you possibly," she asked them, "help me to show my son the truth about his wife?"

One of the brownies, whose name was Wee Tintilinkie, suggested that the old woman visit Stribor, the Forest King, to see if he might have a solution to her plight. "He always knows what to do," he said. His companions nodded enthusiastically and so the old mother agreed. She pulled on her coat and boots, followed the brownies outside, and just as she was closing the cottage door behind her, Wee Tintilinkie gave a piercing whistle. A stag and twelve squirrels appeared in front of them. The brownies set the old woman on the stag, climbed onto the squirrels, then off they went, deep into the enchanted forest.

Eventually, they came to an enormous old oak tree at the center of the forest. At its base was a polished wooden door; Wee Tintilinkie opened it and led the old woman inside. To her astonishment, she saw before her an entirely new landscape, with seven golden castles and a silver-fenced village that looked strangely familiar. They made their way to the largest castle, which was the home of the Forest King; inside it sat Stribor, on a beechwood throne entwined with living green vines.

The old woman approached the Forest King and, at his invitation, told him all that had happened to her. Stribor gestured to the village that lay beyond the castle walls. "Look!" he said. "Forget all about your daughter-in-law. Do you see? There's the village in which you were born, and there's your mother, your father, and all your childhood friends. If you'd like, you can join them, and then you'll be young and fit again — just as you were fifty years ago. All you have to do is clap, and then climb over the silver fence that surrounds the village."

The old woman's face lit up as she thought about her childhood and the prospect of returning to her happy, youthful self — but then the smile vanished from her face. "What about my son?" she asked. "What will become of him?"

"You won't have any memory of him, of course," Stribor replied, "because you'll be returning to your youth — to a time before he was born. And he will be left to his own fate."

The old woman knew what she had to do. "No," she said. "I can't possibly forget the many, long years of my life, and I certainly can't forget my son. I can't forget all the things that have happened to me, and all the things I was and have become. Thank you, but I think I'll just go back home, after all."

The whole forest rang loudly, as if suddenly possessed by thousands of silver bells. And there was an end then to the magic in Stribor's Forest — including the magic that had allowed the snake to become a woman — and all because the old mother preferred the sorrows of her life to all the joys of another world. The forest quaked, and the huge oak with its castles and silver-fenced village sank into the ground. Stribor and the brownies vanished, and the old woman found herself alone in a silent forest. She retraced the path back to her cottage and her life.

When the old woman arrived home, she found her contrite son waiting there, alone. After she broke the forest's spell, his wife had become a snake again, so releasing him from her enchantment; he was ashamed now that he had allowed his mother to be treated so badly by such a creature. He hugged her and begged her forgiveness. And a little while later, when life in the cottage had once again grown affectionate and warm, he married the sweet girl from the village who sold kindling; she remembered the old woman's kindness to her and treated her gently in turn. All three of them are living happily together in that cottage to this day, and on a cold winter's evening when the moon is full and the kindling is piled ready on the hearth, Wee Tintilinkie comes to visit them, and to dance.

The dynamic between the mother and son in this story might be familiar to those of you who've parented teenagers: the many painful ways they invent to sever the umbilical cord, and their single-minded determination to blunder into trouble. The arrival of a child's adolescence often coincides with their mother's entry into perimenopause. Hormones on both sides go haywire and moods swing, crash, and clash against each other, time and time again. Then it's time for the youngster to up and leave; suddenly the nest is empty, and the active part of mothering is done. You're bereft and relieved and maybe a little lost, and just as you're dealing with all of that, the new challenges of the second half of life are rising up in front of you like an unscalable glass mountain.

Whatever the personal circumstances in which we arrive there, it's not easy, growing old: so many of the things that once defined us are slowly but thoroughly stripped away. Our youth, our looks — and, all too often, our power and our voice. If our culture insists that older women are not worth listening to, then however much we might rail against it, we'll be treated as if we are not worth listening to — just like the mother in this story when her son refuses to listen to her. It can be tempting then to live in the past, especially if the present is intolerable and the future seems to hold little hope of improvement. But if we want to live through the second half of our lives in a grounded and meaningful way, we must find ways of fully inhabiting the present — and not in a spirit of resignation but of acceptance.

All of us will face the loss of physical function as we grow into elderhood and, if we live long enough, some degree of frailty is inevitable — but the knowledge and inner strengths we'll have accumulated through the long years of our experience are no small consolation. So it's her discernment that enables the old mother to see through the deceptions of the snake-woman, her strength of character that sustains her in the face of magic, and her integrity that enables her to overcome the offered temptation to return to the lighter days of her youth. For love of her son and her long, rich life, she chooses, instead, the challenges of old age. She chooses to grow, not to regress. She chooses reality over fantasy.

Carl Jung, one of the most influential psychologists of the past century, firmly believed that we wouldn't have the potential to live for eight decades or more if there was no meaning to, or purpose for, that extended life. "The afternoon of human life must also have a significance of its own," Jung wrote.* But so often, in the contemporary discourse around middle age, women are encouraged to cling to fading youth at all costs. Menopause is presented as a medical condition that needs to be managed. Hormone replacement therapy, instead of being a useful and often necessary antidote to the most challenging

---

* C. G. Jung, *Modern Man in Search of a Soul.* Psychology Press (2001), p. 112.

physical consequences of menopause, is offered as an anti-aging medication. We're taught to think of menopause as heralding a time of decline, rather than a natural and necessary entry point into the next stage of life that, like the old woman in this story, we must find a way to welcome, for its new and deeper gifts.

Ride a Cock-Horse to Banbury Cross

ENGLAND

This well-known nursery rhyme more commonly sets a "fine lady" on the white horse. Most nursery rhymes have regional or local variations, though, and this one happily makes an old woman the subject of the rhyme.

Ride a cock-horse to Banbury Cross,
To see an old lady upon a white horse.
Rings on her fingers, and bells on her toes,
She shall have music wherever she goes.

The Giantess's Burden

In the old times, there was a giantess who lived high in the mountains of Eryri in North Wales, and she was built just as craggily as those great peaks of Cambrian rock. Her hair was like a forest of stag-headed oaks, entwined with lengths of trailing ivy; her eyes were as dark and as deep as the pools that nestle in the high cwms. And her skin — well, it was rough as a cliff face, and mottled with lichen and moss on account of her great age.

One morning, on waking, she stretched and yawned, sending tremors throughout the land. It came to her mind that it might be a good day to build a bridge across the Menai Strait — that deep crevasse of churning, swirling, sucking water that separates the Isle of Anglesey from the mainland — so that she could more easily visit the giantesses who lived there. And so she took herself off to search for suitable boulders with which to build the bridge. She crossed great distances with each stride; fast-flowing rivers were no more than trickles tickling her gigantic toes, and Llyn Padarn was just a puddle splashing around her ankles as she strode through it. Her skirts swept swathes of leaves from the ancient woodland that clung to the mountainsides and the giantess brushed away soft clouds from her eyes so that she could see her way more clearly through the vast and undulating landscape.

She pressed on over high mountains and along deep valleys, till finally she arrived at a place called Cwmdwythwch. There, she gathered up the corners of her apron and began to fill it with great boulders that she planned to use to construct her bridge. She filled her apron, then filled it some more. She was strong: she could carry heavy burdens — and so she filled it just a little bit more. Her apron strained under the weight of the enormous chunks of rock, and her arms and back ached as she lifted it higher and began to make her way, slowly, steadily, back toward the coast.

Just as she came down the north side of Moel Eilio, the giantess slipped and slid, and her great heels gouged two deep-water channels in the side of the mountain. She landed on her bottom with a resounding, earthquaking thud — and to this day, that place is known as Gafl y Widdan: the Witch's Lap.

A little shaken and really quite bruised, she staggered to her feet. Undeterred, she gathered up her apronful of stones again and continued on her way. But a few great, heaving strides later — SNAP! — the cord of her apron broke, and her bundle of boulders tumbled to the ground.

So the giantess gave up on building her bridge that day and that week — and indeed, as far as we know, she never built the bridge at all, because that's where the stones lay for a long, long time. And that pile of boulders became known as Barclodiad y Gawres: the Giantess's Apronful.

What happened to the giantess after that? We don't know; the story is lost — or perhaps it was never told. It's possible that this was the same accident-prone giantess who dropped another apronful of stones on the southwest coast of Anglesey, which later were carved and painted by tomb builders of the Neolithic, and which became the spectacular passage grave we also know today as Barclodiad y Gawres. Perhaps she was responsible for the several other cairns and sites known as Barclodiad y Gawres across Wales, which are similarly associated with giantesses in the landscape.

She may also be related to the witch-giantess who lived at Tre'r Ceiri, "the town of giants," an Iron Age hillfort on the Llŷn Peninsula. This giantess, after the people of a local village had offended her, decided to heat up an assortment of great boulders with the intention of hurling them into their fields, which were ready for reaping. As she was carrying the stones up Moel Carn y Wrach ("Witch Cairn Hill"), she was accosted by a knight and dropped them where they remain to this day. What is certain is that the overburdened giantess of this story, along with her sisters, has left a legacy of marks and place-names in the landscape of the hills and mountains of North Wales. Like so many folk tales, this story is bound, rock and root, to the land it arose from, and has left a lasting footprint.

There's no trace in Wales today — nor in England — of a divine old woman like the Cailleach of Scottish and Irish traditions who we will meet later in this book, and who was known to create and shape the land. But the idea of an old woman as the spirit of place has certainly been recorded in other parts of Britain. In Wales, she shows up in the stories of several local giantesses like this one, who similarly embody the landscape and the force of nature.

At one level, this is a funny little tale about a giantess attempting to build a bridge. But if we dig beneath the surface, it might have something to tell us about the gathering of great boulder-burdens as we travel through life. Many of these burdens are of our own making; others are imposed on us and we simply learn to carry them. Sometimes, we deceive ourselves into thinking that we're strong enough and tough enough to bear an ever-increasing load — but at some point it's bound to become too much for us; at some point we will simply break. We might hit mountainous or tricky terrain; we might trip up, slip down, fall flat on our back. If we're lucky, or especially wise, we'll take the hint and sort ourselves out. Other times, we'll pick ourselves up and carry on anyway, in spite of the increasing strain. But then the load will grow heavier. We'll tire, and eventually something will snap — like the giantess's apron string in this story. And out will pour our burdens: the unhealed wounds and unprocessed griefs, the *yes*es that should have been *no*s, the regrets and intense self-criticisms, the toll of care given to others without care for ourselves. Out they'll all pour, crashing down at our feet.

The journey through midlife, menopause, and on into elderhood is a walk through uneven, often craggy, and sometimes mountainous physical and emotional terrain. However strong we might imagine ourselves to be, it's no surprise that the weight of these burdens should become increasingly hard to bear. This story invites us to examine what it is that women carry, and why; to identify the parts of our load that we can safely lay aside; to leave a boulder or two behind us as way markers in the dusty landscape of our past. Maybe then we can journey on, bearing only what's needed, to enjoy a lighter and freer second half of life.

My Grandmother's Cottage

WALES

Grandmother lives in a cottage next to a grove of trees
Lives in hearty contentment, at eighty years of age

Chorus:
She has an orchard and a neat little homestead
With countless chickens, a cow, a cat, a dog, and a pig in a sty

And when the children of Earth cannot live in harmony
Grandmother lives peacefully, at ease in her little world

Tending Eden

ENGLAND

Many moons ago, near the banks of the fast-flowing River Tavy on Dartmoor, there lived an old woman who loved to garden. Her cottage was next to a pixie field, in which — as the flat green rings in the grass indicated — the little folk loved to dance. The old woman's garden was a sight to behold. There was lavender and hollyhock, blue-button and gillyflower, forget-me-not and rue — there was a procession of color and scent from early spring to late autumn. But the finest of all the flowers were her tulips: a riotous bed of tightly packed, brightly colored blooms that the old woman tended with special care. Neither you, nor I, nor anyone who might ever pass her garden could prevent themselves from stopping to peep over the gate when the tulips were in flower. Well, of course the pixies loved that spot. They enjoyed the garden, and they loved the gentle old woman who nurtured it.

One clear night, as moon shadows stole around the garden and tiny lilac-blossom petals shone pale as a galaxy of stars, the old woman started up out of her sleep. At first, she thought the strange sound that had woken her was the call of the tawny owl who sometimes frequented the ancient elm tree, but as she strained her old ears to listen, she realized that what she was hearing was no owl. It was a very much sweeter and more melodic sound.

It sounds for all the world like a lullaby, she thought, and lay still in bed listening for a while. Then, curious to know what manner of creature was creating it, she slipped her feet into cozy slippers and shuffled over to the window to look out at the midnight garden below. Everything was still except for the moonlit tulips, which were swaying gently and nodding their flower-heads in time to the sweet music. For a moment, it seemed to her that the tulips were singing.

The next night, the same thing happened — and then again the next night, and the night after that. The old woman finally realized that the pixies were bringing their babies to her garden each night and placing each one in a tall tulip flower to keep them safe and sheltered while their parents danced. "Well, I never! They're lulling their little ones to sleep!" she said to herself, delighted. And as she peered more closely, she saw them: pixie babies tucked up tight, fast asleep among the cupped petals. And out in the field, where dewdrops on the long blades of grass lit up the land like tiny spotlights, their parents were gathering to dance. She sat at the window and watched until, just as the sun was heaving itself up out of the eastern sky, the pixies returned to the garden to fetch their babies. A broad smile stretched across the old woman's face.

"Bless my soul! If those little dears aren't kissing their babies before they pick them up," she said to herself. "What loving little beings they are."

That spring, the tulips didn't fade as quickly as the other spring flowers in her garden; it seemed as if their leaves would never wither and their petals would never fall. And as she bent over to tidy the flower border one afternoon, the old woman noticed something else about those tulips: the pixies, by breathing over them, had made them even lovelier, so that now they smelled just as sweet and fragrant as lilies and roses. From that day on, she declared that neither she, nor anyone else, should ever pick a single tulip from her garden. They would all be kept for the pixies' delight, and for the comfort and safety of their little ones.

So it continued for a good many years — until at last, the kind old woman died. It was a sad day for the garden, and the tulips hung their heads in sorrow. Not long afterward, the cottage passed into other hands, but the new tenant cared little for pixie lore. He was only interested in the fruit trees and berry bushes — for, after all, gooseberries, raspberries, and greengages made very tasty pies. But he could hardly wait for the fruit to ripen before picking them, causing one of his neighbors to warn him, "You shouldn't gather those gooseberries out of season — the pixies can't abide being robbed of their own, so you're sure to be courting bad luck!"

"Pah! Pixies!" the man said. "I've never heard such nonsense."

Then, one day, another neighbor walked by the cottage, casting a forlorn glance at the garden, which was now in dire need of love and care, when she spotted the man digging up the tulips.

"Surely you aren't taking out the tulip bed!" she cried. "They were the old lady's delight. What do you mean to grow in their place?"

"I'm planting a bed of parsley — though what business it is of yours, I don't know."

"Parsley!" the woman said. "Upon my soul. Don't you know it's unlucky to plant a bed of parsley in such a place? The last man I heard of who did that was bedridden forever afterward!"

"What a lot of stuff and nonsense," the new tenant muttered, and that was the end of those glorious blooms. But the pixies were so offended that they caused the parsley to wither and rot; try as he might, the man could grow neither herb nor vegetable in that bed, and soon enough, the entire garden became a desolate wasteland.

Though no more lullabies were ever heard in the flowerbed that once had doubled as a pixie nursery, the little folk still dwelled in the neighborhood. And on the night before every full moon, they gathered by the old woman's headstone to sing sorrowful laments; while they sang, they tended her grave. Not a single weed was ever seen there, and from spring to autumn it bloomed with a procession of the old woman's favorite flowers: lavender and hollyhock, blue-button and gillyflower, forget-me-not and rue. And, of course, tulips.

This story arrived like a breath of fresh air, with its wonderfully positive image of what a happy, ordinary elder woman might be like. She isn't a gnarly old goddess, a wily old witch, or a wise woman who sees deep into the heart of things that others cannot: she's just an everyday old woman living in an everyday little village, enjoying her garden, perfectly in tune with the world around her.

There's something very special about this old woman, though, and perhaps it derives precisely from her ordinariness. She's kind, she's content; she's the type of old woman that most of us would like to have as our neighbor, and possibly the type of old woman we might one day want to grow into. You'd feel safe with a woman like this as your grandmother, for sure. She unwittingly creates a sanctuary for the pixies, then maintains it for their benefit and, for all their otherness, fully accepts them as part of the land and her life.

This elderly gardener is one of the oldest of the women in this book, very close to the end of her life — and indeed, by the time the story ends, she has died. As the natural processes of aging slow us down, we too might adopt a more contemplative approach to the world. We might find ourselves taking joy in the simple beauty of a flower bed, and in the cycles and seasons of the natural world around us. Or we might find ourselves sitting at the window to watch pixies dancing in our gardens at night — because this growing capacity for stillness and contemplation makes us more porous, and so more receptive to the numinous and Otherworldly.

Our gentle old woman tends her garden right to the end: she never gives up on it. It's so very tempting, today, to beat ourselves up for humanity's catastrophic plundering of the natural world — and indeed, at some level, we probably should. We might not be able to save the world, but each one of us, like the protagonist of this story, is capable in some way of valuing and caring for it. Myths and folklore from all around the world tell us how important it is to live in balance and harmony with the natural world — and also with the denizens of the Otherworld that animate it. If we give to nature with love and care, we receive its gifts of abundance and joy. And there's a lovely lesson about the beauty of such reciprocities in this story: just as the old woman tends the garden that is loved by the pixies, the pixies in return mourn her and tend her grave.

Baubo

Baubo is a bawdy old woman in Greek mythology who appears in the story of Persephone. Persephone's mother, the goddess Demeter, is brokenhearted because her daughter has been abducted by Hades and taken to the Underworld to be his wife. She wanders the Earth in search of Persephone and eventually comes to the town of Eleusis. She refuses all food and drink and rejects all efforts to help her — until she encounters an old woman called Baubo. Baubo approaches Demeter, lifts up her skirts, and displays her genitals; Demeter bursts into sudden laughter and, after she has recovered from her merriment, accepts the drink that Baubo offers her and so breaks her fast. As a consequence, Demeter's long period of grief and stasis is ended, and she becomes herself again.

Earthenware figurines identified with Baubo, which were found in the ruins of the fourth-century BCE Temple of Demeter and Kore in Ionia, offer some insight into the reason for Demeter's amusement. In each of the statues, the head and female genitals are merged together, with the vulva on display immediately below the figurine's mouth, blending into her chin.

Old Woman Song

ENGLAND

I am an old woman, you know
Four-score years and one,
Yet for that, you know,
I can mark so straight as a gun
Then lawk-a-massie what fun
I pray to my soul I'd never grow old
If kissing had never been done.

I am an old woman, you know
Four-score years and two,
Yet for that, you know,
I can stoop to buckle my shoe.

I am an old woman, you know
Four-score years and three,
Yet for that, you know,
I can gather above my knee.

I am an old woman, you know
Four-score years and four,
Yet for that, you know,
I can cock my leg higher or lower.

I am an old woman, you know
Four-score years and five,
Yet for that, you know,
I can keep the game alive.

I am an old woman, you know
Four-score years and six,
Yet for that, you know,
I can stoop to pick up sticks.

I am an old woman, you know
Four-score years and seven,
But for that, you know,
I do pray to go to heaven.

I am an old woman, you know
Four-score years and eight,
But for that, you know,
I can bend my leg crooked or straight.

I am an old woman, you know
Four-score years and nine,
But for that, you know,
I can toss a glass of wine.

I am an old woman, you know
Four-score years and ten,
But for that, you know,
I do love to kiss the men.

Kissing the Witch

Chances are that if you were to ask your friends and family whether they remember any older women in fairy tales, their first thoughts would be of wicked witches. The old witch in "Hansel and Gretel" who wanted to eat the children; the witch who keeps Rapunzel captive in her tall tower. In many such stories, a witch is a malevolent old woman above all, and an ugly and frightening one too. And throughout history, all the way up to the period of the European witch trials (between the fifteenth and eighteenth centuries) and beyond, the word "witch" was almost always used specifically to refer to someone who caused harm to others by magical means.

Over the past century, though, we've come to think of the Witch archetype more as something that we might aspire to, that will teach us, and maybe even save us. The Witch archetype has come to embody our longings for what we now imagine to be the old pagan ways of our ancestors: a reverence for the natural world and the other-than-humans who are part of it; a wild, green spirituality that links contemporary feminism with environmentalism. Today, to identify as a witch is to identify as a woman who holds herself apart from "civilization" and chooses instead to live by her own deeper values — someone whose magic is derived from the natural world and who lacks the malicious intent of the classic storybook witch.

Because this revisioning of the Witch archetype is relatively recent, it's a rare thing indeed to find a benign witch in older folk and fairy tales. Nevertheless, two such stories are included here that are not nearly as well known as the stories of wicked witches that so many of us remember from our childhood. These are for sure the kind of witches who are worthy of a kiss rather than a curse.

The Nixy

ENGLAND

Back in the old times, there was a miller who, after many years of plenty, fell on hard times. Things became so bad that he could no longer make a living; all that remained to him were his pregnant wife, his home, and the mill. He passed his days aimlessly, full of worry and despair; when he went to bed each night he lay awake sunk in sorrowful thoughts.

One morning, he heaved himself wearily out of bed just before dawn and stepped outside, imagining that his heart might feel less heavy in the open air, surrounded by the beauty of the breaking day. As he wandered up and down along the banks of the millpond, listening to the growing chorus of early birds, he heard a rushing sound in the water; a strange, spectral woman was rising up from the center of the pond. Water weeds wound through her hair, and pond slime clung to her pale, almost fishy skin; she was both hideous and utterly captivating. He realized that this must be the nixy who was known to live at the bottom of the millpond. His heart began to race, and he made to hurry away, but then the nixy spoke gently to him, calling him by his name and asking why he was so sad.

Her friendly tone reassured the miller, so he plucked up courage and told her his troubles: how prosperous he had been all his life up till now, when suddenly he didn't know what to do with himself for poverty and misery. The nixy comforted him and promised that she would make him richer than he had ever been in his life — if only he would give her in return the youngest thing living in his house.

The miller thought that surely she must mean one of the puppies that his hound had recently whelped, or a kitten from the new litter hidden behind the grain sacks in the mill; so he promised the nixy that he would give her what she asked for, and returned home full of hope. But on the threshold, he was greeted by an excited maid with the news that his wife had that very hour given birth to their first child: a boy. The poor miller, who ought to have been delighted, instead was horrified; he went to see his wife and newborn son with a heavy heart. He sat down on the bed beside her and confessed the fatal bargain he had just struck with the nixy. "I would gladly give up all the good fortune she promised me," he said, "if I could only save our child." His wife was heartbroken, but neither she nor any- one else in their appalled household could think of any advice to give him, other than to make sure that the child never, ever, went near the millpond.

The boy thrived and grew up strong and tall, and just as the nixy had promised, the miller began to prosper again; in a few years, he was even richer than he had been before. But he couldn't fully relish his good fortune, because always at the back of his mind was the memory of his contract with the nixy: he knew that sooner or later, she would demand that he fulfill it. Still, the years passed, and the miller's son grew up and became a great hunter. The lord of the land took him into his service, because he was as smart and as bold a hunter as you could ever wish to see. Soon enough he married the young woman he loved, and they lived together on the lord's estate in great peace and happiness.

One day, when he was out hunting, a hare sprang up at his

feet and ran for some distance in front of him in the open field. The hunter pursued it for some time, until at last he managed to shoot it dead. He took out his knife and proceeded to skin it — and so intent was he on his work that he never noticed he was close to the millpond, which from childhood he had been taught to avoid at all costs in case he should encounter the nixy. After he had finished the skinning, he went to the water to clean the knife and wash the blood off his hands. He had hardly dipped them into the pond when the nixy sprang up from the water and seized him in her cold, white arms; she dragged him down with her into the murky depths.

When the hunter didn't return home that evening, his wife grew anxious and went out to see if she could find him. She came across his game bag near the millpond and at once guessed what had happened to him. Beside herself with grief, she roamed round and around the pond, calling her husband's name. At last, worn out with sorrow and fatigue, she sank to her knees and fell asleep on its banks. She dreamed that she was wandering through a flowery meadow, at the end of which was a small, simple hut. Inside the hut was an old woman wrapped in a heavy plaid shawl, puffing on a long-stemmed clay pipe. Her unruly gray hair was barely restrained in a knot at the top of her head; it was loosely pinned with hazel sticks and raven feathers. Bunches of drying herbs hung from the rafters, and potion bottles, stones, and feathers littered the shelves. From this, the dreaming woman knew the old woman to be a witch. But the witch was kind and comforted her, and promised to restore her husband to her.

The hunter's wife woke the next morning feeling certain that the witch in her dreams was real, and so she determined to set out and find her. She wandered through the land for many a day, till at last she came to a flowery meadow, at the end of which she found the hut where the old witch lived. Everything was just the same as it had been in her dream. The old woman invited her inside, and the hunter's wife told her everything that had happened, and that in a dream she had seen that the witch had the power to help her. The witch said that indeed she did, and advised her to go to the millpond at the next full moon. There, she said, she should comb her black hair with a golden comb, then place the comb on the bank of the pond. The hunter's wife gave the witch a handsome gift for her kindness, thanked her with all her heart, and returned home.

Time dragged heavily till the moon waxed full, and as soon as it rose the young wife went down to the millpond. She combed her black hair with a golden comb, and when she had finished, she placed the comb on the bank; then she watched the water impatiently. Soon she heard a rushing sound: an enormous wave rose from the center of the pond and swept the comb off the bank. The next moment, her beloved husband's head emerged from the water, and he gazed sadly at her. But another wave surged up and his head plunged back into the dark depths of the water without having uttered a word. The pond lay still and motionless, a silver mirror for the moon, and the heartbroken hunter's wife wasn't the slightest bit better off than she had been before.

In despair, she wandered again through the land for many days and nights until at last, worn out by fatigue, she fell into a deep sleep. She dreamed about the old witch, just as she had before. So, the next morning, she found her way back to the flowery meadow and came to the witch in her hut. She told her of her continuing grief. The old woman comforted her; she advised her to go again to the millpond at the time of the next full moon and to play a golden flute, and then to lay the flute on the bank of the pond, just as she had the comb.

As soon as the moon grew full again, the hunter's wife went to the millpond and played a song on her golden flute; when she had finished, she placed it on the bank. All at once, there was a rushing sound, and a huge wave swept the flute off the bank. Moments later, the hunter's head appeared — and rose higher and higher, till he was halfway out of the water. He gazed sadly at his wife and stretched out his arms to her — but another wave gathered itself and dragged him under again. The hunter's wife, who had stood on the bank full of joy and hope, sank to her knees in sorrow when she saw her husband snatched away again before her eyes.

That night she dreamed the now-familiar dream for a third time, and she traveled once more to the old witch's hut at the edge of the flowery meadow. This time, the old woman told her to go to the millpond on the next full moon and to spin there with a golden spinning wheel. Then, as before, she should leave the spinning wheel on the bank.

The hunter's wife did as she was advised: on the first night of the full moon she sat and spun for a while with a golden spinning wheel, and then left the wheel on the bank. After a few minutes she heard the all-too-familiar rushing sound in the waters, and a wave swept the spinning wheel from the bank. Immediately, the head of the hunter rose up from the pond, higher and higher, till finally he was free. He took a step onto the bank and fell into his wife's arms.

But the waters of the pond surged and crashed over the bank where the couple stood, dragging them both under. In her despair, the young wife cried out for the old witch to help her — and, in a flash, the hunter was turned into a frog and his wife into a toad. But the sucking, tumbling force of the water tore them apart. When the flood abated, the hunter and the hunter's wife were relieved to discover that they had regained their own human forms. But the witch's swift magic had had an unforeseen effect: when they pulled themselves out of the millpond, each of them stepped out into a different daylit country that was strange to them, and neither knew what had become of the other.

The hunter looked around him at a large valley with small stone farmhouses and creamy-white sheep dotted across green hills; he decided to take work as a shepherd. By chance, his wife too became a shepherdess in the country where she had now settled. They each herded their sheep for many years in solitude and sadness. Then, many years later, the shepherd had cause to travel to the country where the shepherdess lived. He liked the landscape very much and saw that the pasture was rich and would provide perfect grazing for his flocks. So he brought his sheep there and continued to herd them. The shepherd and shepherdess met on the hills and became great friends, but after all these years they had of course changed so very much, and they did not recognize each other.

One evening, though, they sat together beneath a full moon watching their flocks, and the shepherd played his flute. The shepherdess remembered the moonlit evening when she had sat by the millpond and had played on her own golden flute; the memories of loss and grief were too much for her and she burst into tears. The shepherd asked her why she was crying, and she told him her story. All at once, the scales fell away from the shepherd's eyes: he recognized his wife, and she him. They returned joyfully to their former home and lived there together with their sheep in peace and happiness for the rest of their days.

This rather poignant old story offers us a flower-meadow witch who is a savior, not a slaughterer. This witch can penetrate the dream worlds — the Otherworld — and draw to her those who need her assistance; with her deep vision, she is also able to use her magic from a distance, when the hunter's wife calls out to her for help. Although it seems as if her magic has unintentionally torn the hunter and his wife apart forever, something in this story invites us to trust the flow of life, and to believe that the path we're taking — though often it will twist and turn — will eventually lead us home.

The folklore of Europe is littered with witches, and few of them are benign. The witch in this story — at least, as we find her — seems to be entirely benevolent, but you'd be hard-pressed, over the past thousand years or more, to find anyone with a kind word to say about a witch. During the long centuries in which the European witch trials were conducted, the charge of witchcraft was levied specifically against women who were seen to be evading or subverting societal (patriarchal) control, and who had the audacity to be different. Women were deeply affected by the cultural repressions that weighed them down during the period of the witch trials, and many of them — especially the aged, the solitary, or the physically and mentally challenged — lived in fear. Many women would have modified their behaviors and presented themselves to the outer world as people they were not, to avoid attracting attention or suspicion.

The psychological residue of the witch trials persists in women today, and what has often been referred to as the "witch wound" is the psychological wound that still prevents so many of us from fully and fearlessly embodying our true selves. The witch wound is a fear of being too different and of not conforming to what society, or our narrower community, expects of us; it's dread at the idea of speaking out against authority or the majority and of not quite fitting in. It's the result of centuries of marginalization by both religious and societal establishments — centuries during which women had no power, no freedom; in which we never felt truly safe and were constantly subjected to abuse.

This story of a benign witch reminds us that to be different, and to live alone at the far end of a meadow, isn't always a sign of moral or psychological deviance. To be different can simply mean that we're uniquely gifted, and that we're able by some rare magic of our own to help transform the lives of others for the better. This tale reminds those of us in the second half of life always to follow our own heart and exercise our unique gifts, so that we can live the life that we always were meant to live.

There Was an Old Woman Toss'd Up in a Basket

ENGLAND

There was an old woman toss'd up in a basket
Ninety-nine times as high as the moon,
But where she was going no mortal could tell,
For under her arm she carried a broom.
"Old woman, old woman, old woman," said I,
"Whither, ah! whither, whither so high?"
"Oh, I'm sweeping the cobwebs off the sky,
And I'll be with you by and by!"

Kissing the Hag

Back in the day, Eochaid Mugmedón was the High King of all Ireland. That fine king had five sons; four of them were from his first wife, Mongfind, and their names were Brian, Ailill, Fiachra, and Fergus. Eochaid's fifth son, Niall, came from his second wife, Caireann Chasdub, a daughter of the king of the Saxons who he'd taken as a hostage. Well, Mongfind hated Caireann. She made her fetch water from the well for the whole household, and everyone was so afraid of the queen that they were fearful of having anything at all to do with Caireann, so they made sure to turn away from her whenever they saw her.

While the ever-lonelier Caireann was pregnant with Niall, Mongfind piled heavier and heavier tasks on her in the hope that she might miscarry. As Caireann was drawing water one day, her labor pains began; she fell to the ground and, all alone and without help or comfort, gave birth to Niall. The baby was taken away at her request to be fostered by Torna, a poet who happened then to pass by; he promised to raise the child in safety, away from Mongfind.

When Niall had grown into a tall, strong young man, he returned to the High King's court at Tara; he introduced himself to his father, who acknowledged him as his own son. Niall then rescued his mother from her continuing servitude and insisted that Caireann should be treated with respect. In time, Eochaid grew to be as fond of Niall as of his other sons, and so even when Mongfind pressed him, he refused to name her eldest — or indeed any one of his children — as his successor.

One day, Niall and his half brothers — with whom he was friendly enough, despite the ceaseless efforts of Mongfind to make enemies of them — were out hunting together, in the oak woods far from home. They gorged themselves on the rich, roasted meat of the fallow deer they had killed and grew thirsty, so Fergus decided to go looking for water. He wandered for a while through the lush, green trees and soon came across a well, but to his surprise, he found it guarded by an old hag. And oh, she was ugly! Instead of a head of hair, she had a gray, bristly mane like the coarse hair along an old boar's back. Her teeth were green, crammed unevenly into a mouth that stretched from ear to ear. Her nose was crooked, and her nostrils gaped. Her skin was spotted with pustules, and her legs were twisted and set at unlikely angles. Her knees were knobbly, her ankles were thick, her shoulders were huge, her nails were filthy, and the stench of her breath was enough to fell a horse.

Fergus stared at her in disgust. "So you're guarding the well, then?" he said.

"I am," she answered.

"Will you let me have some water from it?"

"I will," she said, "but only if you will kiss me."

"I'll be honest with you," Fergus said, backing away, "I'd rather die of thirst than kiss you!" Away he ran, back to his brothers; he told them that he had failed to find any water at all. Ailill set off in his place, happened upon the same well, and in just the same way he denied the old woman a kiss; in just the same way, she refused him access to the well. Brian, the oldest of the sons, had exactly the same experience, and so Fiachra set off in his place. When the old hag asked Fiachra whether he might spare her a kiss, to his credit he did manage a hasty peck on her cheek — but it failed to satisfy her, so he too returned without water.

Finally, Niall set off to try his luck. Like the others, he chanced upon the well, and the old hag asked him for a kiss in return for water. Niall threw back his head and laughed, then roundly declared, "I'll do more than give you a kiss — I'll lie with you, if you like!" — and he drew a deep breath, pulled her into his arms and kissed her heartily. Coming up for air, he drew away and looked down at her — only to find that he held no loathsome hag in his arms but the most beautiful young woman in the world. Her skin was as pale as the moon, her hair soft and golden as a field of buttercups. Her fingers were long, her legs were shapely and, if her ankles were anything to go by, slender too. She wore fine shoes on her dainty feet and a rich purple cloak clasped with a brooch of bright gold. Her teeth shone like pearls when she smiled up at him, her eyes were large and queenly, and her lips — oh, those lips — were soft and red as rowanberries.

"Who on earth are you?" Niall asked, astonished by this metamorphosis.

The much-transformed hag said, "I am the Sovereignty of Ireland. Go back to your brothers now and take some water with you. But I will give you more than water: I tell you that you and your children and your children's children will rule Ireland forevermore. And I tell you that just as you found me — ugly, brutish, and loathly at first, and then in the end, beautiful — so it is with a king's rule. You see, a throne may never be won without frightful battles and fierce conflict; but once a man has attained the throne and become king, his grace and beauty can shine." The woman smiled at Niall. "One last piece of advice: don't give your brothers a single drop of this water till they promise to follow you and to accept you as the next king of all Ireland."

"I'll do just that," Niall said, and reluctantly he pulled himself away and left her. He ran back to his brothers and told them what had happened, but he didn't give them any of the water until they had sworn never to oppose his rule, or that of any of his children in future. Then together the brothers returned to Tara, and sure enough, Sovereignty's prophecy came true: Niall became king after Eochaid, and all the kings of Ireland after that were his descendants.

The protagonist of this story, Niall Noígíallach, or Niall of the Nine Hostages, was a legendary, semi-historical Irish king who was the original ancestor of the royal Uí Néill dynasties that dominated Ireland until the tenth century; Old Irish texts date his own reign to the late fourth and early fifth centuries.

Niall might happen to be a hugely important figure in Irish history as well as the protagonist of this story, but of course it's the shapeshifting old hag who is infinitely more interesting in the context of this book. The story tells us that her name is Sovereignty, and the Old Irish word for sovereignty (*flaithius*) that is used in this context had a very specific meaning. It had nothing to do with personal power or agency, in the way that the word is so often used today; rather, it signified the power of the goddess of the land to bestow kingship on whoever she believed would make the best ruler for it. And the best ruler, in the Old Irish tradition, was always the one who would uphold the covenant of mutual care and respect between people and the land. If that covenant were to be broken, dire consequences would follow. Niall was the only one of Eochaid's sons to show care and respect to the old woman who personified the land; Niall, then, was her chosen king.

The Sovereignty goddess was the personification of the land, but she also came from the Otherworld, and so embodied all the ways in which the two were entangled. Her gifts to the world were the wisdom of the land and the blessing of the Otherworld. In this story, by giving Niall the gift of water from the well she guards, she is also granting him the blessing of the Otherworld, because in Irish myth and folklore, wells were sourced from its animating waters.

Sovereignty was a moral force, a creative force, a nurturing force, and an ecological force. From an archetypical perspective, she can be seen as an example of the archetype of the *puella senilis* — the "maiden of old age" who perfectly combines youth and elderhood in the same body. The young woman who represents one face of this archetype carries within her the strength and wisdom — and the physical decline — of old age, and the old hag who represents the other face carries within her the life force of youth. And as we grow older, we too will bring with us all the faces we once wore and all the selves we once were; we'll stare into the mirror at our aging faces with a still-youthful spirit and wonder how on earth this came to be. But that is what it means to kiss the hag: to acknowledge the unique, eternal beauty of the person inside, in spite of the many ways in which the superficial external mask might have changed.

Old Woman, Old Woman, Shall We Go A-Shearing

ENGLAND

"Old woman, old woman, shall we go a-shearing?"
"Speak a little louder, sir: I am very hard of hearing."
"Old woman, old woman, shall I love you dearly?"
"Thank you, kind sir; I hear you very clearly."

Morgan

Morgan, also known as Morgan Le Fay, is the sorceress and "Lady of the Lake" who haunts the shadows of Arthur's court, weaving magic or guarding the misty margins of Avalon, in the vast body of Arthurian literature and legend. She is a complex character who spans many ages and guises, and traverses both physical and Otherworldly domains; she similarly straddles the liminal realms between good and evil, light and shadow, history and myth.

Her earliest documented appearance is in Geoffrey of Monmouth's *Vita Merlini* (written around 1150). In this medieval bestseller, the fatally wounded King Arthur is taken to Morgan, one of nine magical sisters who inhabit Avalon, the Isle of Apples, for healing. In this tale, as in the early French chivalric romances by Chrétien de Troyes, Morgan is presented as a skilled healer — part goddess, part priestess, part fairy — and a protector of King Arthur. She and her sisters are capable of shapeshifting and flying, and use their powers only for good. Morgan is also said to be a learned mathematician and to have taught math and astronomy to her sisters.

The Romance authors of the late twelfth- and thirteenth-century prose cycles were the first to bind Morgan and Arthur by blood. From this time onward, she is presented as his half sister: the youngest daughter of Igraine, Arthur's mother, with her first husband, Gorlois; she's overshadowed and displaced by her younger brother. As she grows, she becomes skilled in the arts of magic, and in some versions of the stories she's taught by the renowned and powerful magician, Merlin.

By the time Sir Thomas Malory had reworked the Arthurian legends in the mid-1400s, Europe was in the grip of witch hysteria, and within a century the steady flow of witch trials would become a torrent. Unsurprisingly, and probably consequentially, the Morgan of his *Le Morte d'Arthur* was depicted as using her magic to undermine Arthur's power and to bring about his downfall. Now, she had been utterly transformed from the goddess-like healer of the earlier *Vita Merlini* into a shadowy, malicious sorceress, an archetypical medieval representation of the potential dangers of uncontrolled female power. Like so many women who walked the fields and cobbled streets of Europe during the Middle Ages and beyond, Morgan became that thing of equal fascination and revulsion: an independent woman, with some skill in healing and with arcane knowledge, who was a little different from most, and who was therefore to be feared and mistrusted. In short, what many at that time might have called a witch.

The Old Woman and Her Cat

ENGLAND

There was an old woman, who rode on a broom,
    With a high gee ho! gee humble;
And she took her Tom Cat behind for a groom
    With a bimble, bamble, bumble.

They traveled along till they came to the sky,
    With a high gee ho! gee humble;
But the journey so long made them very hungry,
    With a bimble, bamble, bumble.

Says Tom, "I can find nothing here to eat,
    With a high gee ho! gee humble;
So let us go back again, I entreat,
    With a bimble, bamble, bumble."

The old woman would not go back so soon,
    With a high gee ho! gee humble;
For she wanted to visit the man in the moon,
    With a bimble, bamble, bumble.

Says Tom, "I'll go back by myself to our house,
    With a high gee ho! gee humble;

For there I can catch a good rat or a mouse,
    With a bimble, bamble, bumble."

"But," says the old woman, "how will you go?
    With a high gee ho! gee humble;
You shan't have my nag, I protest and vow,
    With a bimble, bamble, bumble."

"No, no," says old Tom, "I've a plan of my own,
    With a high gee ho! gee humble";
So he slid down the rainbow, and left her alone,
    With a bimble, bamble, bumble.

So now if you happen to visit the sky,
    With a high gee ho! gee humble;
And want to come back, you Tom's method may try,
    With a bimble, bamble, bumble.

The True History of Little Golden Hood

ENGLAND

I'm quite sure you'll know the tale of poor Little Red Riding Hood, who was deceived and devoured by the big bad wolf. You'll know about her cake, about her basket, and certainly about her grandmother. Well, what you might not know is that the true story happened quite differently. First of all, the child was actually called Little Golden Hood; second, it was neither she nor her grandmother but the wicked wolf who was, in the end, caught and devoured.

So listen. The true story begins in a way that is similar to the way the other tale began.

There was once a little girl, bright and beautiful as a star in its season. Her real name was Blanchette, but more often than not she was called Little Golden Hood, because of a wonderful little cloak with a hood, gold- and fire-colored, which she always wore. This little hood had been given to her by her grandmother, who was so very old that she couldn't remember her age anymore. Her grandmother told her that the cloak would bring her good luck, for it was made of a ray of sunshine. And since this good old woman was considered to be something of a witch, everyone thought that the little hood was rather bewitched too.

And so it was, as you will see.

One day, her mother said to Blanchette: "Let's see, my

Little Golden Hood, if you know how to find your way to your grandmother's house by yourself. You can take this nice big piece of cake to her for tomorrow's Sunday treat. Ask her how she is and then come back at once, and don't under any circumstances stop to chatter with people you don't know. Do you quite understand?"

"I quite understand," Blanchette replied happily. And off she went with the cake, rather proud of herself and the importance of her errand. But her grandmother lived at the edge of another village, and a deep, dark forest had to be crossed before she could reach it. She came to the threshold of the forest and passed into the trees, and as the road turned sharply to the right, she spotted a movement out of the corner of her eye. "Who goes there?" she cried.

"Friend Wolf." The wolf had seen the child set out on her journey alone and, villain that he was, he was waiting to devour her — but he noticed some woodcutters who might see him doing it, and so he changed his mind. Instead of leaping on Blanchette and bringing her down, he came frisking up to her like a friendly dog.

"It's you! And aren't you a nice Little Golden Hood!" he said. The little girl stopped to talk with the wolf, who, it has to be said, she didn't know at all.

"You know me, then!" she said. "And what is your name?"

"My name is Friend Wolf," he replied, baring his shiny white teeth. "And where are you going today, my pretty one, with your little basket on your arm?"

"I'm going to visit my grandmother, to take her a nice big piece of cake for her Sunday treat."

"And where does she live, your grandmother?"

"She lives at the other side of the forest, in the very first house at the edge of the village, near the windmill. Do you know it?"

"Ah, yes! I know it, for sure," said the wolf. "Well now, and isn't that a fine coincidence: that's just where I'm going. I shall get there before you do, with your tiny little legs, and I'll tell her you're coming to see her. Then she'll be expecting you."

So the wolf cut quickly across the forest, and before five minutes had passed, he'd arrived at the grandmother's house.

He knocked at the door: *Toc, toc!*

There was no answer.

He knocked louder: *TOC, TOC!*

Nobody.

Then he stood up on his hind legs, put his forepaws on the latch — and the door swung open.

There wasn't a soul in the house. The old woman had risen early to go and sell her herbs in town; she had left in such a rush that she'd left her bed unmade, and her great white nightcap was lying there on the pillow.

"Good!" said the wolf to himself. "Now I know just what to do."

So he shut the door, pulled the grandmother's nightcap over his ears and all the way down his great forehead to his eyes, then stretched out in the bed and drew the curtains.

In the meantime, little Blanchette traveled quietly on her way, amusing herself here and there, as little girls do, by picking Easter daisies, watching the birds making their nests, and running after butterflies that fluttered in the sunshine.

At last, she arrived at the door of her grandmother's house. *Knock, knock!*

"Who is there?" said the wolf, softening his rough voice as best he could.

"It's me, Granny — your Little Golden Hood. I've brought you a nice big piece of cake for your Sunday treat tomorrow."

"Press your finger on the latch, then push, and the door will open."

"Why, you've got a cold, Granny," she said as she came into the room.

"Ahem!" the wolf replied, pretending to cough. "Well, maybe a little. Shut the door properly now, my little lamb. Put your basket on the table, and then take off your frock and come and lie down beside me. We'll rest for a while together."

The good child removed her frock but kept her underwear and the golden hood on her head. When she saw what a strange figure her granny cut in bed, the poor thing was astonished.

"Oh!" she said, "you look so much like Friend Wolf!"

"That's just because of my nightcap, child," the wolf said.

"And oh, what hairy arms you've got, Grandmother!"

"All the better to hug you with, my child."

"And goodness, what a big tongue you've got, Grandmother!"

"All the better for talking to you, child."

"But really, what a mouthful of great white teeth you have, Grandmother!"

"That's for crunching up little children!" snarled the wolf — and he turned and opened his jaws wide to swallow up Blanchette.

She quickly lowered her head, crying, "Mamma! Mamma!" and the wolf's teeth missed their aim and only caught her little hood.

Then — oh deary, deary me! — he drew back, crying out and shaking his head as if he had swallowed red-hot coals. Because that little fire-colored hood had burned his tongue all the way back, deep down into his throat. The hood, you see, was made with witchy magic — the kind that in old days was used for casting spells of invisibility or protection.

So there was the wolf with his throat burned, jumping off the bed and trying to find the door, howling and yowling as if all the dogs in the country were at his heels. Just at this moment Blanchette's grandmother arrived, returning home from the town with her long herb-sack empty on her shoulder.

"Ah, you rascal!" she cried when she saw the wolf. "Now just you wait there!" — but the maddened wolf, desperate to find his way to water to cool his burning mouth and throat, sprang toward the doorway. But that old granny was fast: she quickly opened her sack wide and held it across the opening; the wolf dashed in, headfirst. So he was the one who was caught now, swallowed right up like a letter in the mouth of a postbox.

The brave old woman closed her sack and ran outside to empty it into the well. And that scoundrel of a wolf, still howling, tumbled in and was quite drowned.

"Ah, you devil! You thought you would gobble up my little granddaughter! Well, tomorrow I'll make her a muff from your skin, and you yourself shall be gobbled up, because we'll give your carcass to the dogs."

The grandmother returned inside to dress poor Blanchette, who was still trembling with fear in the bed.

"Well," she said to her, "and where would you be now, darling, without my little hood?" She made the child eat half of her cake and drink a good glass of wine, and then she took her by the hand and led her back home again. Her mother scolded her when she found out what had happened, but Blanchette promised over and over that she would never again stop to talk to a wolf, and at last she was forgiven. And Blanchette, the Little Golden Hood, forever afterward kept her word.

In most of the many versions of the story of Little Red Riding Hood (or Little Red Cap, in the variant by the Brothers Grimm), the little girl's grandmother is presented as a passive character — and often a dead one, frail and easily overcome and swallowed up by the big bad wolf. This wonderful and surprisingly little-known revisioning of that story, originally told by French writer and folklorist Charles Marelle in 1888, offers us a granny with agency. This quick-thinking old woman is perfectly capable of trapping the wolf on her own, so that there is no need, as in most versions of the story, for a huntsman — or for any other man — to save them. And, much more interestingly, it presents us with a granny who also happens to be a witch: a witch who is so old that she can't remember her age anymore, and a witch who is thought of by her community as a "good old woman" — not as malevolent or cursed.

It's the mother who sends Little Golden Hood off on her first solo foray into the woods, and so initiates the first stage of her long journey into self-reliant adulthood — but it's the formidable old granny who shows the girl how to survive it. This particular granny-witch is an herbalist who sells her herbs in town, but she is also the kind of witch who can imbue a simple garment with protective power. She had always foreseen the possibility of danger for the girl and had protected her from an early age by giving her the gift of a talisman, in the form of a golden hood.

Even though she and her magic are presented as perfectly benign, you nevertheless wouldn't want to mess with this witch, and quite probably it's the whiff of danger that's associated with crossing a witch in so many old fairy tales that makes her all the more attractive to us as a role model. By the time we've reached midlife, women today are bone-tired of being messed with, and so the idea that we might find ways to be fierce and to protect ourselves has its resonances, for sure. And in this story, it's particularly gratifying that a grandmother who is so old that she can't remember her age still has the power to overcome the big bad wolf.

Gifts for the Young

In most Indigenous cultures around the world, teaching and guiding the young is the business of elders. Here in the West that tradition petered out long ago, though it's a fine thing that intergenerational mentoring, especially in schools, seems to be having a renaissance now. As we grow older, we accrue so much wisdom and experience — as well as networks — that can be shared with young people; mentorship puts those resources to good use, and so the relationship can sustain elders as well as their mentees.

"It takes a village to raise a child," so the saying goes, and the presence in their lives of a range of reliable elders can certainly expand the ways in which a child might experience care and protection. No parents can provide a child with every bit of attention and guidance they'll need to flourish as they grow, and so a congregation of trusted "aunts" and "uncles" (blood relatives or close friends), grandparents, godparents, neighbors, and teachers can offer a diversity of worldviews, draw out young people's gifts, and inspire in them a deep curiosity about the many different ways that humans have of being in the world. Adolescents need adults — other than their parents — with whom they can flex their adulting muscles as they grow, and with whom they can safely try on new skins.

There are many delightful examples in European folklore of elder women who play a critical part in positively transforming a young person's life and helping them to find their way in the world. They might emerge out of the dark heart of the frightening forest with precisely the gift the protagonist needs to change the course of a challenging story. Sometimes, they'll make apprentices of them, instructing them in the difficult but necessary work of discernment and order, developing in them the character traits (usually involving kindness, hard work, and cooperation with the other-than-human world) that will enable them to lead a fruitful and useful life. But they are also living examples, for the young girls under their wing, of the power of women's ways of knowing and being in the world, exhibiting and teaching relationality, empathy, and a fierce compassion for others. From egg-wielding henwives to dangerous old women in the woods, it's a pleasure to introduce you to a few of them in the pages that follow.

The Goose Girl at the Well

Beyond seven rivers and across seven seas, an old woman lived in a pretty little house on a heath, nestled amid stark granite mountains. She had a flock of white geese for company, and every morning, she hobbled over a hill and down into the forest beyond, to fill a bundle and two baskets with grass and wild fruits to feed them. And although her round face was scoured by age, each day she would carry it all home on her back. If ever she met someone along the way, she would greet them with: "Good day, my dear countryman — and what a fine day it is! Ah! You're wondering why I'm dragging this heavy load around with me — but, well, we all have our burdens to bear, don't we?" Despite her cheerfulness, people really would rather not meet her: because she lived alone and outside the village, they thought her eccentric and strange. So if they could, they would take a roundabout way to avoid her house and, as so often happens, parents did what they could to make their children wary of her. "She's a witch," they said. "Beware — there are claws beneath her gloves!"

One morning, a handsome young man was traveling through the forest. The birds were singing, the forest floor hosted a dance of light and shade, and he was full of gladness. He passed into a large clearing and happened upon the old woman, kneeling on the ground; she was busy cutting the grass with a sickle. She had already gathered a huge pile in the center of a large cloth, and two baskets, brimming with wild apples and pears, stood next to her. A wide smile spread across the deep wrinkles of her face.

"My goodness," he said, "are you here alone? But then how could you possibly carry such a heavy load home!"

"Well, simply because I must, sir," she answered. "Rich folks' children don't need to do such backbreaking work, but I have no other choice." She struggled to her feet. "Though perhaps today you could help me?" she asked. "You seem to be young and strong; this load would be a trifle for you to bear. My house isn't so very far from here — it's just over the hill, on the heath beyond."

He was a kind young man and perhaps a little embarrassed by her comments, and so he said, "My father's no peasant — he's actually a wealthy count — but I'll prove to you that it's not only peasants who can carry a heavy burden. Let me take that load of grass from you."

"Thank you," said the old woman. "I'd be very glad of your help, but won't you take the apples and pears as well? It'll take no more than an hour or so to walk to my house."

The young man, who had imagined a much shorter excursion, looked decidedly disconcerted, but the old woman knotted the cloth to create a bundle, tied it onto his back, and hung a basket from each of his arms.

"See, it's quite light!" she said, with a grin.

He staggered and pulled a rueful face. "The bundle feels as if it were full of rocks, and the fruit in the baskets is heavy as lead! I'm sure I can barely breathe."

He made to put the baskets down, but she wouldn't allow it. "Just look at you," she mocked him, hands on her black-skirted old hips. "A strapping young gentleman such as yourself can't seem to manage the burden that I, an old woman, carry

every day! You're full of fine words, but when it comes to actually doing the work, you want to take to your heels. Well,
we can't have that. What are you standing around for? Come
on — off we go."

So off they went, and as long as they were walking on level
ground it was just about bearable, but when they started to
climb the hill that led to the old woman's house, stones began
to shift and roll under the young man's feet as if they were
alive. Beads of perspiration gathered on his forehead and ran
down his back. "Old woman," he said, "I can't go on. I really
must rest a little."

"Not here," she said. "You can rest when we've arrived,
but for now you must keep going. Who knows what good it
might do you?"

The young man stopped, irritated now. "Old woman, you
are shameless!" he said, and tried to throw off the baskets and
the bundle — but they stuck fast to him, as if they'd taken
root in his flesh. He turned and twisted, but however hard he
tried, he couldn't shake them off. The old woman laughed and
danced delightedly around him.

"Don't get angry, dear sir," she said. "Your face is as red
as a turkey's! Carry your burden patiently and I'll repay your
kindness handsomely when we reach my home."

He had no choice but to struggle on, and the more he
shuffled and stumbled, the nimbler the old woman seemed
to become. Then, without warning, she sprang up onto the
young man's back and seated herself on top of the bundle
of grass. However scrawny she might have looked, she was
heavier than the stoutest country lass. The young man's knees
trembled, and he tried to stop again, but she hit him gently
around the legs with her stick, as if he were a horse. Then
finally, as he was on the verge of passing out, they arrived at
her house.

When the geese caught sight of the old woman they stretched out their necks, flapped their wings, and ran cackling to meet her. Behind them came a goose girl, stocky, tall, and outrageously ugly.

"Good mother, what happened to you? You've been away such a long time!" she said.

"Well, my dear daughter, I met this kind gentleman, who has carried my burdens for me all the way home. And, imagine, he even took me on his back when I was tired. We've had such a merry journey home, cracking jokes all the way." She slid down and removed the bundle from the young man's back and the baskets from his arms. "Now, why don't you take a seat on the bench by the door and rest. You've certainly earned your wages, and indeed, they will not be wanting." The young man staggered gratefully to the bench and sat there wiping the sweat from his face.

"Now, my dear," the old woman said to her daughter, "off you go into the house. It's really not becoming for you to be left alone with a young gentleman, and we mustn't pour oil onto the fire, in case he should fall in love with you."

The young count wasn't sure whether to laugh or cry. *A woman like that,* he thought to himself, shaking his head tiredly, *could never touch my heart.* The old woman followed her daughter into the house, and he stretched out on the bench beneath the boughs of a heavily laden apple tree. Lush, green meadow speckled with cowslips, fragrant with wild thyme and a thousand other flowers, surrounded the house on all sides. A clear, sun-sparkled brook rippled on by; the geese honked at each other, wandered here and there, and paddled in the water. *It's quite delightful here,* he thought, *but I'm so tired I can hardly keep my eyes open...,* and in seconds he was fast asleep.

Shortly afterward, the old woman shook him awake. "Sit up, young man; you can't stay here! Well, now: I know I've treated you harshly, but at least you're still alive. You clearly have money and land already, so I have something else for you, to reward you for all that hard work." She placed into his hands a little book, with a single sparkling emerald embedded in its cover. "Here. Make sure you take good care of it; it'll bring you good luck."

So the young man, who by now had quite recovered from his exertions, thanked the old woman and set off again on his travels without a backward glance. For three days and nights he wandered through the forest, till finally he found his way out by following a path that led him to a large town. The people there directed him to the royal palace, where he was brought to the king and queen in their throne room. He dropped to one knee and then, having nothing else of value to offer, took the emerald book from his pocket and laid it at the queen's feet.

The queen told him to rise and hand her the book, but she had hardly begun to examine it when a small pearl rolled out of it and fell to the floor. She fainted; a great commotion ensued, and guards rushed in to seize the young man. As they were dragging him away to prison, the queen opened her eyes and ordered that he should be released. She sent everyone out of the throne room — even the king — so that she could speak with him in private.

The queen looked down at the book again and began to weep. "Once," she told him, "I had three daughters. The youngest was so beautiful: her cheeks were as soft and pink as apple blossom, and her hair was as bright as a sunbeam. And when she cried, she wept tiny pearls instead of tears. It was a strange gift." She sighed. "When my youngest was fifteen, the king asked all three of them to come to the throne room. You should have seen how everyone stared when our youngest entered! It was as if, they said, the sun itself had come into the room. Then my husband spoke to them. 'Daughters,' he said,

'I'm not long for this world, and I need to decide how to split my kingdom and wealth between the three of you. I know, of course, that all of you love me, but the one who loves me best shall receive the greatest portion.'"

The queen shook her head sadly. "And of course, each of them in turn said that she loved him best. 'But won't you tell me,' he said, 'just how *much* you love me, so I can judge which of you truly loves me the most?' Well, the oldest of our daughters replied that she loved her father as dearly as the sweetest sugar, and the second said that she loved her father as much as her prettiest dress — but our youngest daughter was silent. So the king asked her directly how much she loved him. She replied that she could find nothing with which to compare her love for him — but he insisted. She must name something. And so, finally, she said, 'The best food doesn't please me without salt, and so I love you, Father, like salt.'

"Well, that only made him furious. He said that if she loved him like salt, then it was with salt that she'd be repaid for that love. So he divided the kingdom between our two elder daughters, had a sack of salt bound to the youngest's back, and ordered two servants to lead her into the wild forest and leave her there. When she was taken from us, she cried so much that the road to the forest was strewn with the pearls that fell from her eyes. We all begged the king not to do it, but nothing we could say would change his mind. Not long afterward, he grew sorry for what he'd done and had the whole forest searched, but no trace of her was ever found."

The queen wiped the tears from her face. "I'd given up hope of ever seeing her again, but when I opened your little emerald book, the pearl that fell from it was exactly the same kind as those that used to fall from my daughter's eyes. And so tell me — however did you come by that pearl?"

The young man told the queen about his dealings with the strange old woman — who must surely be a witch, he said — but he had no news to offer of her youngest daughter. Nevertheless, when the queen told him the full story, the king agreed that if they could find the old woman, she might have something to say that would help them to understand what had happened to the young princess. And so the three of them set off together, along the road that led into the forest.

A little later the same day, the old woman and the goose girl were sitting beside the fire at their spinning wheels. Transfixed as they were by the rotation of the wheels and the constant whirr of the shuttles, the evening closed in with hardly a word passed between them. Then there was a rustling at the window, and two fiery eyes peered in through the glass. It was a huge owl, and it opened its short, sharp beak and cried "Uhu!" three times.

The old woman said to her daughter, "Well, my dear, it seems that it's time for you to go out and do your work." The girl rose from her stool, and off she went into the night. She crossed the meadows and walked on into the valley beyond, and at last she came to a well that was guarded by three great oak trees. The moon hung full and white above the mountain ridges; you could have threaded a needle by its light. She carefully removed a skin that covered her face, then bent down to the well and began to wash herself. When she had finished, she dipped the skin into the water, then laid it down on the grass so that it could dry in the moonlight.

But how the goose girl had changed, without that skin! Her eyes shone bright as the stars, her cheeks were as pink as apple blossom, and her golden hair spread out now like sunbeams across her shoulders. But there was no joy in her metamorphosis: she sat by the well and wept bitterly, and her tears fell to the ground like pearls. She would have sat there longer if it hadn't been for a sharp crack in the branches of one of the great oak trees nearby. She sprang up like a young doe at the sound of a hunter's shot and, as a cloud slid across the face of the moon and darkened the world, she slipped on the skin-mask and vanished like a candle blown out in a breeze.

She ran back to the cottage and began to tell the old woman everything that had happened, but she held up her hand, laughed kindly, and said, "I already know it all." She sat the girl down by the hearth, set a new log on the fire, then fetched a broom and began to sweep the room. "Everything must be clean and sweet, you see," she said.

"But Mother," the girl said, perplexed, "why are you sweeping up so late at night? Are we expecting guests?"

"Do you know what time it is?" the old woman asked.

"Somewhere between eleven and midnight, I should think," the girl replied.

The old woman nodded. "It's three years to the hour since you came to me, and now your time here has come to an end."

The girl looked up at her, horrified. "But where shall I go? I have no friends and no home to go to. Please don't send me away. Haven't I always done everything you asked?"

The old woman refused to be drawn on the matter, and said simply, "My stay here is over too, but when I leave, the house needs to be clean. So don't stop me from doing my work. And don't worry — there'll be a roof to shelter you, and the wages I'll give you will be more than you need. For now, just go to the chamber and take the skin from your face. Put on the silk gown you were wearing when you first came here, then wait quietly till I call you."

In the meantime, the king and queen and the young man had been traveling through the forest, looking for the way to the old woman's cottage. The young man decided to go for a walk in the moonlight and strayed quite a distance away from the king and queen. Inevitably, he lost his way and decided to spend the night beneath the stars, before trying to find them again in the morning. He climbed into a great oak tree and, as he looked down at the pale, shining landscape beneath him, spotted the goose girl who lived with the old woman walking toward the well in the clearing below. He watched, astonished, as she took off her skin and let down her long golden hair: she was the most beautiful girl he'd ever seen. Hardly daring to breathe, he leaned forward to see her more clearly, and — CRACK! — the branch on which he was leaning snapped, and by the time he'd recovered himself, she'd vanished into the night.

The young count scrambled down the oak tree and hurried away in the direction she'd come from. After a little while, much to his delight, he saw the old woman's house there before him — and then he spotted two figures picking their way across the heath toward the cottage. It was the king and queen, who had noticed the light spilling from its small windows. He ran across and told them everything he'd just seen by the well. When he told them about the pearls he'd seen dripping from the young woman's eyes, they were certain that this girl was their lost daughter.

Hearts filled with hope, they walked on to the cottage together; the geese were sleeping soundly by the door, heads tucked beneath their wings. They peered in through a window, but all they saw was the old woman sitting quietly by the fire, spinning. The room was perfectly clean and quite bare, and the girl was nowhere to be seen.

The king knocked softly at the window, and the old woman called out, "Come on in. I already know who you are." As they walked into the parlor, the old woman said,

"You know, you could have saved yourself a very long journey, if you hadn't so unjustly driven your daughter away
three years ago. Well, here you are, and no harm has come
to her; she's lived with me here for three years, caring for my
geese. And as for the two of you: well, I think you've been
quite sufficiently punished by the grief and anxiety you've
suffered for all this time."

The old woman eased herself up from her stool and
shuffled across the room to the door of the chamber. "Come
out, little daughter," she said. The door creaked open and
out stepped the princess in her silken gown, eyes sparkling
and hair glowing in the firelight. She fell into her parents'
arms and all three of them wept for joy. The young man
stood to one side, watching, and when she caught sight of
him her face grew hot — though, really, she had no idea why.
The king took his daughter's hand and said to her, "My dear
child, I've given my kingdom to your sisters. What can I possibly offer you now?"

"She needs nothing," said the old woman. "I've been gathering up all the pearls she's wept on your account over the
past three years. They're the most precious of pearls, finer
by far than those found in the sea, and certainly worth more
than your entire kingdom. And I'll give her my house too, to
repay her for all her service and companionship." The princess
hugged the old woman and thanked her, and soon she and her
parents were talking and catching up on news — and every
now and again, the princess and the young man would glance
at each other, then turn away, blushing.

Silently, and without anyone noticing, the old woman
withdrew from their circle. She picked up her spinning wheel
and simply melted away. The small company finally grew
quiet, and when they looked around them, the small cottage

had been transformed into a splendid hall. Servants ran everywhere, preparing tables for a feast; fires crackled in two great hearths and a table on a raised dais was covered with golden platters that glinted in the candlelight. Everywhere there were white flowers, as if to celebrate a coming wedding.

But it's there that we have to leave them, for the rest of the story has been forgotten. I shall always believe that the beautiful princess married the fine young count, and that they lived together happily in that palace for a very long time. Whether, as local people said, the old woman's snow-white geese were actually young girls who'd been taken under her protection, and whether they now took back their human forms and stayed there as handmaids to the princess, I don't really know. But I suspect it. This much is clear: that old woman was no witch, but a wise woman who meant well. And I wouldn't be at all surprised if she had been the one, at the princess's birth, to give her the gift of weeping pearls instead of tears.

This old German story offers a telling lesson: in its opening paragraph, we're shown how a wise old woman might find herself taken instead for a wicked witch, through fear of difference and a willingness to succumb to stereotypes and cultural prejudices. Even though the old woman is polite to everyone she meets, she must be a witch because — well, she's an old woman, and a bit eccentric, and she lives alone and outside the village. These few lines are a haunting echo of the fate of so many women — not just in folklore, but in our history.

This characterful wise woman is a mentor or teacher not only to the homeless princess but also to all the others in the story. First, she takes in the princess, keeps her safe until the right time comes for a reunion with her grieving parents, and sets her the task of caring for geese to ensure she doesn't grow up to be idle and pampered. She contrives an introduction to the long-suffering young count — after testing him to see if he might be a worthy suitor. When she finds him to be kind, well-mannered, and (mostly) willing, she rewards him with a magical object that triggers the release of the princess from the old woman's custody, and at the same time sets him firmly on the path to future happiness. The old woman also guides the king and queen: first, she keeps their daughter hidden from them for three years, while the king begins to grasp the seriousness of his error, and anger turns to grief and regret. When finally she meets them, she offers up a heavily weighted basketful of straight talking about their parental failings — but then she helps them, because she sees that they have changed.

Not all of us will have been fortunate enough to benefit from such wise guidance in our youth, but the significance of such a mentor lies in their ability to see us more clearly than we can see ourselves — particularly on difficult days, when we feel lost, hopeless, or worthless, or compelled for our own safety to hide our light from the world. They might provide us with the uncomplicated gifts of presence and belief — and these, of course, are gifts that grandparents have offered throughout human history. As we ourselves grow into elderhood, then, we'd do well to cultivate the qualities of cleverness and compassion that this old woman displays: who knows when we might happen across a repudiated princess, a young man ready for love, or a father needing to redeem himself?

Nevertheless, this old woman is certainly no pushover: she's

quite capable of a trick or two to ensure that the story pro-
gresses as she thinks it should. So she sets up a witty little game
to test the young man's mettle — but when her high standards
are met, she rewards him. In a world that often seems hard
and lonely, this wise old woman's teachings about kindness and
willingness to help others couldn't be timelier.

La Befana

In Italian folklore, the Befana is an old woman who delivers gifts to children throughout the country on Epiphany Eve (the night of the fifth of January), just as Santa Claus or Father Christmas does in other parts of Europe. She is usually depicted as a hag riding a broomstick; she wears a black shawl and is covered in soot, because she slips down the chimney of a house to enter it. She carries a basket filled with sweets and other presents, which she leaves in children's stockings. Some snippets of folklore have her sweeping the floors with her broom before she leaves, in order to sweep away the troubles of the past year. In other traditions, it's said that she sweeps away the troubles of the past year for the entire country, as she flies through the air on her broomstick.

The Christian story of her origins tells us that the Befana was in her cottage sweeping the floor when, through her window, she saw a bright star in the night sky. Soon afterward the Three Kings paid her a visit; they were lost and asked her for directions. They told her that they were following the star and were bringing gifts to honor a baby who would be found in Bethlehem. The Befana didn't go with them on their journey, because she felt that she couldn't leave her work unfinished. But after they'd left, she regretted her decision and changed her mind. She ran after them with her broom and a basket of gifts for the holy child, but she couldn't catch up with them. It's said that the Befana is still looking for that baby today, and leaves gifts for other children as she continues on her long and everlasting journey.

Although these stories have Christian overtones, it's believed that she might originally have been based on a Roman goddess called Sabine (also known as Strenia and Bastrina). In Sicily, the Befana is said to live in the beautiful limestone Grattàra Cave, the water in which was believed by local people to be therapeutic, so associating her with healing. The Befana is celebrated in several festivals throughout Italy at Epiphany; activities include dancing and juggling, singing in the streets — and the appearance of hundreds of women dressed as the Befana, who hand out sweets to children.

Vasilisa the Fair

RUSSIA

Once upon a time, a merchant and his wife lived happily with their daughter. Her name was Vasilisa, and she was so very beautiful that the people in her village called her Vasilisa the Fair. But sadly, when Vasilisa was only eight years old, her mother died. On her deathbed, she called her daughter over to her, took a small cloth doll out from beneath her quilt, and said: "My darling Vasilisa, I'm dying. I'll leave you my blessing — and also this doll. If you keep her with you always, nothing terrible can happen to you. But be sure you don't show her to anyone else or tell anyone about her. If ever you're in trouble, give her food and ask her for advice. After she has eaten, she'll tell you how to manage whatever predicament you find yourself in." She kissed her daughter and then she died.

After his wife's death, the merchant mourned for a good while, but finally he thought of taking a second wife who might also be a mother to Vasilisa. He was a fine-looking man and there was no shortage of potential brides, but he developed a particularly strong liking for a widow. She was no longer young, and she had two daughters of about the same age as Vasilisa. Well, he married her; but it soon became clear that he had made a mistake, because she was not a good mother to his daughter.

Vasilisa's stepmother and stepsisters envied her because of her beauty. They piled as much work as they could on her, trying to make her grow thin and ugly, and to coarsen her skin by exposure to wind and sun. So the child lived a hard life, but she did all that was asked of her without complaining. And she grew more and more beautiful, while her stepmother and her daughters grew uglier because of their spite.

It was the doll who helped Vasilisa to endure her situation. The girl ate little of the food that was given to her but kept the tastiest morsels for the doll. When everyone else had gone to bed, she would lock herself up in her basement bedroom, give the doll some food, and say, "Little doll, eat now, and listen to my troubles. I'm here in my own father's house, but my life is hard. My stepmother is cruel to me. Please tell me what I should do to make my life bearable."

The doll would give her sound advice, console her, and then do all her morning chores for her. She sent Vasilisa out for a walk while she tidied all the flower beds, brought coal into the house, filled water jugs, and heated the hearthstone for cooking. She also taught Vasilisa herb-lore. So, thanks to the doll that her mother had given her, she had a happy enough life and the years passed swiftly by.

As Vasilisa grew up, all the young men of the village dreamed of marrying her. But nobody had any interest in her stepmother's daughters, so the stepmother grew more spiteful than ever and told Vasilisa's suitors: "I absolutely will not allow my youngest daughter to marry before the elders." She sent them all away and, to demonstrate how pleased she was with herself, she beat Vasilisa soundly.

It happened then that Vasilisa's father had to go away on a long, long trip, so the stepmother decided that while he was gone they would go to live in a new house near a dense, dark forest. In the forest there was a meadow, and in the meadow there was a hut, and in the hut lived a mysterious, wild old woman called Baba Yaga. This old woman would allow no one to approach her house, and she had a reputation for roasting and eating men as if they were no more than chickens. Knowing Baba Yaga's reputation, and hoping to put Vasilisa in harm's way, the stepmother took to sending her alone into the wood on one pretext or another; but she always came back perfectly safe, because the doll showed her how to avoid stumbling across Baba Yaga's hut.

One evening in autumn, the stepmother gave all three girls a task to complete. One was to make lace, the other was to sew a stocking, and Vasilisa was to spin. The stepmother put out all the fires in the house and left only one candle burning where the girls were at work. She whispered to her eldest daughter that, when the candle burned out, she should take up another candle as if to light it from the dying flame of the old — but she should instead put the original candle out, and make it look like an accident. Then she went to bed.

Vasilisa and her stepsisters worked on. The solitary candle burned down; the eldest stepsister took up a new candle and went to light it from the spluttering flame. She stood with her back to Vasilisa, so that she would not be able to see what was happening — and, as she had been instructed, she put the old candle out before she could light the new. The room fell immediately into darkness.

"Whatever shall we do now?" the sisters said. "There's no fire in the house and our work isn't finished. We'd better go to get fire from Baba Yaga; she's the only neighbor we have."

"I'm not going," said the eldest sister who was making lace. "I can see well enough by the light of my shiny needles."

"I'm not going either," said the second; "my knitting needles give me light enough too. You must go, Vasilisa. Go to Baba Yaga and don't come back without fire."

Vasilisa went to her room, gave her doll some meat and drink, and said: "Little doll, eat now, and listen to my troubles. They're sending me to Baba Yaga for fire, but the Baba will certainly eat me."

So the little doll ate, and her eyes began to glitter like two bright lamps. She said, "Fear nothing, dear Vasilisa. Do what they say, but take me along too. If I'm with you, Baba Yaga can do you no harm." So Vasilisa put the doll into her pocket and set off nervously into the dark forest.

After she had been walking for a good while, a knight on horseback galloped by. His cloak was white, and also his horse and its reins, and as he vanished among the trees the dark night began to fade into dawn. She carried on, walking tirelessly until another horseman overtook her. This one was dressed all in red, and his horse was red too; as he passed her, the sun rose. Vasilisa walked on through the day and the night and all through the next day too. The following evening, she arrived at the meadow where Baba Yaga's hut stood. The fence around the hut was made from human bones, and glaring skulls with gaping jaws were set on its stakes. Instead of a gate, there were feet; instead of bolts there were hands, and instead of a lock there was a bony mouth with sharp teeth.

Vasilisa grew stone-cold with fright, and started as a third horseman rode by. He was dressed all in black, on a jet-black horse. He vanished abruptly, as though the earth had swallowed him up, and night fell. But the darkness didn't last long, because the empty eye sockets in all the skulls on the fence began to glow red as fire. All at once, a terrible noise was heard all through the forest. The tree boughs creaked and the dry leaves crackled — and Baba Yaga appeared. She flew through the sky in a mortar, brandishing a pestle; a broom behind her swept away every trace of her path. At the door of her hut she stopped, sniffed all the way around it, and cried out, "Fee, fo, fi, fum — I smell the blood of a young woman! Who is there?"

Shuddering with dread, Vasilisa stepped up to her, bowed low to the ground, and said, "Grandmother, I am here. My stepsisters sent me to you to ask for fire."

"Did they indeed?" said Baba Yaga, raising a white, bushy eyebrow. "Well, if you stay with me and work for me, I will give you your fire. If you don't, I'll eat you up." Then she strode to the door and cried out: "Ho! My strong bolts, draw back; my strong door, spring open!" The door sprang open at once and Baba Yaga went inside, whistling and whirring; tentatively, Vasilisa followed her.

When the door had closed behind them, Baba Yaga said to Vasilisa: "I'm hungry. Bring me whatever you find in the oven."

So Vasilisa went outside again, lit a lamp from the fire inside the skulls on the fence, and came back in to fetch food out of the giant oven for Baba Yaga. There was enough of it for ten men. From out of the cellar she fetched beer, mead, and wine. Baba Yaga ate and drank almost everything — and all that was left for Vasilisa was a little bit of soup, a crust of bread, and a morsel of pork.

Baba Yaga lay down to sleep and said: "In the morning when I go away, you must clean the courtyard, sweep the room, get the dinner ready, do the washing, go to the field to fetch a quarter of oats, and sift it all out. See that everything is done before I come home — otherwise I'll eat you up." As soon as she'd finished speaking, she fell fast asleep and began to snore.

Vasilisa put the small amount of food that was left in front of her doll and said, "Little doll, eat now and listen to my troubles. Baba Yaga has set me so many tasks, and she's threatening to eat me up if I don't carry them all out in time. Please help me!"

"Don't worry, Vasilisa. Eat and go to sleep, for the morning is wiser than the evening."

Very early the next morning, Vasilisa awoke. Baba Yaga was already up, and she stood staring out of the window. The glimmer in the eyes of the skulls had dimmed, the white horseman raced by — and all at once the new day dawned. Baba Yaga stepped out into the courtyard and whistled: the mortar, the pestle, and the broom appeared. The red horseman came by, and the sun rose. Baba Yaga climbed into the mortar and flew on her way, driving it with the pestle and removing all traces of her path with the broom.

Vasilisa took a little time to explore Baba Yaga's house, marveling at her wealth; then she wondered where she should begin. But all the work was already finished, and the doll had sifted out the very last of the ears of oats.

"Oh, my dear friend!" said Vasilisa. "You've helped me again, in my great need."

"Now you have only to get dinner ready," the doll said, and she clambered back into Vasilisa's pocket. "Do that now, then sit here quietly and wait."

Vasilisa laid a cloth on the table and waited quietly for Baba Yaga. Dusk arrived; the black horseman rode by and abruptly it grew dark — but, as ever, the eyes in the skulls glowed red with fire. The trees shuddered, the leaves crackled; Baba Yaga flew in, and Vasilisa met her at the door.

"Is it all done?" Baba Yaga asked.

"Yes, Grandmother — look!" said Vasilisa.

Baba Yaga looked round everywhere and was rather angry that she could see nothing to find fault with. "Very well." Then she said: "My faithful servants, friends of my heart! Store up

my oats!" — and three pairs of hands appeared out of nowhere, snatched up the oats, and carried them away.

Baba Yaga had her supper, and before she went to sleep,
she said to Vasilisa: "Tomorrow, do just the same as you did
today, but also take the poppy-hay that's laid out on my field
and clean from it every trace of soil. Somebody, out of spite,
has mixed earth into my fine hay." And as soon as she had finished speaking, she turned her face to the wall and was snoring
in a flash.

Vasilisa fed her doll, who said — just as she had the day
before — "Lie down to sleep, little Vasilisa, for the morning is
wiser than the evening. Everything shall be done."

Next morning, Baba Yaga rose from her bed and stood
staring for a while out of the window, then went out into the
courtyard and whistled; the mortar, the broom, and the pestle
appeared; the red horseman rode by and the sun rose. Baba
Yaga sat herself down in the mortar and flew off, sweeping
away her traces just as she had before.

Vasilisa made everything ready with the help of her doll
and completed all the tasks she had been set. Then Baba Yaga
came home, looked at everything that had been done, and
said: "Ho, my faithful servants, friends of my heart! Make me
some poppy-oil." The three pairs of hands appeared just as
they had the night before, took hold of the clean, dried pop-
pies, and carried them off.

Baba Yaga sat down to supper and Vasilisa sat silently in
front of her. "Why don't you speak?" Baba Yaga asked. "Why
are you sitting there as if you had no tongue?"

"I didn't presume to speak to you, Grandmother, but if I
might, then I should like to ask you some questions."

"You may ask, but bear in mind that not every question
turns out well: too knowing is too old."

"Still, I should like to ask you about some of the things I've seen. On my way to you I met a white horseman, in a white cloak, on a white horse. Who was he?"

"The bright day."

"Then a red horseman, on a red horse, in a red cloak, overtook me. Who was he?"

"The red sun."

"What's the meaning of the black horseman who overtook me as I reached your door, Grandmother?"

"That was the dark night. Those three are my faithful servants."

Vasilisa thought of the three pairs of hands, but she had an instinct that this was a question she should not ask.

"Why don't you ask me something else?" Baba Yaga said, staring intently at Vasilisa.

"I know enough, now — for, as you say yourself, 'too knowing is too old.'"

"It's a very good thing that you asked only about things you saw in the courtyard, and not about things here inside my house. I don't like people to tell stories about me, and I eat up those who are too curious. But now it's my turn to ask a question of you. However did you manage to do all the work I gave you?"

"By my mother's blessing," Vasilisa replied.

"Ah, then you must leave here as quickly as you can, blessed daughter, for no one blessed may stay with me!" Baba Yaga shoved Vasilisa out of the door, took a skull with burning eyes from the fence, put it on a staff, and gave it to her. "Now you have fire for your stepmother's daughters — since that, so they said, was why they sent you here."

Vasilisa ran home as fast as she could, helped on her way by the light from the skull's eyes, but the fire inside it went out when dawn arrived. She reached her stepmother's house on the evening of the following day. She looked at the skull and thought of throwing it away, but then a hollow voice spoke from between its grinning teeth. It said to her: "Do not throw me away. Take me into your stepmother's house." There was no light in any window, so Vasilisa decided to go in. She was received in quite a friendly manner, though the two sisters looked a little surprised to see her; they told her that they had had no fire since she had gone away: nothing they did could seem to keep a log in the fireplace or a candle alight.

"Hopefully, your fire will burn!" said the stepmother.

They took the skull from Vasilisa — but the skull's glowing eyes locked onto the eyes of the stepmother and her daughters, and in no time their eyes burned out. Screaming, they tried to run away, but they couldn't escape the skull, whose red eyes followed them everywhere. By the time morning came, they were all burned to cinders; only Vasilisa was left unharmed.

Vasilisa buried the skull in the earth, locked up the house, and made her way into town. She asked an old woman if she would give her food and shelter until her father returned. The old woman agreed; the next day, Vasilisa said to her, "Mother, sitting here idle makes me feel dull. Please fetch me some of the very best flax; I should like to do some spinning."

The old woman brought some fine flax for her, and Vasilisa set herself to work. The skein she spun was as smooth and as fine as hair, and when she had enough yarn, she turned to her doll, who said: "Bring me some old comb from somewhere, an old spindle, an old shuttle, and some horse mane, and I will weave the thread you've spun."

Vasilisa went to bed, and while she was sleeping the doll made her a splendid spinning stool. By the end of the winter, all the yarn that Vasilisa spun had been woven into linen that was finer than any that had ever been seen before. When spring came, they bleached the linen, then Vasilisa said to the old woman: "Go now and sell the cloth, and keep the money for yourself."

When the old woman saw the cloth, she exclaimed: "Oh, my child! Nobody except the tsar deserves to wear such fine linen; I'll take it to court at once." So she traveled to the tsar's palace and walked up and down in front of it until the tsar noticed her.

"Old mother," he said, "what do you want?"

"Mighty tsar, I've brought you some wonderful cloth, which I couldn't possibly show to anyone but you."

The tsar ordered that the old woman should be given an audience, and when he looked at the linen that she held out before him, he admired it greatly. "What do you want for it?" he asked.

"It's priceless," she said. "I'll only give it to you as a gift."

The tsar was so taken with this that he sent her on her way with many rich rewards. He then wanted to have shirts made from the beautiful linen, but he couldn't find a seamstress skilled enough to undertake the work. He thought for a long time, and finally sent for the old woman again.

"If you can spin this cloth and weave it," he said to her, "perhaps you can make a shirt out of it too?"

"It wasn't me who spun and wove the linen," the old woman said. "It was a girl who's staying with me for a while."

"Well then, have her do this work for me."

The old woman went home and told Vasilisa everything; Vasilisa locked herself up in her little room, set to work, and didn't rest her hands again until, with the help of the doll, she had sewn a dozen fine shirts. The old woman took the shirts to the tsar while Vasilisa washed herself and combed her hair, dressed herself, and then sat down by the window to wait. After a while, one of the tsar's servants came into the house and said to her, "The tsar would like to see with his own eyes the artist who has sewn these fine shirts, and to reward her personally."

Vasilisa the Fair went to the tsar's palace and as soon as he set eyes on her, he fell deeply in love. "Fairest of maidens," he declared, "if you'll be my wife, I'll never part from you." The tsar took Vasilisa's white hands in his own and drew her to him, and he ordered that the bells should be rung at once for their wedding.

Vasilisa's father came back home soon afterward and was delighted by his daughter's good fortune. He stayed with her in the palace, along with the old woman. And the doll? Well, it remained forever in Vasilisa's pocket, of course. Just in case.

Baba Yaga, the archetypal Dangerous Old Woman, appears in many Slavic folk tales, as well as in the visual arts; the story of Vasilisa — of which there are several versions — is one of the most popular. In these stories, Baba Yaga typically flies around in a mortar, wielding a pestle; she lives deep in the dark forest in a hut that is usually described as standing on chicken legs — and so it can turn around, run around, and as a consequence might not always be found in exactly the place where you saw it last. Baba Yaga's domain, then, is the enchanted forest: a traditional symbol of transformation and also a place of considerable peril. But Baba Yaga's forest isn't just any old forest: it is also the Otherworld, the "land of the living dead," known in Russian folk tradition as "the thrice-nine kingdom." Although she's presented in so many folk tales as little more than a dangerous old witch, the suspicion that Baba Yaga would once have been a major deity is reflected in the names of her three faithful servants: the White Horseman, "my Bright Dawn"; the Red Horseman, "my Red Sun";

and the Black Horseman, "my Dark Midnight." They control daybreak, sunrise, and nightfall, showing us that she is associated with the cosmic order, ensuring that dawn, day, and night occur when they must.

Baba Yaga is a decidedly ambiguous character: a trait that is typical of many Mother Goddesses. This ambiguity — sometimes she's nice, sometimes she's not; sometimes she'll help you, sometimes she'll eat you — is characteristic of Jungian psychologist Erich Neumann's representation of the Great Mother Goddess archetype. For every positive, creative, Earth-enhancing force, he argued, there must be an opposing, destructive, "shadow" force. So the Great Mother archetype has two facets: the "Good Mother" but also the "Terrible Mother," who is usually imagined as a force of death and destruction. In the oldest mythic traditions, these two aspects almost always occur together. Baba Yaga is neither straightforwardly good nor straightforwardly evil: she's quite simply a force of nature. If you're the protagonist of a story in which she appears, you never quite know which face she's going to show to you; it depends on how you approach her, and most definitely on your response to the tasks that she'll set for you.

In a still-patriarchal world in which women's worth is so often assessed by how "nice" they are, Baba Yaga offers up a refreshingly different kind of role model. You don't mess with the Baba. And menopause especially isn't a time that can easily be defined by "niceness": for so many of us, it's a time of rising rage, of torched taboos, of giving fewer fucks. We're infinitely more Fury than fairy, more Medusa than Madonna — and perhaps that's why so many eldering women love Baba Yaga. She's fierce, she's elemental, and she takes neither nonsense nor prisoners. By the time we reach menopause, and certainly by the time we reach our elder years, we've had more than enough of all that.

In all the stories in which she appears, Baba Yaga's primary role is as an initiator: she is the one who tests the young men or girls who find their way to her. She's the agent of their inevitable — for better or for worse — transformation. To enter Baba Yaga's house, surrounded by symbols of death, is to submit to that initiatory experience. And the stakes are high: here, you risk everything. If you fail, the Baba will quite simply gobble you up — and so her testing should be responded to, just as Vasilisa does, with both humility and trepidation.

The essence of the tasks and testings that Baba Yaga typically arranges for Vasilisa-like characters is sorting: sorting good corn from bad, picking out the soil caught up in the poppy-hay. Such tasks are to be found in many folk and fairy tales; they require patience, focus, application, and very fine discrimination: useful skills to cultivate for adulthood. Baba Yaga asks Vasilisa to take care of her house and also to feed her, and by doing this work, Vasilisa in a sense is apprenticing herself to her. But, ultimately, it's fire that Vasilisa is seeking from Baba Yaga, and it's fire that she carries away with her. This fire is the ultimate agent of her transformation at the hands of this wonderfully feisty and powerful old woman: an alchemical burning away of the old to leave space for the new.

Glorious as Baba Yaga is, we shouldn't let her make us forget the old woman in the final act of this story. She's a quiet, straightforward counterpoint to the Baba, and decidedly more grandmotherly: a kind benefactor who provides Vasilisa with care and a safe place to live. She might be presented as a simple old woman, but she's sharp, nevertheless: she knows exactly how to engineer Vasilisa's marriage to the tsar, and is rewarded for her service with a place in Vasilisa's now-royal family.

The Little Old Lady of Kidwelly

WALES

The little old lady of Kidwelly
A seller of sweets is she;
Counts out ten for a halfpenny
But always eleven for me.
That was very good news for me, for me
Counts out ten for a halfpenny
But always eleven for me.

Habetrot and the Spinning Sisters

ENGLAND

Once upon a time — and a very good time it was, though it wasn't my time, or your time, nor anyone else's time that I know of, for that matter — a poor and busy woman had a beautiful young daughter. That daughter loved to be outside very much more than she loved indoor work. She loved wandering through the meadows and forests, talking to the flowers, learning the songs of local birds and the ways of woodland creatures. What she did not love was time spent at the spinning wheel or with the distaff onto which she was required to wind the fiber for hand spinning. Her mother was deeply frustrated by this, for in those days no girl had a chance of finding a good husband unless she was a fine spinner. So she coaxed, encouraged, and finally threatened her daughter — but all to no avail: the girl remained, in her mother's opinion, "an idle young fool."

One spring morning, the woman gave her daughter seven bundles of fiber. She firmly told her that she would accept no excuses: they must all be returned to her in three days, spun into perfectly even yarn. The girl noted the hard look in her mother's eye and knew that this time, failure would lead to dire consequences. She dressed her distaff and plied it as well as she could, but her hands were unused to the task, and by the evening of the second day only a very small part of her work

110

was completed. She could hardly sleep that night, and in the morning, after throwing aside the distaff in despair, she snuck out of the door and ran off into the fields, which were sparkling still with dew.

After a short while she reached a stream that bubbled out of a small wood and ran along the foot of a hill that was hedged with woodbine and wild roses. She settled down among the flowers and buried her face in her hands. When she looked up again, she saw an old woman there by the bank of the stream; she was perched on an enormous flat stone with a hole bored through the center of it; she was drawing out thread from a distaff that she held tightly under her arm. There was nothing very remarkable in her appearance, except that her lips were unusually thick and long. Curiosity got the better of the girl, and she walked over to the old woman, gave her a friendly greeting, and then asked, "What is it that makes you so long-lipped?"

"Spinning thread, my hinny," said the old woman, cheerfully. "I wet my fingers with my lips as I draw the thread from the distaff."

"Ah!" the girl said. "I see." And then she sighed. "I'm supposed to be spinning too, but it's all completely pointless. I have no skill at all. I'll never finish the task that my mother set me, and then who knows what will happen to me."

"Well then," said the old woman, "why don't you let me do your spinning for you?" Overjoyed, the girl ran home at once to fetch her bundle of fiber, and when she returned, she placed it in her new friend's hands. She asked her where she should go to collect the spun yarn that evening but received no reply; the old woman walked away from her and disappeared among the trees and bushes. The girl, bewildered, wandered about a little more and finally, exhausted from her troubled night, fell asleep by the side of the flat, holed stone.

When she woke up, she was surprised to find that darkness had gathered around her. Causleen, the evening star, was gleaming with a silvery light that was fading as the brightness of the full moon asserted itself. And then she was startled by the sound of a rough voice that seemed to issue from below the holed stone. She laid her ear to it and heard: "Hurry up, Scantlie Mab, for I've promised the yarn tonight and Habetrot always keeps her promise." The girl peered down through the hole in the stone and saw the old woman pacing up and down inside a deep cavern. She alone was standing, among a group of other old women — each of whom was seated on a great white river stone and busying herself with a distaff or spindle. They were a strange company, all dressed in black, with crisp white aprons, and their lips were disfigured like old Habetrot's. One of the sisterhood, who sat in a distant corner reeling the yarn, was marked in addition by a long hooked nose and gray eyes, which were so prominent that they seemed to be popping out of her head.

As the girl looked down in bemusement, she noted that it was this woman that Habetrot was addressing by the name of Scantlie Mab. She said to her, "Bundle up the yarn; it's time for the young lassie to take it to her mother." Delighted to hear this, the girl stood up from the stone, but she found Habetrot standing right behind her. The old woman placed the yarn in her hands.

"Oh, thank you! And what can I do for you in return?"

"Nothing — nothing at all," the old woman said. "But mind you don't tell your mother who spun the yarn."

Scarcely able to believe her good fortune, the girl went home. Her mother had been busy making sausages and had hung up seven hanks of them in the chimney to dry; then, tired out, she had taken herself to bed. Famished after her long day by the hill, the girl took down link after link, fried them, and ate them, and at last she went to bed too.

Her mother was the first one up the next morning, and when she came into the kitchen and found her sausages all gone, and the seven hanks of yarn lying beautifully smooth and bright on the well-scrubbed table, she ran out of the house, crying:

"My daughter's spun seven, seven, seven,
My daughter's eaten seven, seven, seven,
And all before daylight."

A young nobleman who happened to be riding by heard the exclamation but could not understand it; curious, he rode up and asked the woman what was the matter with her. But she had no answer for him, other than to break out again:

"My daughter's spun seven, seven, seven,
My daughter's eaten seven, seven, seven,
And all before daylight;
And if you don't believe me,
Why then come in and see it."

The nobleman dismounted and strode into the cottage, where he saw the fine yarn lying there on the table. He admired it so much that he begged to see the spinner, so the mother went upstairs and dragged her daughter out of her bed and down into the kitchen. The nobleman declared that he was lonely without a wife, and indeed, he said, he had been in search of one who was a good spinner. So it was agreed at once that the two would be married, and the wedding took place soon afterward — though the new bride was greatly afraid that she wouldn't prove to be quite as clever at her spinning as her new husband expected. But old Habetrot came again to her aid.

"Bring your bonny bridegroom to my cavern," she said to the girl just after her marriage, "and he will see the consequence of spinning. I promise you that never again will he tie you to the spinning wheel."

The next day, the bride led her husband to the hill and told him to peer down through the stone with the hole in the middle. He was greatly surprised to see a strange old woman dancing and jumping over a large, white river stone, all the while singing this ditty to her sisters, while they kept time with their spindles:

"We who live in dreary den,
Are both rank and foul to see;
Hidden from the glorious sun,
That teems the fair earth's canopy:
Ever must our evenings lone
Be spent on the colludie stone.

Cheerless is the evening gray
When Causleen has died away,
But ever bright and ever fair
Are they who breathe this evening air,
And lean upon the self-bored stone
Unseen by all but me alone."

When her song ended, Scantlie Mab asked Habetrot what she meant by the last line, "Unseen by all but me alone."

"There's someone," Habetrot replied, "who I decided should come here at this time, and I'm the only one of you who knows it. And now, he's heard my song through the hole in the stone." Then she rose, opened a door that had been concealed by the roots of an old tree, and invited the newly-weds to come inside the cavern to meet her spinning sisters.

The nobleman was astonished by the strange-looking company, and asked each one of them what was the cause of her disfigured lips. Each in a different tone of voice, and each with a different twist of the mouth, answered in turn that it was all caused by spinning. At least, they tried to say so, but one just grunted out "Nakasind," and another muttered "Owkasaand," while a third spluttered "O-a-a-send." Every one of them, though, made the cause of their strange appearance quite clear to him.

Habetrot cunningly hinted that if his wife were allowed to spin and spin, her pretty lips would grow out of shape too, and her pretty face might be quite significantly changed. So before he left the cave he vowed that his wife should never again touch a spinning wheel, and he kept his word through all their long life together. Instead, the young woman took to wandering in the meadows by his side and riding behind him over the hills. And all the flax grown on his land was sent to old Habetrot to be spun into the finest of yarns.

Stories of an old spinning woman named Habetrot seem to belong equally to England and to Scotland; they occur most frequently in the borderlands that straddle the two countries. But variants of this story exist in most areas of Europe. In *Grimm's Fairy Tales* there's a version of it called "The Three Spinners," and rather than featuring one senior old woman and several sisters, it's focused on three old spinning women. This motif reflects the three Fates of Greek mythology or the three Norns in the Norse tradition who, together, spin the world into being.

Inherent in these threads of European tradition is a belief that the act of spinning tends to be a catalyst for magic and attracts magical beings — but not all of those beings are easy to be with and often their help comes at a high price. At one level, then, we can see the story of Habetrot as a "helper" story: one of those common tales in which an Otherworldly being helps a young person to complete an impossible task. But unlike Rumpelstiltskin and similar "helper" characters in so many other tales, this old woman doesn't want the girl's firstborn child in return. Indeed, Habetrot asks for nothing at all — just that the secret of her existence should be kept.

The most interesting image in this story is that of the stone with the hole in the middle, through which the young girl peers into Habetrot's underground cavern: effectively, into the Otherworld. In her song, Habetrot calls it a "colludie stone," but in most parts of Britain stones with naturally formed holes in the center — commonly found on beaches — are called "hag stones," and in our folk traditions it's said that if you look through the stone with an open heart and good intent, you can see into the Otherworld. In the north of England, they might also be hung on the back of a door to protect the occupants of the house against witches.

Many stories of this kind stress the virtues of hard work, and spinning is certainly hard work. Heroines like Vasilisa often fail at the tasks that are set them — and so require help — not because they're lazy but because the task facing them is quite simply one that couldn't possibly be completed by the average human. This story is rather different, and almost all opinion about it and commentary on it focuses on its "moral ambiguity," because, it is argued, the girl is perfectly capable of spinning but is shown instead to profit from laziness and deception. However, just as old Habetrot herself does, it's very possible to see the story rather differently.

Perhaps this old woman knows that there's a time and a place for hard work — but there's also a time for simply *being* in the world and discovering its natural magic. In this story, Habetrot isn't rewarding laziness: she's freeing the young woman from a life of drudgery. She is challenging the prevailing assumption here in the West that virtue lies in learning to do precisely the things we dislike doing, and that only by overcoming our resistance and doing hated tasks well — being, by this definition, a "good girl" — will we be rewarded. Unlike the girl in the Grimms' tale of "The Three Spinners," this girl isn't actually described as idle: spinning just isn't a skill that comes naturally to her, and so of course she hates it. In contrast, what she loves is simply being outdoors in nature. She refuses to be confined in the straitjacket of overdomestication and to settle for too small a life.

The girl in this story loves life — and Habetrot is determined to give it to her. When we see the girl in nature, we see a wilder world that brings her great joy. She instinctively stumbles across magical places; she finds herself constantly in the liminal — by the side of running water, at twilight, on the threshold of two worlds. She's no lazy fool: she's friendly and curious and grateful. She is in her element. Habetrot sees this and clearly accepts her for who she is, because only those who are invited can see or hear Habetrot. This old woman, then, understands that we can grow into authenticity only by, as American mythologist Joseph Campbell put it, "following our bliss." Perhaps she understands that the girl's refusal to spin is in service to her own authentic self, rather than idleness. In encouraging her to be exactly who she is, Habetrot is offering her the greatest gift of all: acceptance.

Spinning Wheel Song

ISLE OF MAN

Spin, wheel, spin!
Turn, wheel, turn!
And ev'ry leaf upon the trees,
Spin above my head!
With myself the spinner,
And with the King the Wool;
Help me get my spinning done,
Before the Weaver come!

Ah, Ah, Ah

Spin, wheel, spin!
Sing, wheel, sing!
And ev'ry slate upon the house,
Spin on my behalf!

Tra la la la la

Else Old else Old Trit Trot will never get the thread!

Ah, Ah, Ah

Spin, wheel, spin!
Hum, wheel, hum!
And ev'ry wave upon the shore,
Spin along with me!
With myself the spinner,
Spinning the gray wool;
Help me get my spinning done,
Before the Weaver come!

Fair, Brown, and Trembling

IRELAND

Fadó, fadó — long ago, long ago — in a time when Ireland was a place of many kingdoms, there lived a king called Hugh. He ruled over the far western land that then was called Tír Chonaill, though now we know it as Donegal; he was a widower and had three daughters whose names were Fair, Brown, and Trembling. Fair and Brown always had a fine array of new dresses and were allowed to go out to church every Sunday, but Trembling, the youngest, was kept at home to do the cooking and housework. Her older sisters wouldn't let her out of the house at all, because she was more beautiful than them and they dreaded the possibility that she might marry before they did.

Well, this state of affairs continued for a good few years — until the son of the king of Ulster fell in love with Fair, the oldest of the three sisters. Then, one Sunday morning after Fair and Brown had gone to church, the old henwife who looked after King Hugh's poultry came into the kitchen where Trembling was scrubbing the table and said, "You ought to be at church today, instead of working here at home."

"How could I possibly think of it?" Trembling replied. "I have no clothes good enough to wear to church — and besides, if my sisters were to see me there, they'd punish me severely for daring to leave the house."

"Don't you worry about all that," said the henwife, who understood many more things than the keeping of the king's poultry. "I'll give you a finer dress than either of them has ever seen. So tell me, now — what kind of dress would you like?"

"Oh," Trembling said, closing her eyes to conjure up an image of herself as she'd never been seen before. "I'd love to have a dress as white as snow, and green shoes for my feet."

The henwife put on her magical cloak of darkness and snipped a piece of cloth from the old frock that Trembling was wearing. Gathering the cloak around her, she whispered a request for the whitest dress in the world and the most beautiful that could be found, and a pair of green shoes too. When the edges of her cloak fell open again, the garments lay in her hands; she gave them to Trembling, who put them on.

When Trembling was dressed and ready, the henwife said to her, "I have a honey-bird here to sit on your right shoulder, and a honey-finger to put on your left. By the front door you'll find a milk-white mare with a golden saddle for you to sit on, and a golden bridle and reins to hold in your hand." Trembling went outside and found that everything was just as the henwife had told her. She climbed up onto the golden saddle and the henwife said, "It's important that you don't go inside the door of the church: just wait outside it. And as soon as everyone stands up at the end of Mass, you must ride home at once, as fast as the mare will carry you."

When Trembling rode up to the door of the church, everyone inside it turned away from their prayers and stared. They were desperate to know who she was, and when they saw her hurrying away at the end of Mass, they poured out of the church and ran along the road to see if one of them could overtake her. But there was no use running: she was away over the hill before anyone could come near her. The horse ran so fast that she overtook the wind before her and outstripped the wind behind. When Trembling arrived home, she found that the henwife had dinner ready. She took off her beautiful snow-white dress with more than a little reluctance, and her old dress was on her again in a twinkling.

When the two elder sisters came home the henwife asked them, "Have you any news today from the church?"

"Astonishing news!" they said. "We saw a wonderfully grand lady at the church door, and we'd never seen the like of the dress she was wearing — not on any woman, ever before! Our dresses were nothing by comparison, and every man at the church, from our father the king to the beggar, just stood there and stared at her, desperate to know who she was."

Well, the sisters wouldn't rest till they each had a snow-white dress like the one worn by the strange lady at the church, but honey-birds and honey-fingers were not to be found anywhere in the land.

Next Sunday, the two older sisters went to church again and left Trembling at home to cook the dinner. After they had gone, the henwife came in again carrying eggs and asked her, "Will you go to church today?"

"I would go," said Trembling, "if only it were possible."

"It's possible," the henwife said. "What kind of dress would you like to wear today?"

"The finest black satin that can be found, and red shoes for my feet."

"What color do you want the mare to be?"

"I want her to be so black and so glossy that I can see my own reflection in the gleam of her dark coat."

So the henwife put on the cloak of darkness, drew it around her, and whispered a request for the dress and the shoes and the mare. Again, when the cloak opened, the beautiful clothes lay in her hands. When Trembling was dressed, the henwife put the honey-bird on her right shoulder and the honey-finger on her left. The saddle on the mare was silver this time and so was the bridle. When Trembling had mounted, the henwife reminded her not to go inside the door of the church, and to hurry home on the horse as soon as everyone stood up at the end of Mass, before anyone might be able to stop her.

That Sunday, the churchgoers were more astonished than ever; they stared and stared, desperate to know who this grand and beautiful lady was. The priest completely lost the attention of his congregation, and at the end of Mass they elbowed each other out of the way in their efforts to be out of the church door to see the mysterious woman. But they had no luck, because she was flying off down the road again before anyone could even talk to her.

The henwife had the dinner ready; Trembling took off her satin dress with a sigh and had on her old clothes again before her sisters arrived home.

"What news have you today?" the henwife asked the two sisters when they came back from the church.

"Oh, that grand, strange lady came again! And no one even noticed our dresses after they saw the fine robes of satin that she had on! Every single member of the congregation had their mouths open, gawping at her, and no one so much as glanced at us."

The two sisters gave neither rest nor peace till they were given dresses as close to the strange lady's dress as they could find. But of course they were not nearly as fine, for the like of that dress could not be found in the whole of Ireland.

When the third Sunday came, Fair and Brown went to church dressed in black satin. As always, they left Trembling at home to work in the kitchen and told her to be sure to have their dinner ready when they came back. After they were out of sight, the henwife came to the kitchen with a basket of warm, freshly laid eggs and said: "Well, my dear, are you away to church today?"

And Trembling replied, with a twinkle in her eye, "I would go if I had a new dress to wear."

"I'll get you any dress you ask for. What will it be today?"

"A dress red as a rose from the waist down, and white as snow from the waist up; a cape of green on my shoulders; a hat on my head with a red, a white, and a green feather in it, and shoes for my feet with the toes red, the middle white, and the backs and heels green."

Well, the henwife put on the cloak of darkness and whispered her wish for all these things; when the edges of the cloak were parted, there they were in her hands. When Trembling was dressed, the henwife put the honey-bird on her right shoulder and the honey-finger on her left. She pinned the hat securely to her head, clipped a few hairs from one lock and a few from another with her scissors, and suddenly the most beautiful golden hair was flowing down over the girl's shoulders. Then the henwife asked her what kind of mare she would like to ride. Trembling replied that she would like a white mare, with blue-and-gold diamond-shaped spots all over her body. She should have a saddle of gold and a golden bridle.

When she went outside, she found the mare she had asked for standing there by the door. A bird that was sitting between the horse's ears began to sing as soon as Trembling was in the saddle, and it didn't stop for a moment till she came back home again from the church.

The fame of the beautiful, grand, and strange lady had now traveled beyond Ireland and all through the world, and princes and great men came from all corners of it to the Donegal church that Sunday — each one of them hoping that he would be the one to carry her away home with him after

Mass and make her his wife. Even the son of the king of Ulster was there; by this time he had forgotten all about Fair, and he decided to wait outside the church to catch the mysterious lady before she could hurry away.

The church was bursting at the seams, and there were three times as many people outside it as there were inside. The bird between the mare's ears announced Trembling's arrival as surely as any herald, and so, even before the final "Amen" of Mass was close to being said, everyone who had found a spot inside the church was pushing and shoving their way through the door. Seeing the crowd surging toward her, Trembling turned the head of her glorious mare, put heel to flank and swept away ahead of the wind. But all at once the prince of Ulster appeared at her side and, seizing Trembling by the foot, he ran alongside them for half a mile. He didn't let go of her till the shoe he was holding slipped from Trembling's foot, and he was left with it in his hand as she galloped away. She flew home as fast as the mare could carry her, worrying that the henwife would scold her for losing the shoe.

Seeing her so vexed, the older woman asked, "What's the matter with you?"

"Oh! I've lost one of the shoes off my feet," cried Trembling.

"Don't you worry about that," the henwife said. "It just might be the best thing that ever happened to you."

So Trembling gave all the beautiful clothes back to the henwife, put on her old dress, and went as usual to work in the kitchen. When her two sisters returned home, the henwife asked, "Have you any news from the church?"

"We have indeed," they said, "for we saw the grandest sight today. The strange lady came again, in even finer array than before. The richest colors of the world were on her and the horse she rode, and between the ears of the horse was a bird that never stopped singing from the time she came till the time she went away. The lady herself is certainly the most beautiful woman ever to be seen in Ireland."

Now, after Trembling had disappeared from the church, the king of Ulster's son, brandishing the red, green, and white shoe in his hand, declared to the other princes who were gathered there: "I will have that lady for my wife."

They shook their heads, and said to him, "You didn't win her by taking the shoe off her foot! You'll have to win her by the point of your sword. You'll have to fight for her with every one of us before you can call her your own."

"Well," said the son of the king of Ulster, "when I find the lady whose foot that shoe will fit, I'll fight for her, never fear, rather than leave her to any of you."

All the kings' sons were anxious to know who it was that had lost the shoe, and they traveled together all over Ireland to see if they could find her. The prince of Ulster joined the company, and they wandered north, south, east, and west. There was not a house in the kingdom that they did not search, looking for the one woman the shoe would fit. They didn't care whether she was rich or poor — they were simply determined to find her.

The prince of Ulster held on to the shoe, never letting it out of his sight. Each young woman who saw it was filled with hope for, beautiful as it was, it was of a normal size, neither large nor small. No one, though, had any idea about the material it was made from. Well, the shoe didn't fit a single one of them. One thought it would fit her if she cut a little bit of flesh from the tip of her big toe; another, with too short a foot, stuffed something inside the tip of her stocking. But it was no use: they only spoiled their feet and had to treat them for months afterward.

The two elder sisters, Fair and Brown, heard that all the princes of the world were searching Ireland for the woman who the shoe might fit, and every day they babbled excitedly about trying it on. One day, tired of it all, Trembling spoke up and said, "Maybe it's my foot that the shoe will fit."

"Don't be so ridiculous!" they said. "How can you say so, when you were at home every Sunday?" So they waited, and scolded their younger sister, and poked at each other, and primped until finally the princes drew near. On the morning of the day that they were due to arrive, the sisters put Trembling in a cupboard and locked the door on her. When the company of princes arrived at the house, the prince of Ulster gave the shoe to the sisters. But though they tried and tried, it would fit neither of them.

"I remember you have a younger sister. Where is she?" the prince asked Fair.

"I'm here!" said Trembling, speaking up in the cupboard.

"Oh! She's just a serving girl who we keep to take care of the ashes," the sisters said. But the prince and his companions refused to leave the house till they had seen her, so the two sisters had to open the cupboard door. When Trembling came out, the shoe was put to her foot — and it fitted perfectly.

The prince of Ulster looked at her and said, "You are the woman the shoe fits, and so you are the woman I took the shoe from."

Trembling smiled at him. "Stay here till I return," she said, and ran to the henwife's house as fast as her feet would carry her. The older woman was waiting, with the cloak of darkness already around her shoulders. She whispered a request for everything that Trembling had worn that first Sunday at church and sat her on the white mare in the same fashion. Trembling rode along the highway to the front of the house, and as she passed by, everyone who'd seen her the first time cried out, "That's the lady we saw at church!"

Then she galloped to the henwife's house a second time

and came back on the black mare, wearing the second dress the henwife had given her. All the people who'd seen her the second Sunday cried, "That's the lady we saw at church!"

A third time she urged the mare back to the henwife's house, and soon she returned on the mare with blue-and-gold diamond-shaped spots all over her body, and wearing the third dress. By now an enormous crowd had gathered, and all of those who had seen her the third time cried, "That's the lady we saw at church!" And so everyone was satisfied, quite sure that Trembling was indeed the woman they'd all seen.

But it wasn't over yet: the princes came together to the son of the king of Ulster and declared, "You'll have to fight for her now."

"I'm ready for you," the prince replied, and drew his sword. So first, the son of the king of Lochim stepped forward. The struggle began, and a terrible struggle it was. They fought for nine hours and then the prince from Lochim dropped his sword, gave up his claim, and left the field. Next day, the son of the king of Spain fought for six hours before yielding his claim. On the third day the son of the king of Nyerfói fought for eight hours and then surrendered. On the fourth day the son of the king of Greece fought for six hours, then gave up. On the fifth day, it seemed that no more princes from overseas wanted to fight the prince of Ulster. None of the sons of the kings of Ireland were willing to fight with a man of their own land; the strangers had had their chance, they said, and since no one else had come to claim the woman, she belonged of right to the son of the king of Ulster.

The wedding day was set, and invitations were sent out; the celebrations lasted for a year and a day. When it was over, the king's son brought home his bride, and when the time came a son was born. The son of the king of Ulster and Trembling had fourteen children together, and they lived happily till they died of old age. Or so the story goes.

This story is included here because it furnishes us with a fine example of a character who regularly appears in fairy tales from around Europe, but especially in stories from Britain and Ireland: the henwife. She is usually depicted as a mature woman, around midlife. The henwife does indeed keep hens, but her remit goes far beyond the selling of eggs: she has attributes both of a fairy godmother and a wise woman. Unlike most wise women, who tend to live in the woods or on the farthest fringes of a town or village, the henwife is almost always presented as an integrated member of the community; she lives in the center of the village, or sometimes in the grounds of the castle. Her wise-woman specialty is advice in the areas of life we might call "women's mysteries"; in particular, she points young women in the direction of their future husbands. She's more than just a matchmaker, though: she seems to know — and arguably to attract — the one husband who will best suit the young woman she's assisting.

Usually, the henwife's primary role in these stories is to act as a helper to the younger protagonist; in most stories, though, she is rather more than that: she is the instigator of the action. She gladly disrupts convention — in this case, by helping the younger sister to marry ahead of the older sisters — in order to achieve her aims, or, as in this story, to redress an unjust situation. Here, she is the one who decides that it is time for Trembling to marry, and specifically that she should marry the son of the king of Ulster. She takes it upon herself to arrange things so that this happy event might take place, making the decisions and understanding that it is a sense of mystery as much as the grandeur of her clothing that will draw the young man to Trembling. The henwife in this story, as in so many others, offers practical advice — and even makes the dinner — as well as performing magic.

The most striking image in this story is the magical "cloak of darkness" that the henwife puts on in order to successfully cast her spells. Her requests are for dresses and shoes and mares — but we don't ever know who, or what, she is asking. This is almost always the way of things in fairy tales. The cloak of darkness in itself has no particular significance; it's simply a magical object, symbolizing the henwife's transformation from keeper of poultry to keeper of the mysteries. The honey-bird and honey-finger are equally mysterious, but are certainly there to convey a sense of magic and otherness — and so are the wedding celebrations that lasted "a year and a day," a common motif in fairy tales for conveying the magical nature of the tale. Nevertheless, as we see with other wise-woman characters who haunt the pages of this book, the henwife is clearly on intimate terms with what we might think of as the "Otherworld": the place from which magic naturally and inevitably arises.

Mother Holle

GERMANY

In the time before this time, there was a widow who had two daughters. One was beautiful and hardworking; the other was ugly and lazy. The mother loved the ugly and lazy girl more because she was her own daughter: the other was her stepdaughter. Since her father died, the stepdaughter's life had become miserable. Her stepmother required her to do all the housework and other heavy chores, and each morning she was sent out into the yard with her spindle, to sit by the well at the side of the road and spin till her fingers bled. One day, some of the blood fell onto the spindle and as the girl reached over the stone wall to draw up some water to wash it clean, the spindle seemed to spring out of her hand, and it fell down into the darkness of the well.

She walked back to the house, fearful of what her stepmother might say or do — and indeed the woman scolded her harshly, saying, "Since you were clumsy enough to let the spindle fall into the well, you'll have to go down there and fetch it out yourself."

The stepdaughter made her way back to the well, distraught. She had no idea what to do. For a little while, she sat on the wall with her feet dangling over the edge, and at last, closing her eyes in despair, she heaved herself off and let herself fall into the well. She remembered nothing more till she

131

opened her eyes to find herself lying in a glorious meadow, lavish with many-colored wildflowers, which danced in a gentle breeze. The sky was the brightest of blues, with a scattering of cotton-wool clouds; the golden sunshine warmed her skin and lifted her spirits.

She started to walk across the meadow and hadn't gone far before she happened upon a black-iron baker's oven full of bread. No one seemed to be there to tend it, and the loaves cried out to her, "Take us out! Oh, please take us out or we'll be burned to a cinder. We were baked through long ago!" So the girl picked up the bread shovel that lay by the side of the oven, carefully pulled out every last one of the loaves, and laid them out next to it. Then she went on her way.

After a little while, her path took her past a tree so heavy with bright-red apples that the overburdened boughs bent low to the ground. "Shake me, shake me," the tree pleaded. "My apples are rosy and ripe and my limbs ache with their weight." So the girl shook the tree and the apples fell down on her like rain, but still she shook and shook till there wasn't a single apple left on it. Then she carefully piled up the fruit by the side of the tree and went on her way.

At last, she came to a little thatched house with a bright-blue door; an old woman was peering out through one of its windows. She had huge teeth and was quite terrifying to look at. The girl took fright and was ready to turn on her heel and run, but the old woman called out to her. "Dear child," she said, "what are you afraid of? Why don't you stay with me for a while? If you will do the housework, and do it all properly, then I'll make you very happy. But you must be careful to make my bed exactly as I tell you. Always shake the mattress thoroughly, so that the feathers fly about. And then, out there in the world beyond, it will snow. Because I am Mother Holle."

Despite her fearsome teeth, the old woman spoke kindly, so the girl — imagining that doing Mother Holle's housework could be no worse than being her stepmother and stepsister's skivvy — summoned up her courage and agreed to stay and work for her. She always took pride in her work, taking care to do everything according to the old woman's liking. She would take the bed to the window and shake it with all her strength till feathers flew about like snowflakes. And the old woman was true to her word: she never spoke harshly, and fed the girl well each day.

Days turned to weeks, weeks into months, and the months stretched ever closer to a year. For a good long while the girl was happy enough, but eventually she grew sad and lonely. Despite the abundance and beauty of this world and the fact that she was much better off in it with Mother Holle, it wasn't home. It just wasn't the place where she belonged. Eventually, the girl had to tell Mother Holle how she was feeling. "I'm homesick," she told her, "and although you've been so very kind to me, and I've been happy here, I'm longing to return to my own people."

Mother Holle smiled warmly. "I'm delighted that you feel you're ready to return," she said. "You've worked diligently and faithfully, so I'll take you up again myself." She led the girl to an enormous gate at the back of the house; it opened as they approached. As the girl stood in the doorway a shower of golden rain fell upon her, clinging to her till she was covered with it from head to foot. "This is your reward for all that hard work," Mother Holle told her, and then she gave the girl the spindle that had fallen into the well.

The gate closed behind the girl, and she found herself up in her own world again, close to her home. As she entered the courtyard, an old cockerel who was perched on the well called out:

"Cock-a-doodle-doo!
Your golden daughter's come back to you!"

The girl entered the house, shimmering and shining in her golden coating. Her stepmother and stepsister were quite dazzled, and it took them a moment to realize who she was. As she was so richly covered in gold, they welcomed her warmly, of course; they sat her down by the fire and pressed the girl to tell them all that had happened to her. When her stepmother heard how she'd come by such great wealth, she decided that her own daughter must try her luck down the well too, so she urged her to go out right away, to sit by the well and spin. The ugly, lazy daughter dragged her feet all the way there, but instead of spinning, she thrust her hand into a thornbush to make herself bleed. A few bright drops of blood fell onto the spindle, then she threw it into the well and jumped in after it.

Down into the darkness she fell until, just as her stepsister had done, she opened her eyes to find herself in the beautiful, flower-filled meadow. She walked until she arrived at the baker's oven. "Take us out! Oh, please take us out or we'll be burned to a cinder. We were baked through long ago!"

But the girl just pulled a face. "Why should I burn my hands for you?" she said, and then she went on her way.

After a little while, her path took her past a tree laden with a crop of bright-red apples, so heavy with fruit that the boughs bent low to the ground. "Shake me, shake me," the tree pleaded. "My apples are rosy and ripe and my limbs ache with their weight."

"Huh!" the girl said. "And risk an apple falling on my head? I really don't think so!"

On she went and at last she came to Mother Holle's little house. She had heard about that old woman's large teeth from her sister and so she wasn't in the least afraid. "Mother Holle," she called out, "please may I stay a while and work for you?" And although Mother Holle raised one hairy white eyebrow just the tiniest of fractions, she welcomed the girl in. On her first day, she was obedient enough and did the chores that were required of her, thinking only of the gold she would receive in return. But the next day, she grew tired of it all and began to dawdle and linger over her work. On the third day, she slept late and refused to get out of bed when Mother Holle called her. Worse still, she neglected to make Mother Holle's bed as the old woman had instructed, and so no snow fell in the world above.

Mother Holle had now lost patience with her, and the next morning told the girl that she must leave. The lazy girl was delighted: her hard work was over, and her golden reward was sure to come. The old woman led the girl to the gate — but just as it opened before her and she began to walk through, a great bucket of tar spilled all over her. "That is just reward for your service," Mother Holle said, and she shut the gate behind her.

So the lazy girl returned home covered from head to toe in sticky black tar, and the cockerel on the well called out to her mother when he saw her:

"Cock-a-doodle-doo!
Your tarry daughter's come back to you!"

Try as she might, the idle young woman could not remove the tar: it stuck to her for as long as she lived.

The folkloric character known as Mother Holle — sometimes called Mother Hulda or Old Mother Frost — derives from an ancient Germanic goddess who ruled over the weather. In

many parts of Germany, when it's snowing, it's said that Frau
Holle is shaking out her feather bed. Holle also protected ag-
riculture and women's crafts. In the visual arts, she was often
portrayed holding a distaff or drop-spindle, or sometimes she
sat at a spinning wheel — and spinning (along with weaving)
is, as we've already seen, connected in myth and folklore to
women's magic, and especially to the mysteries of transformation. In this story, Mother Holle is presented as a strange,
Otherworldly old lady. The hardworking heroine has already
experienced sadness and misfortune by the time she drops her
spindle into the well: the loss of her parents, abuse at the hands
of her stepmother, and her relegation to the role of servant
in her own home. When she is forced then to recover the lost
spindle from the well, she is understandably fearful and heavy-
hearted. Her descent into the well, then, is ambiguous: her
evident despair before she pushes herself off the wall and lets
herself fall suggests that, in some sense, she is embracing the
abyss, relinquishing the cares that threaten to overwhelm her.
Sometimes we have to let ourselves fall, in order to kick-start
the process of transformation. We have to let go of old ways of
thinking, of old limits — because once you've stepped across
that threshold between world and well, it is for sure a kind of
death: you can never go back to what you were before.

Happily, the girl's long fall into the well ends not in tragedy
but in opportunity. When she unexpectedly finds herself in another world, she responds to the tests she encounters along her
path with grace and diligence. Mother Holle's primary role in
this story, then, isn't so much as mentor — but as savior. She
saves the girl from despair by offering her kindness as well as
purpose, and by furnishing a final reward that totally trans-
forms her fortunes in the "real" world. It doesn't always take
gold to change a life, though: sometimes, it's enough just to take
a young person seriously, to offer them work or pastimes that

reflect their gifts and their loves, so enabling them to cultivate a stronger sense of self-worth. In a fairy-tale world, this work — especially when the protagonist is a young woman — is often as simple as keeping house. This might seem rather hackneyed on the surface, but the teachings of this common housework motif stretch far beyond gender stereotypes: we need to regularly sweep our spaces, and the ability to keep your house in order — both literally and metaphorically — is a skill that is certainly worth instilling in the young. It isn't the only accomplishment that's worth cultivating — creativity and more fluid ways of being in the world of course are important too — but without the landmarks we create by attention to a grounded daily practice, it is all too easy to become hopelessly disorientated out there on the infinite ocean of the imagination.

Old Mother Goose

ENGLAND

Old Mother Goose, when
She wanted to wander,
Would ride through the air
On a very fine gander.

Mother Goose had a house,
It was built in a wood,
Where an owl at the door
For sentinel stood.

She had a son Jack,
A plain-looking lad;
He was not very good,
Nor yet very bad.

She sent him to market,
A live goose he bought:
"Here! mother," says he,
"It will not go for nought."

The Groac'h of the Well

BRITTANY

In a time now long past, when it was still of use to cast a spell, there was a girl whose mother was...well, complicated. One autumn night the mother took to her bed, pretending to be ill, and sent her young daughter out into the darkness to fetch fresh water from the spring well in the nearby wood.

When she arrived at the well, bucket in hand, the girl became aware of an old woman approaching out of the gloom. Her long gray hair was matted and wild, her clothes were gray and ragged, her eyebrows were dense as thorn thickets and her nose was huge and crooked. There was no mistaking it: this was a groac'h. But her mother badly needed a drink of water, so the girl plucked up her courage, nodded at the old woman, reached over the stone wall, and made to lower her bucket into the well.

"Who gave you permission to come to the well at this late hour?" the groac'h snapped.

"Th-there's not a drop of water at home," the girl said, her heart pounding. "My mother is ill and thirsty, and who knows what might happen to her during the night if she can't find anything to drink."

The groac'h rubbed her long, hairy chin with bony fingers; she fixed the girl with eyes as dark and fathomless as the depths of the well. "Hmm...well, this time I'll forgive you, since you're a fine girl and well mannered. But don't you ever come back here again at night."

"It's the first time, and hopefully the last," the girl replied, hastily splashing her bucket into the water. When she got back home, shaking and tired, she told her mother about meeting the groac'h. She said that the hag had warned her never to go to the well again at night, otherwise that would be the last time she would see her mother. Her mother nodded her head, wearily.

A few days later, in the evening, the girl's mother again pretended to be ill. She sent her daughter outside on an errand, then poured away all the water they had in the house. When the girl returned, her mother was in bed and calling for a cup of herbal tea. The daughter went to the kettle but found it empty of water. She went to the bucket where they kept water for the house: it too was empty. "Mother," she said, "just a little while ago the kettle and the pail were full of water, and now there's none."

Her mother shrugged her shoulders and complained about her parched throat. There was nothing for it but to return to the well — but now it was dark, and the girl vividly remembered the groac'h's warning. Nevertheless, she gathered her courage, picked up the bucket, and walked to the threshold of the woods, crying all the way. As she approached the well, she could see the groac'h standing beside it, hair writhing like snakes in the breeze. She began to shake with fear. The groac'h hissed, "Didn't I warn you never to come back here at night?"

"My m-mother is ill again," the girl said, "and there's no water to make any herbal tea."

The groac'h fixed her dark eyes on the girl and stared at her for what seemed like an eternity. "Well, now," she said finally, her voice a little softer than before, "your mother will just have to do without. You won't see her again, and you'll stay here with me until you're set free." With that, the groac'h picked up her staff and tapped the stone wall behind the well with it. The wall opened, revealing old stone steps that wound deep into the darkness. The groac'h led the young girl down into a surprisingly warm and cozy cave.

Given all that had happened to her, the girl thought: *Well, if no one is unkind to me and if no one beats me, it's quite possible that I could be happy here.*

A long time passed. It could have been days or weeks, she couldn't tell — but in all that time, the girl wanted for nothing. There was a cupboard full of cakes and delicious treats, and another filled with game and cheese and good bread. There were jugs full to the brim with sweet, clean water from the well, and a great hearth in which three fires could be lit at the same time. One day the old groac'h said to her, "I'm going to visit my two old sisters, because my heart tells me that one of them is unwell. No one will come here, and when I leave, I'll close up the cave so you'll stay safe and sound."

In the world outside the cave, two moons waxed and waned. Then, one night, the cave entrance opened and a younger groac'h stood there. Her hair was long and wild and gray, and her eyes were just as dark as those of the old groac'h, but she was slightly less stooped. "I've come to tell you that your mistress died while she was staying with her sisters," she said. "Before she died, she asked me to come here and tell you that, although you were here as a punishment for disobeying her, she knew that you were happy in the cave. And so her last wish was that you might be offered a choice: if you'd like to stay you'll want for nothing, but if you would prefer to leave, then you may."

By this time, the girl had spent a lot of time alone, thinking about her predicament, reflecting on her old life and this unusual situation in which she found herself. And so she had a ready answer: "I'll stay," she said. "But could you give me the key to come and go, because it can be a little stuffy in here? I won't go very far: I'll just walk around the well."

The younger groac'h thought for a moment. "I can't give you the key to this cave until the oldest of the three sisters dies," she said. "She's ailing, so be patient for another month. I'll be on my way now and will lock you in as usual, but the day after her death, I'll come back to you."

It seemed like a long time, and yet not such a long time, till the night came when the cave was unlocked. True to her word, the younger groac'h stood in the doorway; in the outstretched palm of each hand she held a key. One shone brightly, but the other was dull and gray. "Here are two keys for you," the groac'h said. "One is made of gold and will unlock the cave from the inside, so you can go out into the sun. The other is made of stone; it opens the door from the outside so you can return to this cave. You can go out whenever you want to, but make sure you don't ever stay outside after sunset."

The girl took the keys from the groac'h. "Thank you," she said. "And I'll remember always to return before sunset."

"Make sure that you do," the groac'h replied. "Don't lose track of time, because once the sun has set, you'll find no cave by this well. It will have disappeared completely, as if it never had been."

From that day on, the girl came and went as she pleased, but she never strayed very far from the well. Days turned to weeks and weeks to months, and the girl grew bolder. One day, she walked a little farther than usual and she met another girl, who spoke to her and tried to keep her talking. But she grew afraid as the sun slipped ever lower in the afternoon sky, and ran away back to the well. She had just put the stone key in the hidden place in the rock when the sun disappeared beneath the treetops. *I won't go so far again*, she thought, *because surely I'll always come across some gossip or other who'll hold me up, and then what would I do if I couldn't live here anymore?*

The next day came and went, and she didn't venture out. Then, for a few days afterward, she packed herself some lunch and enjoyed it on the grass by the well before hurrying back inside as the afternoon drew on. She was careful never again to stray too far from the well.

Then came a morning when she went among the trees for a short stroll and a young man appeared. He threw her a smile as bright as the sun itself and wondered if he might join her on her walk. He asked her name and talked of all manner of things, and the sun rose to its zenith and began its slow slide down toward the western horizon. Eventually, looking a little bashful, he said, "I've been walking here for three days and it's the third time I've seen you emerge from the same place. So today I waited for you, hoping you would come."

The young woman blushed. "I would invite you to my home," she said, "but no one else can go into the place where I live."

They fell deeper into conversation, deeper into liking, and very soon found themselves in love. As the sun's bright glow began to fade fast, the young man asked the girl to marry him. She had had many long years to daydream of such a thing and so didn't hesitate. "I'd like that very much," she said, "because I'm weary now of being alone. But I don't think I can take a husband into the place where I live. In any case, it's getting dark and I'm afraid I really have to go now."

He took her hand and kissed it. "I'll wait for you here tomorrow and we'll see each other again."

That night, the younger groac'h came to visit; they sat together by the great fire. The young woman told her what had happened and spoke of her dilemma.

"Marry him," said the groac'h. "He's a fine boy. Together, you'll be able to go wherever you like and you'll want for nothing. Your life is calling, and you won't have to fear the setting of the sun anymore. It's time."

And so, the next morning, the young woman used the golden key to unlock the cave one last time. She climbed the stone steps up into the morning sunlight, and she did not look back.

The groac'h is a kind of "water fairy" in the Breton tradition; they live in caverns under the beach or the sea or, like this groac'h, they're associated with wells. Usually, they're seen only at night and, generally, they're presented as old women, sometimes with walrus teeth and hunchbacked. Although the groac'h, like so many old women in European stories, is often depicted as malign, there are a number of stories that, like this one, draw attention to their generosity. A groac'h might allow humans to enter her solitary home and then offer them treasure, magical objects, or healing cures. They can be overbearing but are full of good intentions.

Water, of course, is the reason why the girl first comes to the well, and water is the groac'h's element — an element that is rich with metaphorical meaning. In many symbolic systems around the world, water represents the realm of the feminine and the emotions. The catalyst for this story is that there isn't enough water at home, just as there seems to be little emotional sustenance for the girl in the house of a mother who seems — for reasons we are not told — intentionally to put her daughter at risk. In contrast, the cave-beneath-the-well offers a place of safety for the care-starved young girl, and the groac'h offers a great gift in providing shelter for her.

The groac'h doesn't give the girl an easy ride at first, though, and that's quite appropriate: she disobeyed her instructions to stay away from the well at night. Those instructions were likely given because a groac'h only goes out at night, and this is her place. So, as is typical in fairy tales, there are consequences for infringing the privacy of an Otherworldly being — and certainly for disobedience. But the original punishment turns into nourishment as the girl adjusts to her new and very much easier life with the older woman, and as the cave that once was presented as a prison becomes a sanctuary.

In the end, the refuge of the cave and the care and protection of two older women enable the young girl to pass safely into adulthood. When she's ready, she makes new connections in the world above and finds her way back into the human community. She has used the gold key to unlock the door of her adult life, and so has no more need of the stone key: there's no need now to reenter that womb-like cave in which she has been able to safely grow.

The cave, though, was originally a refuge for the solitary groac'h — and, like her, as we grow older, we might increasingly find that we too need a quiet place like this. In such a refuge, we might create space for new insights and understandings, for our imagination to be unshackled. A greater tendency to introspection is a consistent thread in many women's experiences during and after menopause; we might find ourselves desperate to draw back from all the frantic busyness of life, longing for rest and renewal. We might need more time to simply just be: time in which we can make ourselves comfortable in the deep container of soul, taking time out in a silent, low-lit "she-cave" to reflect and nourish ourselves.

The Earth Itself

British and Irish folklore offers us an abundance of hags who are ancient and imminent in the land, who represent the cycles of the seasons, and who can summon storms and talk to animals. In a sense, they are the Earth itself. Stories of these mythic old women originated in eras when the Earth was symbolized as a woman's body: caves were thought of as wombs, rivers as veins, hills as breasts....Now, so many old ways of perceiving the world have vanished from everyday life — but the stories of these women have not. They've lived on, just as the ancient women in them live on, through all the long epochs of the Earth. These magical tales, then, teach us that to be elder is to be strong and hard as the oldest rocks of this

Earth, which so many of our mythical old women personify. To be elder is to be powerful and to stay the course: not just to endure, but always to remain fully alive and engaged, till our work here is done.

The elder-woman tales included in this part of the book show us what it might look like to understand the language, cadences, and exigencies of the natural world, because these gnarly old hags exist in the wider flow of life, fully enmeshed in it. Today, we have constructed an almost exclusively human world for ourselves, and in so doing we've cut ourselves off in so many ways from the land and the other-than-humans who occupy it with us. These stories lead us back to a sense of kinship and belonging to an Earth that is animate and full of soul. And, ultimately, they remind us that there's a further intimate relationship between elder women and the Earth: one way or another, in the end, we all return to the land.

Beira, Queen of Winter

It was that time again. Beira stood ankle-deep in the narrow strait between the islands of Jura and Scarba, her coarse gray hair fading into gathering storm clouds. The icy salt water ebbed and flowed around her feet, and her gnarled toes were rooted deep in the sand below. Beira was doing her washing, watching her vast autumn-brown shawl swirl in the whirlpool named Corryvreckan like some crazed, tentacled creature of the deep. No wonder that the people, over many lifetimes, had come to call it Beira's washing-pot.

She stood there and summoned late-October winds; off they flew to sweep and swoop across the isles, to rip the last desiccated leaves from scattered trees and sparse hedgerows. The relentless tug of tide and time pulled at her old body. Now her work here was almost done, and she could return to Ben Nevis to take up the throne of Winter and rule the season with ice and biting storm.

It was twilight on the third day when she reached into the dark heart of the foaming chaos to withdraw her now-white shawl and wring it out. It was midnight when she laid it across the great mountains of the Highlands to dry. It was dawn when the first glimmers of light revealed a thick cast of snow on the peaks, signaling to all that her reign had begun. Winter was coming.

Now it was well past Samhain, and the resting moon had turned her light from the world. In the high places, among the snows and squalls, Beira sat firm. She was the cold of the craggy rock, the howl of gale, and the bite of ice. Through the darkening days, she contemplated the great epochs through which she had lived. Her memories were those of the land, and they must be renewed year after year — for what would the hills and mountains, lochs and rivers be without their memories? And who would the people be without the stories of their places?

Beira reached deep into her store of memories, excavating for the time when she had roamed the empty land, shaping and forming it with her great hammer. She had brought it down with all her might to form vast valleys, sending violent tremors down through the great tectonic plates of the Earth. Other times, tired from her work, she had sat on the ground and used her hands to fashion hills and mountains from clay. They each, she believed, deserved their own shape and spirit, so she struck with the edge of her hammer to carve unique peaks and ridges into every one of them.

There was that time when the relentless pounding of her hammer had caused the artesian waters to rise and flood the land. She remembered the day she had hefted a great creel onto her back, filling it with boulders and rocks as she traveled across the land through the surging water. The basket would sometimes tilt, then drop some of its load to form an archipelago of small islands. Other times, when she stumbled or bent over, weary from her work, all the rocks and stones would fall from the basket in a great pile. In this way Ben Wyvis and other mountains were formed, and when the work was done and the water had settled, some of it remained in the valleys and birthed the first lochs.

In those days, of course, she had had some help. Eight fine giantesses had also carried baskets and spilled their burdens onto the earth, helping to shape the high places where her giant sons had made their homes. Eventually, people had come to the land; she had watched as they learned the stories of the rocks and trees, the mountains, and the rivers. They had given her names: Beira, Cally Berry, the Cailleach, the Carlin, Great Hag, Winter Queen. But that was long ago. Now, her hag-sisters were all gone, and her sons too. She had outlived them all, cycle after cycle, an everlasting loop of renewal and decay.

Midwinter approached, and the dark days darkened even more. Beira, capricious now and at the height of her powers, summoned gales from grief and snowstorms from old rage. When her passions were spent, she withdrew, and rested for long days in glacial silence. Though she was powerful, she was beginning to tire. She sat on her throne of ice and gave way to the bittersweet memories of her youth. Oh, the days when she would range across the land with her retinue of wild animals! How the foxes had barked when they saw her, how the wolves had howled to honor her, and the great golden eagles had shrieked like heralds, announcing her approach. All these creatures and more were hers: nimble-footed deer, high-horned cattle, shaggy gray goats, black pigs, and mountain sheep with snow-white fleece. She would charm her deer to protect them from the huntsmen and would milk the hinds in early winter; their milk flowed into the mountain creeks and turned them frothy and white. She grew lonely in the depths of winter, when cold sent them to shelter and graze in the deep valleys away from her freezing snows. That was her most solitary time, when only an occasional eagle or raven would visit, to fetch up secrets from below.

But there had been that hard winter long ago, when a fine young druid had visited her lofty realm. "Tell me your age, O sharp old woman," he had asked. And for a moment she had regretted her winter form: her long rust-red teeth; her dull slate-blue complexion; her wild hair, white and coarse as a mare's tail; her one glaring, glacial eye. "I have long ceased to count the years," she had said, "but I will tell you what I have seen. Far beyond this land, in the middle of the sea, is the seal-haunted rock of Skerryvore. I remember when it was a mountain surrounded by fields. I saw the fields plowed, and the barley that grew in them was rich and juicy." She had pointed in the opposite direction. "Over there is a loch; I remember when it was a small round well. In those days I was a fair young girl, and now I am old and tired."

She had told him more stories to delay his leaving. He reminded her of seasons past, when her body had been ripe with the soft bloom of summer. But in spite of all his magic, he grew cold; she cut a path through the snow to guide him safely back to the valley below, to carry his tale to the firesides of the people.

February came, and with it Imbolc. The return of the light, they called it, but down in the frigid valleys, people still kept their fires burning all day. Beira was aging rapidly now, spine twisting and bones aching more and more with every new moon. Her mind drifted like winter snows.

Beira had lived through all the long ages of the Earth; she was the oldest of the old — and yet, each spring, she was renewed by drinking from the Well of Youth that bubbles up on the Green Island of the West. This enchanted summer isle floats on the silver tides of the Atlantic. It drifts and dreams; sometimes you can spot it off the western coast of Ireland, and at other times close to the Outer Hebrides. Sailors, mermaids, and minke whales have caught a glimpse of it, from time to time.

Beira always knew where to find the Green Island, and soon it would be time. Time to make her slow, painful way there; to release her tight grip on winter. To drag herself down from the crags of Ben Nevis and walk abroad again. To keep to the shadows and twilit edges, away from the growing strength of the sun.

April danced toward Bealtaine Eve. On this last night of her reign as Winter Queen, Beira sat alone. She kept her dark vigil beside the Well of Youth and waited for the May Day dawn. When the first faint glow pushed up above the eastern horizon, she would drink the water that bubbled from the crevice in the rock. She must take care to drink it before any bird should visit the well and before any dog should bark. If she did not, the enchantment would be broken, and the cycle of cycles — the wheel of life, age upon age, epoch upon epoch — would fail. And Beira would crumble to dust.

In the darkest hours of the night, just before dawn, hope fades fast. Cold seeps deeper into bones and morning feels like an empty promise. But as she sat there, her memory-sifting at an end, Beira felt the tide shift again. There it was: the palest glimmer of a solitary and blessedly silent dawn. She cupped her gnarled, age-marked hands under the bubbling spring and drew the sweet elixir to thin, cracked lips. The coolness of it, as it trickled down her old, parched throat, as it slipped down into her winter-empty stomach, suffused her with new life.

She had participated in this miracle every year, down all the long ages of the Earth, but it never failed to fill her with awe. Before the sun had clawed its triumphant way above the horizon, she was young again. She jumped to her feet and shook off her drab, gray cloak; beneath it, her dress was a vivid green. She waded back across the sea to Scotland,

and as she strode across the land the soft, mossy shadow of her mantle cast a green, growing blessing on the earth. The slumbering seeds stirred in their dark soil caves, and it was time for her now to lend herself to the rising of sap, the running of herds, the weaving of dreams. She walked the hills now as a beautiful girl with long hair, yellow as the blossom of broom; with milky skin and cheeks pink as a soft, summer rose. But her eyes...her eyes would always hold the ice-blue promise of winter.

In the mythology of Britain and Ireland it wasn't a bearded, transcendent father god up in the sky who made and shaped this world. It was an old woman who was the land itself: a giant woman called the Cailleach (which literally means "old woman" in the Gaelic languages and is pronounced "kal-yach"). She is perhaps the best-known example of a multitude of legendary giant women scattered through the myth and folklore of Europe. Stories about the Cailleach (who is given the name of Beira in some parts of Scotland, and Cally Berry in Northern Ireland) are deeply embedded in the landscape, because she's the one who created and shaped it through all its long ages, since the beginning of time. "When I was a young lass, the ocean was a forest, full of trees," she says, in a couple of stories about her — stories that are firmly embedded in the oral tradition of Scotland and Ireland — and indeed, she is the grandmother of all the grandmothers, the one who knows the ancient history of this planet and preserves its stories for the ones who come after her.

Her landscapes are wild and rocky places, and the place-names that are associated with her are usually attached to mountains, or to locations where ancient dolmens and cairns are to be found. The Cailleach is consistently portrayed as a profoundly elemental force: a wilderness, and sometimes a seasonal, spirit. Her embeddedness in the land is another facet of the Great Mother archetype originally outlined by analytical psychologist Erich Neumann. To Neumann, the Great Mother was above all a transforming force, representing the feminine as the creative principle; he also noted that the worldview of those who once honored the Great Mother considered the Earth itself to be sacred. But the "Terrible Mother" face of the Great Mother can also be seen in folklore about the Cailleach that presents her as harsh and inimical to humans, and as the bringer of winter, with its fierce storms and cold weather.

The story of Beira inspires aging women to fully experience all that the wintering seasons of life offer. Winter is hard, but it's necessary. We need the fallow times in which we withdraw into ourselves to rest and regroup, and in which we care for ourselves and lick accumulated wounds. Winter is a time for much-needed retreat, but it's far from a passive season: under the surface, seeds are building up strength for the coming of spring.

In the extensive body of folklore about the Cailleach, she grows beyond her wintering self to reflect the cycles of death and rebirth in nature: many stories report her ability to renew herself each year. All cycles in nature renew themselves constantly: the tide ebbs and flows, the moon waxes and wanes, the year cycles through each season in turn. But we seem somehow to have forgotten that this perpetual motion applies to humans too. As we sit with Beira at the well, waiting for a new dawn, perhaps we can find comfort in that — because these stories of a divine old woman who is so profoundly entangled with the seasons and cycles of nature, can help us learn to dance to the shifting rhythms of our own lives too.

Berrey Dhone

Berrey Dhone is a Manx figure who is very similar to the Scottish and Irish Cailleachs. Folklorist Walter Gill suggests that Berrey was a woman of the mountains: a witch, prophetess, hag, or giantess. In addition to her hauntings of the central hilltops, her name and her oracular presence are attached to a pool or ford at a highland stream in South Maughold, at which divination was commonly practiced.

Art thou within, Berrey Dhone?
Where walkest thou,
Unless thou art in a green strip
On the side of Barrule?

Let us go to the mountain
To lift up the turf,
And to see will Berrey come
Home to-night.

I walked upon Carraghyn
And I walked upon Snaefell,
But Berrey was behind the door
And the slab on top of it.

I walked upon Carraghyn
And I walked upon Slieu Beg;
Berrey was behind the door
As safe as a rock.

I walked upon Pennypot
And I walked upon Slieu Ouyr;
Berrey was behind the door
'Mid a circle of the treasure.

The Bush Grandmother

GERMANY

The Buschgroßmutter ("bush grandmother") is a legendary old woman from German folklore. She's an ancient forest spirit who shows herself to humans just once every hundred years and is depicted as small and hunched, wrinkled and ugly. She has wide, staring eyes, and her hair is a long white tangled mess, ridden with lice. She often holds a gnarled stick, and her feet are covered in moss. She manifests herself in a series of natural phenomena: when the mountains are smoking with fog, for example, then the Bush Grandmother is said to be cooking.

Like so many old women in European folklore, she's an ambivalent character. She often asks people to comb or delouse her hair; those who willingly do as she asks are rewarded with a never-ending spool of yarn, or with green or yellow leaves that will turn into gold if they're not thrown away. But if someone should sneer at her, the Bush Grandmother will take revenge by breathing onto the perpetrators; her breath causes them to become ill. Normally, she's presented as a solitary figure, but occasionally she is seen leading a group of Moosfräulein ("moss ladies"), who are her daughters.

In traditional folk tales of Transylvania, there is also a Bush Grandmother (the Baschgrîs): an old wood spirit with shaggy hair, large fiery eyes, and enormous teeth. A similar being, called the Baschmôter or Waldfrau ("forest woman"), has the habit of revealing herself to woodcutters; she'll drive them away if they are littering the forest or smoking there. She might offer a stern warning at first but will punish persistent forbidden behavior by causing a landslide.

Grandmother Snow

SIBERIA

On the plains of the far north, where Arctic marsh grass, creeping sedge, and saltmarsh starwort bind a thousand scattered lakes to the edge of the icy sea, an old Nenets man lived with his three daughters. They were reindeer herders, and every year they followed a thousand miles of ancient migratory routes all across the vast tundra. Now, a pelt of snow lay across the permafrost. They had brought their reindeer to the moss and lichen pastures of the taiga and were hunkering down there for the long season ahead.

The family's conical tent stood ragged at the edge of the camp, its skin walls so thinned with age and use that it barely kept out the cold air that crept in and overwhelmed the fire's meagre heat. In the darkest days of that winter, a great snowstorm gathered and growled across the tundra. For three wicked days and three merciless nights, winds tore at the tent's brittle seams and blizzards stung the air. Not one of these bold and hardy nomads dared to venture outside; they huddled around their fires, fearful that their homes might blow away or the camp should be buried beneath the fast-falling snow.

The father and his daughters shivered with cold and fear. "We're certainly going to die," he said to them, "if Kotura, Lord of the Winds, stays angry with us."

One of the daughters asked, "How can we placate him, then, and save our camp?"

"We'll have to send him a wife." But his daughters were the only young, unmarried women in the camp, and he turned a sad and weary face to the oldest of the three. "And so you must go to Kotura. Make him happy, and then beg him to stop the storm."

"But how will I find him, Father?" she said. "I have no idea where he lives."

"Turn your face to the north wind," he said. "Just push your sled forward and follow wherever it leads. The wind will tear apart the laces of your coat, but don't stop to tie them. Snow will fill your boots, but don't stop to shake them out. You'll come to a steep hill; don't stop till you've climbed to the top of it. Then, a little bird will land on your shoulder. Don't brush him away: caress him gently, then get on your sled and slide down the other side of the hill. You'll find yourself at the door of Kotura's tent. Go inside, but don't touch anything. Just wait until he comes — and then, do exactly as he tells you."

The eldest daughter put on every threadbare scrap of clothing she owned till she could hardly draw together the lace fastenings of her long reindeer-skin coat. She braved the twilight world and the whirling storm and, just as her father had predicted, the wind soon prized apart the lacings of her coat and clumps of snow filled her boots. She was so cold that she stopped, fastened her coat and shook out the snow from her boots. At last, she came to a steep hill and climbed to the top of it. A ragged scrap of feathers careered out of the gloom and would have landed on her shoulder but, tired now and irritable, she shooed the little bird away. It ducked, circled three times, and disappeared. The eldest daughter sat on the sled and rode it down the hill till she arrived outside an enormous tent.

She went inside; it was warm and dry, with great beds of soft skins piled around the fire that blazed in its center. A chunk of roast venison was set down next to it. Hungry as a polar bear in summer, she threw off her mittens and coat, sat down next to the fire, and picked up the meat. Piece after delicious, juicy piece, she ate till her belly was full and her cheeks and fingers were slick with grease. Now she was tired, but just as she lay down on one of the skin beds, the door flap drew back: in strode Kotura, Lord of the Winds, in all his youthful glory.

He raised one of his thick, dark brows. "Who are you, and what are you doing here?"

"My father sent me to be your wife."

He sighed, then frowned as he took in the half-eaten bones that once had been a tasty venison joint. He looked at her again with winter-cold eyes. "I've been hunting, and I've brought back some more meat. You'd better set to work now and cook it for me."

The eldest daughter did as he asked, and when the meat was cooked, Kotura cut it into two halves. "You and I will eat one part," he said to her, "and you'll take the other half to my neighbor. But make sure you don't go inside her house: just give her the meat and then wait for her to come out again with the dish."

So out into the storm she went, holding the plate tight against her chest. She struggled through knee-deep snow for a while, but she couldn't see another tent, and it was so cold and she was so tired that she just threw the meat into the snow and turned back to Kotura's warm fire.

"Did you do as I asked?"

"I did," she said.

"Then show me the dish and let me see what she gave you in return."

The eldest daughter showed him the empty dish. Kotura said nothing; he ate his share of the meat, then stretched out by the fireside to sleep. He rose at dawn and brought the eldest daughter some reindeer hides.

"While I'm out hunting, clean up these hides and make me a coat, a pair of shoes, and some mittens. I'll try them on when I get back, and then we'll see whether you're as clever with your hands as you are with your tongue."

The eldest daughter set to work. While she was cleaning and preparing the skins an old woman came into the tent, wrapped from head to toe in a voluminous sealskin coat. One of her eyes was shut, and the other was a pale shade of icy blue. "Child," the old woman said, "I have something in my eye. Could you help me remove it?"

The eldest daughter carried on with her work. "I've no time," she said. "I'm far too busy making clothes today."

The old woman left the tent.

The eldest daughter worked all day. She began to hack at the hides with a cooking knife, but she had no time to properly shape the garments, and no patience at all with the sewing. Late that evening, the handsome Lord of the Winds returned. "Are my clothes ready?" he asked.

"They are," the young woman said, laying them proudly at his feet.

Kotura fingered skins that were rough to the touch and poorly cleaned. He examined the seams, poked his fingers between the careless stitches — and saw that all of them were badly shaped and far too small for him. Kotura tossed them to one side, picked up the eldest daughter with one hand, and threw her out of the tent; she landed heavily in a snowdrift and lay there, unconscious, till she froze to death.

Back in the camp, the wind blew more fiercely and more icily than ever. The old father understood that Kotura was displeased and turned sorrowful eyes on his two remaining daughters. "Your elder sister didn't heed my warnings," he said to them. "Kotura is even angrier. And so, my second daughter, you're going to have to go to him now."

The old man gave the girl her instructions and sent her on her way. Unfortunately, just like her elder sister, she didn't do as he told her to — and she didn't follow Kotura's instructions either. She didn't take the meat to his neighbor or help the old woman with her eye when she came the next day to the tent, just as she had before; nor did she make Kotura fine clothes that fitted him. So the same fate befell her, and she too met a cold death in the snow.

Back in the Nenets camp, the storm whipped itself up to a wild, maddened frenzy. In the ragged tent at the edge of the village, tears rolled down the old father's cheeks and froze as they hit the floor. He turned to his only remaining daughter. She was so young and so beautiful, with her raven hair and eyes the color of the polar night sky. "Neither of your sisters followed my instructions," he said to her. "They've only succeeded in angering Kotura even more. Though it breaks my heart to send you to him, you're the only hope of our people. If you can't stop this storm, we'll all die."

The youngest daughter wrapped herself up as warmly as she could and followed her sled into the north wind. The storm raged about her; the snow blinded her, and the icy wind toppled her into the deep snow. But even when the laces of her coat tore loose and her boots filled with snow, she remembered her father's words and staggered on till she reached the top of the hill, where the sled finally came to a halt. A little bird tumbled out of the storm and landed on her shoulder; comforted, she gently stroked its breast feathers; a few breaths later, the bird flew off into the storm. The youngest daughter climbed on the sled and rode down the hillside till she came to Kotura's tent.

She gathered her courage and went inside the home of the Lord of the Winds. She sat down on a bed of skins and waited patiently until the door flap was lifted and Kotura strode in with a sack of jointed venison. When he saw the lovely young woman, the smallest of smiles softened his solemn face. "Who are you, and why are you here?"

"I'm the youngest of my father's daughters. You met my sisters. My father sent me to be your wife, and to ask you to calm the storm, because if you don't, all our people will die."

"Stoke up the fire and cook me some of this meat," Kotura said. "I'm hungry, and since you've touched nothing since you arrived here, I expect you are too."

The youngest daughter did as she was told. She cooked the meat he gave her; when it was ready, she put it on a plate and handed it to Kotura. He cut it in two and instructed the girl to take one half to his neighbor.

She went out into the storm again — but where was she to go? How could she possibly find the neighbor's tent in this blinding blizzard? Suddenly, a tiny bird flew out of the heart of the storm and fluttered in front of her face: it was her little friend from the hilltop. It flew away for a couple of feet and then back to her again; she realized that it was trying to get her to follow. So she struggled on behind the bird, clutching the plate of meat to her chest, till eventually a ragged plume of smoke caught her eye. But as she grew nearer, she realized that the smoke wasn't rising from a tent but from a mound, all covered with snow. She walked around it, looking for a door, but none was to be found. She prodded the mound with her foot and a door appeared; it opened to reveal a gray-haired old woman. "Who are you?" the old woman asked her. "And why have you come here?"

"Grandmother," the youngest daughter said, "I've brought you a gift of meat from Kotura, Lord of the Winds."

The old woman looked the youngest daughter up and

down with her strange, pale-blue eyes. "Kotura, you say? Very well then; you wait here." And she took the dish of meat and closed the door. The girl waited by the strange snow-house. She waited, shivering, for a long time. Just as she thought she was going to turn to ice, the old woman reappeared and gave the dish back to her. There was something in it, but she couldn't see what it was. She thanked the old woman and retraced her steps to Kotura's tent.

"What took you so long?" Kotura asked her. "Did you find Grandmother Snow's place?" The girl shook the snow from her boots and coat and nodded. "Then let me see what she's given you," he said, and held out his hand. When he looked in the dish, he saw that it contained two sharp knives, a handful of strong bone needles, and a set of scrapers for dressing hides. Kotura laughed. "She's given you some fine gifts, and you're going to find them very useful."

The next morning, Kotura rose at dawn and brought the girl a bundle of skins; he told her to make him new shoes, mittens, and a coat — and all by nightfall. "If you make them well," he said, "I'll take you for my wife."

As soon as Kotura left, the youngest daughter washed the skins and set to work with the fine tools. The scrapers made the skins soft and pliable enough to cut and sew, but she worried nevertheless that she wouldn't be able to finish in time. She worked so hard and so fast that her hands began to blister. Then the door flap lifted and in came Grandmother Snow, wrapped in a coat made from polar bear fur.

"Will you help me, child? I have something caught in my eye and I can't get it out." At once, the youngest daughter set down her work, examined the old woman's eye, and removed from it a pale eyelash.

"Ah, that's better," said Grandmother Snow. "Now, child, look in my right ear and tell me what you see."

The girl did as she was told and gasped in surprise. "There's a girl sitting inside your ear!"

"Then why don't you speak to her? She'll help you make Kotura's clothes."

So the youngest daughter called out to the girl and, along with her three sisters, she jumped out of Grandmother Snow's ear, and they applied themselves to the task at hand. Soon, the clothes were ready. The young woman thanked them for their help, then Grandmother Snow took the four girls back into her ear and left with a nod and a smile.

As night fell, Kotura returned. "Are my new clothes ready?" he asked.

"Yes," she said, and held out the newly made garments.

Kotura passed his great hands over each of them. The skins were soft and supple, the stitches fine and tight, and each item fitted him perfectly. He smiled.

"I like you, youngest daughter. And my old mother and four sisters seem to like you too. You're brave and you're kind. You faced up to the worst of my storms so your people wouldn't die, and you did everything you were asked to do. Will you stay here and be my wife?" The youngest daughter happily accepted his proposal and, all at once, the winds stilled and the snow stopped falling.

Back in the camp, the girl's father tentatively poked his head out of the tent. The sky had cleared. There was the moon, and there were the familiar, guiding stars. The people were safe. One by one, they drew their reindeer-skin coats around them and stepped out into the bright, silent land. And in a snow-covered mound far, far to the north, Grandmother Snow laughed.

Like the Cailleach in Scottish folk traditions, the old woman in this Siberian (Nenets) story personifies winter. She's the mother of the Lord of the Winds, who brings storms to the world, and so she seems to preside over a family with decidedly elemental inclinations. The Finns, the Saami people of Lapland, and the Samoyed people of Siberia also honored as deities old women who embodied the Earth and its cycles and seasons.

Like some of the other older women in this book, Grandmother Snow's primary role in the narrative is to test the mettle of the young. She assesses the three girls to get to the heart of them: to see who they are, and what they will do under pressure. But in contrast to some of the kindlier mentors in the "Gifts for the Young" part of this book, when Grandmother Snow finds her subjects lacking, there's a ruthless inevitability to the trajectory of the fate that follows. Like winter itself, she's uncompromising. She rewards kindness and courage handsomely when eventually she finds it, but she has no truck with laziness, lies, callousness, or self-centeredness. But those are exactly the qualities she finds in the first two daughters in this story: they disobey their father, slap away a tiny bird caught in a storm, throw food away rather than bother taking it to someone who might need it, and refuse to stop what they're doing for a couple of minutes to help an old woman remove a painful mote from her eye. In the clear-cut, elemental world of the fairy tale, the unfortunate consequence for such behavior is death.

After emerging from the purging fires of menopause, most women find themselves profoundly changed. From the beginning of our perimenopausal years, the hormones that are associated with what we think of as "feminine qualities" — relationality, emotion, the drive to nurture and to avoid conflict — are in serious decline. And so, as we pass through menopause and grow into elderhood, we're likely to have considerably less patience with those who are economical with the truth or who try to take advantage of us, and we suffer fools much less gladly. After decades of taking care of others or of deference toward them, we begin to realize that the maintenance of their happiness and self-esteem at the cost of our own is no longer our raison d'être. Being nice is no longer a life goal.

That doesn't, of course, mean that kindness and compassion have entirely fallen away from us: rather, they are more selectively bestowed on those who are deserving. It's wise to forgive genuine mistakes and understandable failures of courage, and we would all, where we can, benefit from instructing rather than destroying. But it's also important to reward the wide range of behaviors that serve life and not to reward the behavior that doesn't. In that way, older women become flagbearers for the positive moral qualities that have always enriched the world.

The Carlin of Beinn Bhreac

SCOTLAND

"Carlin," a slightly disparaging Scots word for an old woman, is another name given to the Cailleach in parts of Scotland, and there are many songs and stories about a Cailleach who lived on Beinn Bhreac (anglicized to Ben Vreck), a twin-peaked mountain in the Cairngorms. In the seventh verse, the carlin is explaining that she never wore shoes, just short socks.

The carlin of Beinn Bhreac ho,
Bhreac ho, Bhreac ho,
The carlin of Beinn Bhreac ho,
The tall carlin of the mountain spring.

I would not let my herd of deer,
My herd of deer, my herd of deer,
I would not let my herd of deer
Go nibble the gray shells of the shore.

They had rather their own cress,
Their cress ho, their own cress,
They had rather their own cress
That grew on the spur of the high hills.

I am a carlin ranging bens,
Ranging bens, ranging glens,

170

I am a carlin ranging bens,
Trying to see the best glen.

Climbing up the mountaintop,
The mountaintop, the mountaintop,
Climbing up the mountaintop,
I found not the white pin.

I found not, I lost, I found,
I found not, I lost, I found,
I found not, I lost, I found,
I found not the white pin.

I never wore an upper shoe,
An upper shoe, an upper shoe,
I never wore an upper shoe,
What I got was the short hose.

I never wore a garment,
A garment, a garment,
I never wore a garment,
Until the fair-haired gallant rescued me.

I never set a fetter,
A fetter, a fetter,
I never set a fetter
On black or red cow in the herd.

I am the carlin who is light,
I am the carlin who is light,
I am the carlin who is light,
Alone on the spur of the cairns.

The Green Man of No Man's Land

WELSH GYPSY

Back in the good old days, there lived a handsome young miller called Jack; he was so clever a gambler that nobody could beat him, no matter how hard they tried. One day, a tall stranger knocked on Jack's door and challenged him to a game of cards. "If you can beat me," the stranger said, "you may ask me for anything you want. But if you lose, your life is mine."

Jack thought this was very peculiar, but he happily agreed to the tall man's terms; after all, no one had ever beaten him before, so why should he worry now? They took themselves down to the village inn, sat down at a table, and played. As he had expected, Jack easily won the first round.

The strange man scowled. "Right, then — what do you want?" he said to Jack, and Jack thought for a moment, then asked for a castle. The stranger waved his hand at the open door of the inn and Jack rushed outside. A beautiful castle, made of warm, brown stone studded with glittering diamonds, had appeared in the field behind Jack's house.

Jack was delighted with the way his day had gone and wanted to hurry away to his castle to see what he might find inside. But the stranger held up his hand. "You really are as great a gambler as I'd heard," he said to Jack. "Won't you play just one more round with me? Surely there must be more things you'd like to have." Jack, flushed with success and full of confidence, declared that he would be delighted to play another round, and he began to think of all the wonderful things that he could demand from the strange man when he won. So another round of cards was played — but this time, Jack lost. The strange man smiled and heaved himself up from the table. He stretched this way and he stretched that way, until he grew even taller and very much stouter, and his skin began to turn a shade of bright emerald-green.

"I am the Green Man of No Man's Land," he said in a deep, booming voice to an open-mouthed Jack, "and now your life is mine. But I'm a generous man, and I'll offer you a chance to win it back. I'll give you a year and a day to find my castle in No Man's Land. Unless you can do that, I'll come and find you, and I'll chop off your head when I do."

Too much time passed before Jack applied himself to his task, because he had no idea where to begin. No one in his village had ever heard of No Man's Land, and even though he asked every traveler who came through, no one else had heard of it either. Finally, when winter arrived, the increasingly despondent Jack realized that he'd better try to find the Green Man's country, so one frigid morning he set off into a land that was blanketed in snow. He left the still-sleeping village before the cocks had started to crow and he passed into the forest beyond, trudging wearily through the deepening snow.

Eventually, the forest opened out into a country that was new to him, and as he looked around him, Jack spotted a small stone cottage by the side of a fast-flowing river. He made his way down to it, knocked on its door, and an ordinary-looking old woman with gray hair, swathed in a paisley shawl against the cold, opened it. She looked Jack up and down and shook her head when she saw his face, which was blue with cold, and his cloak, which was covered in snow, and then she invited him inside. She sat him down at her table and offered him a bowl of barley soup and lodging for the night.

Jack accepted gladly, and while he was tucking into the delicious soup, he asked the old woman if she knew of the Green Man, or where in the world he might find No Man's Land.

"I've lived on this Earth a long time, and I've come to know many things, but that I don't know," she said to Jack. "But if a quarter of the birds in the world know, then I'll be able to tell you."

In the morning, when Jack had woken up, the old woman climbed onto the roof of the cottage. She lifted a great horn, put it to her lips, and blew it three times. The sky grew dark and the air quivered with the beating wings of a quarter of all the birds in the world; they quickly settled on the trees around her cottage. She asked them whether they knew of the Green Man, or where in the world No Man's Land might be found — but they didn't, so the old woman told them they could leave, and off they went. She clambered down from the roof and told Jack not to worry; he should go to visit her elder sister, she said, because she knew more things and was much wiser. So she lent Jack her horse so that he could make the long journey, and that's precisely what Jack did.

After a hard and seemingly endless three days, Jack came to the cottage of the old woman's older sister; he found her outside, chopping logs with a great axe. The old woman straightened and tucked long wisps of steel-gray hair behind her ears. "It's a long time," she said to Jack, "since I've seen my sister's horse. You'd better come inside." She offered him food and lodging, and Jack accepted gladly. While eating a bowl of delicious stew, he asked the old woman if she knew of the Green Man, or where in the world he might find No Man's Land.

"I've lived on this Earth a long time, and I've come to know many things, but that I don't know," she said, her gray eyes sparkling; "but if half of the birds in the world know, then I'll be able to tell you."

In the morning, when Jack woke up, the old woman climbed onto the roof of the cottage and blew three times on a great horn. With a sound like thunder, half of the birds in the world flew in and settled on the trees around her cottage. She asked them whether they knew of the Green Man, or where in the world No Man's Land might be found — but they didn't know, and so the old woman told them to fly away again. She slid down the thatched roof and landed on a pile of fresh hay destined for the stable. Jack shouldn't worry, she told him, but he should go and visit the oldest of the three sisters, who knew more than she did and was very much wiser. She took her sister's weary horse and presented Jack with her own, then gave him directions to find the eldest sister.

Finally, after a long and hard three days, Jack came to the cottage of the oldest of the three old sisters. He was met at the door by a wizened old woman with flint-sharp eyes. "It's a long time," she said, "since I've seen my sister's horse." She invited Jack inside and offered him food and lodging. Again, Jack accepted gladly, and as he was eating a plate of delicious pie with thick, brown gravy, he asked the old woman if she knew of the Green Man, or where in the world he might find No Man's Land.

"I've lived on this Earth a long time, and I've come to know many things, but that I don't know," she said to Jack; "but if all the birds in the world know, then I'll be able to tell you."

In the morning, when Jack was awake, the old woman climbed onto the roof of the cottage and sat on the ridge. She lifted a great horn and blew it three times — and in an instant, the sky darkened and rained feathers, and all the birds in the world flew in and settled on the trees around her cottage. She asked them whether they knew of the Green Man, or where in the world No Man's Land might be found — but they didn't know. Just as she made to turn away and climb down from the roof, though, the old woman stopped and frowned. She turned back to look carefully at the gathered birds. After a moment she nodded and told the birds to stay right where they were; then she went into her house and rifled through the pages of an enormous leather-bound book that was lying in a corner of the kitchen table. She consulted a long list of birds — pages and pages long — and eventually she turned to Jack and told him that there was an eagle missing. So she climbed back onto her roof with her horn, took a deep breath and blew one long, last blast, and after a few minutes a great golden eagle flew out of the forest and settled on the thickest branch of the oak tree in front of her house. The old woman scolded him for not responding to her first summons, but the eagle said that he had been far, far away and had come as fast as he could. She asked him where he had been, and he told her that he had been near the castle of the Green Man of No Man's Land.

The old woman thanked the birds and made her way down from the roof. She took her sister's horse and lent Jack her own, and then she told him to travel west till he came to a vast, crystal-clear pool, at the edge of which he would see three large white birds. She told him to hide there, and then to rush over and steal the feathers of the last bird that went into the water.

So Jack traveled west for nine hard days and nine cold nights, till finally he came to a great pool of crystal-clear water, at the edge of which were three large white birds. They were the most beautiful birds he had ever seen. On the other side of the lake was a castle all made of bright emerald-green stone, and Jack realized that this was the castle of the Green Man of No Man's Land. He hid behind a bush and watched as, one by one, the great white birds entered the water — but as the last one went to step in, Jack ran out from his hiding place and plucked the feathers from her tail. The bird cried out and demanded that Jack return her feathers. But he refused to return them till the bird agreed to carry him across the lake to the green castle on the other side.

The bird reluctantly agreed. Jack gave her back her tail feathers and she flew across the great gleaming lake with Jack on her back. But when she set foot on the other shore and he stepped off, she was suddenly transformed into the most beautiful young woman he had ever seen, and she told him that she was the youngest of the three daughters of the Green Man of No Man's Land.

Jack walked up to the castle and knocked on its great green door. It opened, and the Green Man stood there with his hands on his broad hips. "So you've found my castle, Jack," he said.

"I have," said Jack.

The Green Man reminded Jack that he owed him his life. But, he said, since Jack was a gambling man and all, he would offer him a second chance to win it back. He would set Jack three tasks, but if he failed at any single one of them, he would lose his head.

The first task he set Jack was to clean the stable, but whenever Jack threw out a shovelful of dirt, three shovelfuls returned. He was on the verge of giving up, but then the Green Man's daughter brought his dinner into the stable, and she finished the task for him. But she warned Jack not to tell her father.

The Green Man accused Jack of receiving help, but Jack denied it. So a second task was set for him: Jack must climb a glass mountain in the middle of a lake to the north of his castle, and bring from the top of it the egg of a bird that lays only one egg. The task was to be completed by the end of the day. Well, Jack set out north till he came to the lake in question — and, much to his relief, he found the Green Man's daughter already there. She smiled at Jack and told him to make a wish: he should wish for her shoe to become a boat. Jack closed his eyes and wished, and the shoe promptly turned into a boat with gleaming white sails; they sailed in it together across the great lake.

When finally they reached the mountain in the center of it, Jack tried to climb it — but every time he clutched at its sides, he slipped down again. The Green Man's daughter told him to make another wish: that her fingers should form a ladder. He made his wish, and the girl's fingers flew off her hands and bored into the side of the great glass mountain so that Jack could use them as steps. She warned him to tread on every step and not to miss a single one, but Jack was so keen to complete his task that he forgot her words, and he stepped over the last finger in his haste to take the egg. When he returned to the ground, the girl's fingers flew back onto her hands — but one of them was broken. Again, she warned Jack not to tell her father that he had had help in obtaining the egg.

When they got back to the castle, the Green Man snatched the egg, glowering, and then set the final task: Jack must guess which of the Green Man's three daughters was the youngest, as they flew three times over the castle in the shape of great white birds. At first, Jack was unable to tell them apart — until he noticed that one of the birds had a crooked wing, and then he knew that this was the youngest daughter, whose finger had been broken at the glass mountain.

When Jack identified the correct daughter, the Green Man flew into a rage — but he too was a gambling man, and eventually he accepted that, on this occasion, Jack had won. He asked Jack what he most desired in the world as reward for his win, and Jack asked for the hand of the Green Man's youngest daughter. So they were wed at once, and returned to Jack's village to live in the beautiful stone castle that was waiting there for them. And if they're not yet dead, they're living there still.

This story from the Welsh gypsy tradition contains a common motif in European folklore: encounters with three witchy sisters of increasing age who help the protagonist to achieve his or her heart's desire. The youngest of the old women is wise, the middle sister is wiser still, and the oldest is always the wisest of all. Wisdom, these stories tell us, matures and deepens with advancing age.

In this story, the three old sisters have the ability not only to summon birds and to speak their language but also to know every single bird in the world and to identify any one of them who might be missing. The sisters convene the birds to access knowledge that they themselves don't possess, and in the days when stories such as this one made their way into the oral tradition, animals were very much more than simply creatures that we might hunt and eat: they were teachers and allies, and sometimes they were even gods. Some of our oldest stories involve powerful elder animals who embody a kind of wisdom that is different from (but entirely congruent with) the ways of knowing that humans have. And in these ancient tales, the oldest animals of all were often repositories for the kind of knowledge that humans long ago renounced.

From early Classical times, literature offered up an image of the witch as, like the three older sisters in this story, firmly situated in the natural world. The tools of the witch, and especially the ingredients she needed for her magic potions, came from nature and were all tied up with the cycles and seasons of the year: herbs, for example, must be gathered in specific places and at specific times of the day or night. Witches were closely associated with animals, and so Homer and Ovid both tell us that Circe's house was guarded by wolves, lions, and bears. Witches would commonly transform themselves or other humans into animals: according to the Roman writer Apuleius, for example, Thessalian witches could transform themselves into birds, dogs, mice, or flies.

The closeness of women to animals and the natural world is a strong thread that runs throughout our native European myth and folklore, then, but it's one of many feminine qualities that has gradually been driven underground over the last two thousand years. Today, we face the devaluation of all that is wild and instinctual in our own natures, but stories such as this one remind us that older women's deep ways of knowing are not gone forever: they're just lying dormant, waiting for a new dawn. As we let go of the strivings of the first half of life, space can be created for a deeper kinship with the natural world to emerge.

What Are Old Women Made Of?

ENGLAND

What are old women made of?
What are old women made of?
Bushes and thorns
And old cows' horns,
That's what old women are made of.

The Witch of Beinn a' Glò

SCOTLAND

The story is still whispered in the cold, dark heart of the Highlands of the two poachers who set out from Braemar one winter day, in search of red deer. The weather had been worsening for a good few days, and clouds the color of Payne's gray had softened into mist that masked the distinctive shapes of the mountaintops. The temperature had fallen too, but at least that meant the gamekeepers would be spending more time at home sipping whiskey by their fires, and so it was less likely that they'd be caught.

Just as dawn broke the hold of the night, the two men crept out of town and made their way up and over the hills to the southwest. There was no more than a light breeze and they walked for miles without incident, but when they arrived at the Falls of Tarf, the wind whipped up and they were overtaken by a snowstorm. It turned out to be little more than a shower, though, and after it had cleared up they carried on walking in the same direction. Soon, they spotted a herd of deer in the Forest of Atholl. They spent a couple of hours creeping around the herd, and finally they set their sights on a hind and shot her — but they had only succeeded in wounding her, and she ran off before they could take aim again.

Cursing their bad luck, the poachers tracked the hind over a long distance, following her blood-drops on the snow. But as

day dissolved into evening, the wind scoured the hollow corries and battered the ridges, and snow fell thick and heavy.
They had been so intent on following the bloody traces of the
wounded deer that they hadn't taken much notice of where
they were going, and now they were utterly lost. So they piled
up a few stones and turfs for shelter, and tucked themselves up
tight in their plaids. Fortunately, they'd brought some oatcake
and whiskey with them, and they huddled down, cold and wet
but in no immediate danger.

When they woke from a restless, shivering sleep at dawn,
they realized that they'd landed themselves in serious trouble.
The wind howled, cold and bitter, and the snow was still tumbling down; they couldn't see more than a few feet in front of
them. The task ahead of them wasn't about killing deer anymore but staying alive.

The wind, which continued to blow from the frigid north,
was their only guide. They turned their back on it and so
avoided the brunt of the storm; they hoped they might soon
reach Glen Tilt or the Strath of the Tay, where they could take
their bearings and find their way to shelter. But the snow had
drifted in such lofty masses that they were unable to pursue
anything resembling a straight course, and it was so deep that
their advance was slow and laborious. Soon, the small stock of
provisions they'd brought with them was exhausted. The wind
had turned to the east, but in their windings and wanderings
they were quite oblivious to the fact; they continued to turn
their backs on it, and so traveled west instead of south.

Eventually, when night was setting in again, the snow
slowed for a moment and the two men saw a deep, empty
glen ahead of them. They had no idea which glen it might
be — they felt certain they'd never seen it before — but they
made their way down into it, to escape the bleak winds on the
icy summits. Their plan again was to gather a few stones and

turfs around them for shelter during the dark hours. To their great relief, while they were looking around for a convenient spot, they came upon an old shieling of the kind that would be used by shepherds to tend their roving flocks in summer. They imagined that it would be deserted, because huts in such remote places would never be used in the winter. But the door opened as they approached it: an old woman stood there, silhouetted on the threshold. She told them she had been expecting them, and that their supper and heather beds were ready.

As they walked into the warmth of the shieling, with its peat fire glowing in the hearth and oil lamps flickering in the corners, they discovered that they had indeed been expected. A pan was simmering over the fire, and bannocks and oatcakes were laid out on the table — along with two plates. They sat down at the table, but they could hardly focus on the food before them: now that they could see her properly, there was something so extraordinary about this old woman that they could hardly tear their eyes away. She was wild and haggard, and dressed in ragged plaid; she had long, tangled gray hair, an enormous nose and chin, and deeply set gray eyes. While she was pouring out the soup for them, she stood on one leg and chanted a wild song in a language they didn't recognize. Exhausted and famished as the two poachers were, the whole scenario was so bizarre that they could scarcely bring themselves to eat.

Then she waved her long, sinewy arms at them and said that she had power over winds and storms. They grew fearful. She snatched up a rope from the table and held it out to them; three knots were tied in it. "If I should loose the first knot," she said to them, "a fair wind will blow: the kind of wind that every poacher might wish for. You'll remember that wind, on the morning you set off on your journey." She grinned, showing a mouth filled with neat, yellowed, and oddly sharp teeth. "If I loose the second knot, a stronger blast will sweep over the hills. You'll remember that wind, at the Falls of Tarf. And if I loose the third knot, such a storm will break out that neither man nor beast could survive it. Its blast will yowl down the corries and the glens, and the pines will fall and crash into the swollen rivers. This bare arm of mine will guide the course of the storm as I sit on my throne, Cairn-Gower, on the top of Beinn a' Glò. You experienced my power today, when the wind was cold and deadly and everything hidden in snow."

The old woman put the rope back down on the table and glared at them, bony hands on her hips. "You can see that you were expected here, and yet you've brought no venison with you. What kind of guests are you? Well, then — if you mean to live, and if you'd like to continue your poaching habit while I loosen only my first knot in the hills and glens you're stalking, this is the way to guarantee it. Place a fat stag or a barren hind in the braes of Atholl, by Eraser's cairn, at midnight on the first Monday in every month, for as long as winter lasts. The laird's ghost won't pay any attention to you. But if you don't do as I say, you'll be sorry. You'll perish on the crags; the raven will croak your dirge, and your bones will be picked clean by the eagle."

Needless to say, the poachers agreed. They gulped down their soup and ate their bannocks and oatcakes; they spent the night in a deep, exhausted sleep, and it was late before they rose from their beds of heather. But when they looked around them, their strange hostess had vanished and the shieling was empty and deserted. Much to their relief, the storm had abated; they found their way to Glen Tilt and took the road back home. You can be sure that they followed the strange old woman's instructions to the letter, and never again did a wild winter storm disrupt their poaching.

Beinn a' Glò is a range of hills with three high peaks in the heart of the Cairngorms: it's known as the witch's mountain. The witch in question — the witch of Beinn a' Glò — is depicted in local folklore as a mischievous, occasionally malevolent being. She was also said to have the power to take the shape of an eagle, raven, hind, or any other animal that might suit her purpose. In this story, the witch is more manipulative than malevolent: this is her land, her throne sits up on the highest mountaintop, and she expects tribute from those who come calling. The poachers are hunting for deer on her territory, and she's not going to let them get away with taking unless they acknowledge her and offer something in return.

The story of this old mountain-witch, like so many similar Scottish stories, is akin to many tales about the Cailleach. Several of them portray the Cailleach as a guardian of the natural world's balance — especially when it comes to the need to protect it against humans. And so one story tells of her preventing Donald Cameron, a hunter in Lochaber, from killing a herd of hinds that she was driving. Seeing him raise his gun, she called to him: "You are too hard on my hinds, Donald! You must not be so hard on them!" Donald, quick-witted, answered her immediately, saying: "I have never killed a hind where I could find a stag." He allowed the hinds to pass, concentrated ever afterward on taking the occasional stag, and the old woman never bothered him again. The witch of Beinn a' Glò is similarly careful to instruct the poachers only to leave her a stag or a barren hind, so that the herds might thrive and balance be maintained in the land. Earlier in this section, we encountered similar guidance from the Bashmôter or Waldfrau ("forest woman"), who will cause a landslide if woodcutters persist in littering the forest or smoking there.

This large body of folklore about powerful elder women who stand against the exploitation of animals and the land, who are the guardians and protectors of the natural world, offers us a selection of strong role models — so that we too might be inspired to fight for nature in the face of environmental catastrophe. In these troubled times and challenging environmental conditions, we women need to embrace our inner Cailleach: to stand up for the integrity and health of the wild places and creatures of this world. These old women in the Gaelic tradition are our allies in this work, teaching us that we are the land and the land is us; reminding us also that to grow into an elder is to become strong, as enduring as the beautiful old bones of this Earth.

The witch of Beinn a' Glò has a second useful attribute: her ability to control the weather, and specifically, the wind. Folklore throughout Britain and some parts of Europe tells of "wind witches": wise women who could bind up the wind in knotted ropes. That wind could then be set free when it was needed, by loosening the knot. Sailors would buy these ropes from the wind witches and, when wind was required to fill their sails, a knot would be untied and they would be blown on their way. A fragment of folklore from the Isle of Man, dating back to 1350, reported that the release of one knot brought a gentle, southwesterly wind; the release of two knots at the same time would whip up a strong north wind, and the simultaneous loosening of three knots would conjure up a tempest.

Our failure today to fully embrace aging is in good part because, in the years since the so-called Enlightenment, we have cut ourselves off from nature, and so from the natural cycles and rhythms of our human life. This story, along with the others in this section, reminds us that, once upon a time in Europe, elder women were seen as forces of nature. They were revered — and sometimes they were feared. Today, it's more than time to make our voices heard again, and to stand up for this beautiful, animate Earth on which we depend.

Don't Mess with Old Women

Chances are that most of us, at some time in our lives, will have known a formidable old woman or two: great-aunts, grandmothers, teachers, neighbors — women whacked by the harsh winds of life but never flattened by them. Such women aren't afraid to bite back when biting is precisely what's needed, and their courage lies in standing up for themselves — and for others.

European myths and folk tales also offer us a fine array of older women who allow themselves to express their anger when it's needed: women who show us all the ways in which our often suppressed, but righteous, wrath can be a powerful force for necessary change in the world.

Above all, though, the women in the stories that follow are strong, and their strength of character has grown through a lifetime of trials and tribulations. They're undaunted by injustice and stand firm when confronted by dangerous opponents. They're the custodians of deep and sometimes dark knowledge, and the wielders of curious powers. When the times require it, they're not afraid to use their skill — but the joy of them lies in their refusal to take themselves too seriously: they're not above dishing out their judgments with a good-sized helping of humor. These stories inspire us to imagine feistier, funnier, and braver versions of elderhood: stories to live by that are infinitely more desirable than those imposed on us by a culture that really would rather we just stayed quiet.

The Furies

GREECE

In Classical mythology, righteous wrath was the province of three old women: the Furies (the Erinyes, in Greek). Fragments of stories in which the Furies appear are found in the very earliest Greek texts, indicating that the three sisters were much more ancient than any of the better-known Olympian deities. The Furies responded to complaints brought to them by humans about behavior that was immoral or unlawful. This could include relatively minor misdemeanors, such as the incivility of the young to their parents or to elders, and hosts who offended their guests — and it could also include crimes that were much worse, such as murder. It was the job of the Furies to punish such crimes by relentlessly hounding their perpetrators.

The Greek poet Hesiod named the three sisters as Alecto — "unceasing in anger," the punisher of moral crimes; Megaera — "jealous one," the punisher of infidelity, oath-breaking, and theft; and Tisiphone — "avenger of murder." He presented them as the daughters of Gaea (the goddess who personified the Earth), who was said to have conceived them from the blood of her husband, Uranus, after he had been castrated by Cronos, his son. The Furies were portrayed as foul-smelling old hags with bat-like wings, black snakes adorning their hair, arms, and waists, and blood dripping from their eyes; they also carried brass-studded scourges.

The wrath of the Furies would be expressed in various ways, appropriate to the crime: a tormenting madness would be imposed on the murderer of a parent, other killers might be inflicted with a serious disease, and countries or states that sheltered such criminals could be stricken with famine and plague. The Furies could be placated only with ritual purification, and with the completion of a task that they handed out to lawbreakers so that they might atone for their crimes. Although the Furies were certainly fearful, they were also respected and believed to be necessary: they symbolized justice and were defenders of the moral order, so helping to keep the world in balance.

Watching for the Milk-Stealer

ENGLAND

There was no doubt about it: the cows weren't producing nearly as much milk as usual. The farmer glared at the half-empty pail, took off his cap, scratched his balding head, and ran through it all again. The pasture was as lush as it had ever been around Commondale in May and the cows looked to be in fine fettle — just as good as any of the prize milking cows he'd seen at the mart the week before. But still, they just weren't responding to the milker's fingers as they should be, and it was well past time to get to the bottom of it.

Another possibility nagged at the back of the farmer's mind, and that was witches. There were witches galore in the neighborhood and everyone knew full well that if the fancy took them, they would happily steal milk or dry up udders. A few of his neighbors had suffered in such ways due to unfortunate encounters with witches, but as far as he could tell, neither he nor his wife had done anything to upset them. Still, he wondered how he might find out whether some hocus-pocus of theirs was causing this low yield of milk. He decided that there was nothing for it but to set a watch on the field at night.

That same afternoon, he instructed a young farmhand to watch the meadow in which the cows were turned out to pasture at night, and to report back on anything unusual he might see. One uneventful night followed another, and each morning the lad came back to the farmer and said that there was nothing to tell. The cows hadn't been approached by anyone, and there were no signs of wily old crones — nor even of a furtive maid with a bucket and stool. And yet, morning after morning, the cows gave little or no milk.

One morning, a neighbor happened to be passing while the young farmhand was making his report, and he stopped a while to lean over the gate and listen as the farmer questioned the young lad. The farmhand was adamant, swearing on his granny's life that nobody had even come into the field, let alone gone anywhere near the cows. Then something occurred to the neighbor, and he interrupted the farmhand. "Aye, well," he said. "I know you're saying that no *person* ever came into that field with the cows, but is it true that nothing at all went into it overnight?"

The young lad gazed down intently at his boots as he thought hard about the question. After a moment, he remembered seeing a hare come and go a few times through a gap in the dike; it had hopped over to where the cows were feeding or standing, and it had seemed to enjoy grazing among them. The neighbor asked him whether the hare always came from the same side and entered the field the same way, and the lad looked up at him in surprise. "Aye, it does."

At that, the neighbor and the farmer exchanged knowing glances. "That's the side handiest for Old Mally's house," the neighbor said, and the farmer nodded slowly: that old woman had an uncanny reputation. "I reckon she's the one who's been stealing your milk, while taking the form of an old dewhopper," the neighbor said with a self-satisfied smile.

Now that they had a hypothesis, how to test it was their next dilemma. After much deliberation, they decided that the farmer himself would take the watch that night. He would carry his gun with him, which would need to be loaded with silver slugs instead of lead pellets, to combat any tricksy hocus-pocus. But it wasn't so easy to come by silver slugs in an out-of-the-way place like Commondale, and besides, they didn't want to draw attention to what they were up to. In the end, they decided that the farmer would cut up a few silver buttons and load the gun with the pieces.

That evening, as the sun was setting, the farmer took his shotgun and sat under a hawthorn tree in the far corner of the field; he'd be hidden from view but still have a good view of the gap and the grazing cows. He would watch very carefully, because he didn't want to waste his precious shot on just any old hare: it was Old Mally that he needed to catch — if she was indeed the villain — and to shoot her in the act of sucking the milk from the cows.

The moon rose high over the woods, casting long shadows across the field. The farmer, alert to every sound, almost jumped out of his old tweed jacket when an owl hooted in a tree behind him, but eventually he settled down to his vigil. Midnight came and went, but there was neither a whisker nor a whisper of hare anywhere nearby. The chill night slowly slipped by as the constellations came and went overhead. Dog foxes barked, vixens screamed, bats swooped from tree to tree, and in a hedge nearby a lone nightingale sang his hopeful song to lure a mate. And still there was no sign of any intruder into the pasture. The farmer was just about to give up hope when he caught sight of a hare approaching stealthily from the other side of the dike. Her black-tipped ears were pricked and her eyes bulged as she sat up on her haunches every couple of minutes to listen for suspicious sounds.

The farmer's heart beat faster when the hare stood up again and seemed to glower at the spot where he lay on his belly now, hidden in the shadows. Soon, though, apparently

reassured by the stillness in the pasture, she resumed her lei-
surely advance; she hopped right through the gap in the dike
and on into the moonlit field. But instead of bounding across
to the feeding cows, she took a direct course toward the farmer.
Ever so slowly, he moved his gun into position at his shoulder
and took aim; he closed one eye and, with the other, sighted
the hare. Her eyes grew larger and larger with every jump. The
farmer watched, startled, until, almost upon him now, the hare
reared up, growing taller and taller and all the while glaring
right at the place where he sat — and finally she was right
there in front of him, standing on hind legs, belly pale as the
moon, towering over him with shining eyes as big as saucers.
With a scream of utter terror, the farmer sprang out of his
hiding place, flung his gun away from him, and ran headlong
across the field. He didn't stop till he reached the farmhouse
door, hurled himself inside, and double-locked and bolted it.

And so ended the farmer's attempt to bring the milk-
stealer to account. Never again did he mention the hare, or his
suspicions about Old Mally, and never again was he heard to
complain about his cows' milk yield — though his neighbors
would swear blind that it didn't ever improve.

British and Irish folklore is abundant with accounts of witches
stealing milk and butter or drying up cows' udders. In this context, museum cases across Europe display crocks and jars unearthed at field corners and pasture edges that once contained
scraps of lead, fabric, or wood marked with protective symbols
or fragments of prayer to ward against witchcraft. Not surprisingly, then, stealing milk (along with blighting crops) was among
the most common accusations leveled at women denounced
for witchcraft by their communities. This is undoubtedly a

consequence of the fact that the rural poor relied on the kindness and generosity of their neighbors, especially as they grew old. When times were hard and there were many mouths to feed in the parish, much of the burden landed at the farmer's door, and strange or solitary, not-especially-beautiful older women would likely have been the first to be turned away. It's easy to imagine that, when refused a drop of milk or a crust of bread, an occasional woman might have muttered a threat or hurled a curse. If nature then colluded with a spell of particularly inclement weather, or a sudden outbreak of disease, they could easily develop a reputation for malevolent magic.

Many tales of witches reflect a suspicion that they could shapeshift into hares. This belief was undoubtedly inspired in good part by the hare's remarkable speed and agility, which make it seem capable of appearing and disappearing by magical means. These solitary creatures also often stand on their hind legs and, in distress, can utter a strange, almost humanlike cry. All of that was enough to endow the hare with supernatural qualities, and to perpetuate the belief that it could become host for a witch's spirit, or her familiar. And indeed, Isobel Gowdie, who was accused of witchcraft in Scotland, offered up a range of different spells in the course of her "confession" during the witch trials in 1662. When she wanted to turn into a hare, she stated that she would say:

> "I shall go into a hare,
> With sorrow and sych and meikle care;
> And I shall go in the Devil's name,
> Ay while I come home again."

In most of the folk tales about witches who shapeshift into the form of a hare to steal milk, it ends very badly for the witch. The farmer shoots the hare and injures it, and a day or so later the shot is found embedded in a corresponding wound on a witch's body. This old North Yorkshire story ends so very differently, with the cunning old witch gaining the upper hand. Old Mally isn't going to be scared away by a mere man with a gun: instead, she is the one who frightens off the farmer and continues to claim her share of the land's bounty.

The Farmer's Curst Wife

ENGLAND

There was an old farmer in Sussex did dwell,
(Chorus of whistlers)
There was an old farmer in Sussex did dwell,
And he had a bad wife, as many knew well.
(Chorus of whistlers)
Then Satan came to the old man at the plow:
"One of your family I must have now.
It is not your eldest son that I crave,
But it is your old wife, and she I will have."
"O welcome, good Satan, with all my heart!
I hope you and she will never more part."
Now Satan has got the old wife on his back,
And he lugged her along, like a peddler's pack.
He trudged away till they came to his hall-gate;
Says he, "Here, take in an old Sussex chap's mate."
O then she did kick the young imps about;
Says one to the other, "Let's try turn her out."
She spied thirteen imps all dancing in chains,
She up with her pattens and beat out their brains.
She knocked the old Satan against the wall!
"Let's turn her out, or she'll murder us all."

Now he's bundled her up on his back amain,
And to her old husband he took her again.
"I have been a tormentor the whole of my life,
But I ne'er was tormented so as with your wife."

Elli

NORSE

Elli is the personification of old age in Norse mythology. She appears in "Gylfaginning," one of the four parts of the *Prose Edda*, written in Iceland during the early thirteenth century. It tells the tale of Thor and his companions Loki and Þjálfi, who are in the hall of the giant Útgarða-Loki, where they meet difficult challenges that test their strength and skill. The hammer-wielding, mighty Thor has been humiliated in a drinking challenge and wants to restore his reputation. He calls for anyone who wishes to wrestle with him to come forward. His host, the giant Útgarða-Loki, suggests that Elli, the old woman who was his nurse, might make a good opponent. Elli is summoned to the hall, and she wrestles with Thor. The more Thor tries to grip Elli and topple her, the faster she stands, rooted and unmovable. Then Elli takes ahold of Thor, who immediately becomes unsteady on his feet. They grapple hard with each other, but it isn't long before Thor falls to his knee. The match ends and, once again, Thor is humiliated — and worst of all, it is at the hands of an old woman.

Later in the tale, Útgarða-Loki explains to Thor that Elli was a far more formidable opponent than she appeared, and that the outcome of the match was not such a surprise because "there has been none, and there will be none who can abide 'Old Age' without her causing him to fall."

Big Kennedy and the Glaistig

SCOTLAND

Big Kennedy from Lianachain was a fine, strong, black-haired young man and a talented and hardworking blacksmith. One day, when all his work was finished, he climbed up onto his horse to ride home from the smithy. It was a soft autumn evening, and the moon rose high and full. He rode steadily across the moor toward his parents' small cottage, and just as he was approaching the ford to cross the river, a gray-faced, white-haired old woman cloaked in green suddenly appeared before him. She cast a stone across his path, so that he was forced to draw the horse to a halt. He understood at once that she was the Glaistig who, back in the day, had tended her herds of deer on the moor and in the hills around it. She nodded and said to him:

"Hail to you, Big Kennedy. Can I get a ride with you?"

"Of course you can," Kennedy said to the Glaistig.

"Then where would you prefer that I sit: behind you or in front of you?" she asked.

"Oh, in the front, for sure," he said. And then he drew her up onto the horse, pulled the wizard belt of Fillan out of his saddlebag, bound her with it, and buckled it tight. No one knew how he had come by it, but no other magic could overcome the powers of that belt. He kept a firm grip on her, just to be sure, and after he had crossed the river, the old woman cried out:

"You're holding me too tightly. Let me go!"

"I will not," he said. "No one has seen you for years, and plenty of people have argued that you're dead. So I'm going to carry you back to the village and show you off to everyone, to prove that you're still around."

The Glaistig uttered a single, harsh wail. "Let me go," she spat, "and I'll offer you a field full of speckled cattle: white-bellied, black, white-headed. They will bring great wealth to you and to your children after you."

Big Kennedy grinned. "That's not enough," he said, "for me to set you free."

The Glaistig bared a set of disturbingly sharp teeth. "Well then, let me go, and I will build you tonight, on that field over there, a big, strong, stone house for you and your bride. A house that fire will not penetrate, nor water, nor arrow, nor iron. And it will keep you warm and comfortable, free of dread and fear, and it will be charmed against poison and the fairies."

This was more like the kind of bargain that Kennedy had been hoping for. "All right then," he said. "I'll set you free — but you'd better be sure to fulfill your promise." He dismounted from his horse and pulled the old woman down after him — but he kept tight hold of the wizard belt of Fillan that bound her to him.

When her feet were planted again on the moor, the Glaistig let out a shriek so loud that the moon shuddered and hid itself behind a cloud. It was heard across seven hills; it was as if the Horn of Worth itself, the great horn that was owned by Fionn Mac Cumhail, had sounded throughout the land. Every fairy dwelling in the valley echoed with her wailing, and from every mound and every hill, from every cliff and every cave, out of the mist and out of the shadow, the fairies came flowing across the moor like flecks of white foam on rolling waves. They gathered around the Glaistig, awaiting her orders.

She set them to work — speedily, calmly, orderly. They brought flags and stones from the shore of the loch by Clianaig waterfall and passed them from hand to hand in a long line down to the site. From the small wood by the same shore, beams and rafters, and thick, straight supports were cut from rowan wood. The old woman herself stood firm and strong as a rock in the field as they built, saying over and over:

> "One stone above two stones,
> And two stones above one stone;
> Fetch stake, clod, thatching pin,
> Fetch every timber in the wood
> But mulberry.
> Alas for him who gets not what he sows,
> And sows not what he gets!"

All night, Kennedy stood and watched with the Glaistig, and when the next morning dawned gray and chill, there was a chimney on the fine turf roof of his new house and smoke billowing out of it. Because the Glaistig's promise had been fulfilled, he released the buckle on the wizard belt of Fillan and told her that she was free to go. He went inside his grand new home and put an iron blade in the fire to keep himself safe, since he had heard about the pranks and enchantments of the fairies, and fairies were still lurking around the edges of the field. Iron was the only thing that he knew would keep them away.

Shortly afterward, the old woman walked up to the open front window, stretched her crooked arm through it, and held out her hand to him, to bid him farewell — but Big Kennedy was a suspicious young man as well as a cunning one, and he believed that her true intent was to steal him away and take him into the fairy mounds. So he took the red-hot iron blade from the fire and put it through the window. Expecting his hand to reach out to accept hers, the old woman grabbed hold of it and the skin of her palm stuck tight to it. She screamed three times and then she sprang up onto a gray stone in the center of the field to pronounce his doom.

The Glaistig raised her crooked arms to the sky and brought down the curse of the fairy folk on him, and the curse of the goblins:

"Grow like rushes,
Wither like fern,
Turn gray in childhood,
And die in the prime of manhood.
I ask that not a single son may succeed you.
I am the sorrowing Glaistig
Who lived in the land of the Meadow.
I built a big house on the field,
Which caused a sore pain in my body.
I will pour out my heart's blood
High on the peak of Finisgeig,
Which will be red evermore."

And then she leaped up in a bright-green flame and flew off across the shoulder of Sgurr Finisgeig. It is said that her curse came true, because not many Kennedys after that — and indeed, there were many of them, for they grew like rushes — lived longer than forty years of age. Big Kennedy himself grew gray and withered, then white and worn before his prime, after mourning the passing of his wife and three children, each at an all-too-young age. The high peak of Finisgeig still glows red in the blazing evening sky — but the Glaistig has never again been seen in Lochaber.

A Glaistig (pronounced "glashtig") is a character in Scottish folklore who is also known as the Green Lady; she often appears as an old woman. Like the Cailleach, the Glaistig is a protector of wild places, and particularly of deer and forests. Although she can be depicted as benevolent, fond of children, and a protector of old people, in other tales she is shown to have little love for humans, who she believes threaten the heart of the wild.

British and Irish folklore is full of stories that tell of all the ways a man might outwit or humiliate a powerful old woman; they couldn't ever, it seems, be allowed to prevail in the face of the patriarchy. But, every now and again, we find a story in which the old woman has the last laugh. The story of Big Kennedy and the Glaistig shows us a woman who refuses to be intimidated or exploited. If something is taken from her, she will take something in return — and so she curses not only Kennedy but his descendants too.

Perhaps, on the surface, this might seem like an excessive reaction. Big Kennedy, a blacksmith who owns a magical belt, clearly has knowledge of fairy lore and the ways it might be possible to gain from it — or be tricked by it — and he lets the Glaistig go free in the end, though only after he's taken what he wants from her. The story doesn't suggest that he has an advance plan to physically harm the Glaistig: he offers her the burning iron because he fears she might be about to entrap him just as he entrapped her, not because he actively wants to burn her.

But the story doesn't suggest that the Glaistig has any evil intentions either, though it would be reasonable to wonder why she wanted to ride with Kennedy in the first place. So the damage is done, and Kennedy must pay the price for his actions. He has taken the Glaistig against her will, bound her with a magical belt, humiliated her, and forced her to work for him.

Then, intentionally — whether or not it seems perfectly reasonable to him at the time — he burns the old woman's palm with a red-hot iron blade.

The moral of the tale, then? By the time women reach menopause and cross the threshold into the second half of our lives, we're bone-tired of being threatened, burned, and browbeaten. Do as you would be done by, or mess with us at your peril.

Hop Tu Naa

Hop tu naa is the Manx name for the festival of Samhain, or Hallowe'en.
Folklorist W. Walter Gill suggests that Jinny the Whinney is similar
to the water-hag Jenny Greenteeth of Lancashire or Peg Powler of Co.
Durham, who, if the fancy took them, would pull people into the water and
drown them. In these verses, Jinny is rather more benign than usual, and
the singer is fortunate enough to eat rather than be eaten.

Put in the pot, put in the pan,
I scalded my throat, I feel it yet.
I ran to the well, I drank my fill.
What did you see there? I saw a pole-cat.
The cat began to grin
And I began to run.
Jinny the Whinney
Came out of the lake
A griddle in her hand
All ready to bake;
Her teeth were green
And her eyes were red,
And a thickness of hair
Upon her head;
Baking bonnags,
Toasting sconnags;

I asked her for a bit,
Guess, the bit she gave me!
A bit as big as my big toe!
I dipped it in milk,
Then wrapped it in silk,
And went home by the light of the moon.

Cundrie: The Loathly Lady

The "Loathly Lady" is the name given to a common character in medieval literature: usually, a woman who is first presented as old and ugly but undergoes a transformation when a man approaches her, kisses her, or agrees to marry her in spite of that — at which point she turns into a beautiful, desirable young woman. We encountered such a Loathly Lady in an earlier story, "Kissing the Hag." In the medieval Grail literature, though, the Loathly Lady is a little different, because she continues in her loathly guise throughout the story and is the keeper of the Grail.

One of the most vividly drawn Loathly Ladies is Cundrie from German poet Wolfram von Eschenbach's thirteenth-century Grail romance, *Parzival*: "A plait of her hair fell down over her hat and dangled on her mule — it was long, black, tough, not altogether lovely, about as soft as boars' bristles. Her nose was like a dog's, and to the length of several spans a pair of tusks jutted from her jaws. Both eyebrows pushed past her hair-band and drooped down in tresses...." But Cundrie's nickname, we are told, was "The Sorceress"; she spoke all known languages, and had mastered dialectics, geometry, astronomy, and the healing arts. More importantly, Cundrie is a truthteller. Von Eschenbach writes: "Her mouth suffered from no impediment, for what it said was quite enough. With it she flattened much joy upstanding." Cundrie, then, clearly didn't mince her words, and men didn't much like it.

At a critical point in the story, Cundrie curses the hapless knight Parzival because he is lacking in curiosity and compassion — then she turns and simply rides away. But her harsh words create a moral imperative for the devastated Parzival: his challenge now is to transform himself so that his handsome body will also contain a beautiful heart, and so that he might finally become the Grail King. When he has undergone the necessary transformations, Cundrie is the first to congratulate him.

The Loathly Lady character epitomized by Cundrie is reflected in most other Grail stories. In Chrétien de Troyes's *Perceval* she's a hideous old woman with ratlike eyes, long ears, and a beard, riding a mule; she tells Perceval that if he had only had the wit to ask the "Grail question" then the Fisher King would have been healed and the Wasteland restored. Truth-telling Cundrie and her story-sisters, then, epitomize righteous wrath. They are the voices and guardians of the Grail; they demand that people take their quests to attain the Grail seriously, and that they examine themselves and their actions honestly and face up to the truth. The Loathly Lady trips up the questing knights when they fall into complacency or otherwise lose their way: she's the truth that can't be ignored.

The Water Horse of Varkasaig

SCOTLAND

A small, bright river tumbles down the brae to the black sands of Varkasaig on the Isle of Skye, and at one time there was a simple drystone shieling — a hut — not so very far from it. The shieling was used by people in the township when they came to tend their cattle in the summer pastures. A woman and her daughter stayed in it one summer while herding their cows. One night, as they were sitting and talking by the peat fire after their supper, a great storm passed overhead and the pasture and the creatures on it were deafened by thunder, blinded by lightning, and lashed with rain. At the height of the storm, there came a loud knocking at the battered wooden door of the shieling. The young woman found a very hand-some young man standing there in the doorway. He was well dressed in clean, fine clothes, but he was dripping wet, and he begged her for shelter from the storm. Thrilled by this unusual and diverting turn of events, she invited him in and offered him a place by the fire, and some oatcakes and crowdie cheese. He accepted both gladly, then settled himself on the floor near the young woman. After he had eaten, he placed his head on her lap and, entranced, she sang him to sleep.

The older woman had been carefully watching all this from her wooden chair at the other side of the hearth. When the young man seemed to be fast asleep and his breathing had slowed and deepened, she handed her daughter a comb and nodded at the young man's head. Very gently, so as not to wake him, she began to comb his hair. To her own astonishment, but just as the wise mother had expected, it was full of waterweeds, sand, and tiny shells. The daughter froze as she realized what it was that she had given shelter to: it was a *each-uisge*, a water horse, in human form. It was known that such a creature inhabited the Varkasaig river, but there had been no reports of him now for many a year. Back in the day, as is typical behavior for a water horse, he had abducted a girl from the township and dragged her into the river to live for a while as his wife. Perhaps she had died, the young woman thought, and he had come here to find someone to replace her. Unless she could find a way out of her predicament, that someone was certainly going to be her. She raised horror-struck eyes to her mother.

The wise woman shook her head and put a finger to her lips. She rose quietly to her feet and took down a fat bundle of fleece from the shelf above the sink; she brought it over to the frightened young woman and placed it, ever so gently, on the chair beside her. With trembling hands and hardly daring to breathe, the girl moved the water horse's head out of her lap and onto the soft woolen pillow. Then she backed away and slipped silently out of the door. The rain was still pouring down, and thunder and lightning were crashing all around her, but she made for the river, knowing — as everyone did in those days — that no supernatural creature can cross running water in pursuit of its quarry. But the hut was some way from the riverside and the grass was sodden and slippery, slowing her pace. When finally she reached the river, she found it so swift and so swollen that she could find no safe way to cross.

Moments after the girl had left, the young man jerked awake. After he understood that she was gone, he spotted the woman in a shadowy corner and bared his teeth; they grew long and white and strong. His dark hair began to sprout into a long, curling mane, his hands and feet turned into hooves, his nose lengthened and nostrils broadened, and his dark eyes grew white and wild. His pale flesh sprouted thick, glossy black fur, and, snorting and roaring with fury, the great beast crashed through the door of the shieling and out after the young woman, galloping across the storm-struck land in giant leaps and bounds. But somehow the wise woman was there by the riverbank before him, and she threw down an iron knife in his path. He pulled up, hooves skidding through the rain-soaked soil; the woman strode up to him and said: "If you pursue my daughter any further, I will cry your name to the four brown boundaries of the Earth" — and then, to show that she meant what she said and had the power to carry out her threat, she raised her face and whispered his name. Just what the water horse's name was, or how she knew it, no one has ever discovered, but the effect on the creature was instantaneous: he pulled back his ears, bared his great white teeth, and, with a terrible shriek, he raced along the river, plunged into a deep pool by the old stone bridge, and vanished.

Today it is said that, ignorant of the fact that the wise woman has long since died, the *each-uisge* has never again dared to venture far from his river in case she should see him and name him, and so bind him to her. But people who slip quietly down to the river on a fine summer evening might still happen to see a beautiful dark stallion cavorting all alone along its banks or pawing at the black sand at its mouth.

The *each-uisge* (pronounced "yak ooshger") is a water spirit in Scottish folklore: it's a shapeshifter, switching between the form of a fine stallion or pony and that of a handsome young man. In its human form, it can only be recognized as a water horse because of the waterweeds, sand, and mud in its hair. The *each-uisge*, who is always presented as a male, often wants to take a human woman as his wife. In the standard story of this kind, a young woman herding cattle around the shielings encounters a water horse but believes him to be nothing more than the handsome young man whose form he has taken. He sits beside her in the grass, then lays his head in her lap and falls asleep. But, examining him closely, she sees either that he has horse's hooves or that his hair is filled with waterweeds and sand. She bundles a pillow of rushes under his head in the hope of tricking him into believing that he is still resting in her lap, and swiftly makes her escape.

This story offers us a bonus, in the form of a wise and feisty middle-aged woman who outwits and then challenges the water horse in order to save her daughter. Shrewd and attentive, she recognizes what he is long before her daughter even thinks of being suspicious. She's undaunted by his strength and power and, quite unafraid of the beast (though the *each-uisge* is known to have a particularly vicious streak), she confronts him with a knife. But it is her knowledge of his name that stops him, finally, in his tracks. In so many old stories, knowledge of a person's "true name" can give you power over them, because the name, in a sense, represents the essence of the person who bears it. No one could tell how the wise woman had come to know the water horse's name, but it is entirely possible that the store of knowledge and experience we forage from our journeys through the bleak bogs and fertile

townlands of our lives, might one day save us or save others —
and perhaps in the most surprising of circumstances. Or perhaps it's only with the wisdom of age that we can see into the
soul of a person and catch a glimpse of their true self — and
therefore their true name.

Sgàthach

Sgàthach ("the Shadowy One") appears in the Ulster Cycle of Irish mythology; she is a Scottish warrior woman and martial arts teacher who is sometimes referred to as an "Amazon woman." She lived on the Isle of Skye, where her residence, Dún Scáith ("the Fortress of Shadows"), lies. Some stories say that she took her name from An t-Eilean Sgitheanach, the Gaelic name for the Isle of Skye; others say (and of course we like this better) that the island took its name from her.

In the old Irish texts, Dún Scáith is presented as an impregnable castle in which Sgàthach trained Celtic heroes in the arts of pole-vaulting, underwater fighting, and other forms of combat; she also taught them to use a deadly barbed spear called the *gáe bolg*. But Sgàthach, it is said, would agree to train only those warriors who were already clever and brave enough to penetrate the many defenses of her fortress in order to gain access to her. Her best-known student was the great Irish warrior-hero Cú Chulainn. He lived with her for a year, during which he learned the skills that enabled him to win many subsequent battles: he went on, at the age of seventeen, to single-handedly defend Ulster against the armies of Queen Medb of Connacht in the famous *Táin Bó Cúailnge* ("The Cattle Raid of Cooley").

Although it might on the surface seem unlikely that an

older woman should train a famous and accomplished hero like Cú Chulainn, Sgàthach is just one of a long list of female warriors scattered throughout European myth and folklore. In her native Scotland, for example, stories from the island of St. Kilda tell of a gigantic female warrior who inhabited a mysterious structure known as Taigh na Banaghaisgeic: "the Amazon's House." And indeed, the legendary Amazons themselves were a group of female warriors and hunters who were as skilled and courageous as men in physical agility, strength, archery, riding skills, and the arts of combat.

Throughout human history, women of all ages have fought in and led armies; the idea that we must sit at home and knit while the men go off to war is a relatively recent invention. But an older woman's way of being a warrior is about more than brute force: it's about wit and sass and courage. The courage to stand up for herself, and for others; the courage to look death in the face and laugh.

Seeing Deeply

Insight, vision, foresight...all the women in the stories that follow manifest this many-named talent that we cultivate through the long growing seasons of our lives and that ripens for harvesting as we age. Each of our wise women displays it in her own unique way, and each of them is armed with her own unique brand of shrewd, battle-tested knowledge. Each of them sees deeply into the heart of human — and other-than-human — experience and understands how to discern the true nature of events and situations, with all their multiple interconnections.

This sometimes might seem to be a supernatural skill, but it's born from experience and a lifelong commitment to learning and growing. It requires a capacity to reach through the chaos of the tempest to find the eye of the storm: the still point around which the action revolves, the pivot point around which our fates spin. It also requires an acquaintance with strategic thinking, an ease with rapid decision-making, and the capacity to hold the lives of others in the palm of your hand — and never flinch. In seeing deeply, we're employing a curious blend of experience, gut instinct, and judgment, and the good news is that survival into our elder years allows us to exercise this skill with acuity.

The Dream Makers

SCOTLAND

On a fine morning, as the summer grew old, a group of young women from an island at the far western edge of the world set off into the mountains to gather blaeberries. One of them, daydreaming and enjoying the sun on her shoulders, strayed from the rest and climbed up higher and higher in search of larger and finer berries. But all at once the air grew chilly, and a wall of mist tumbled down the slopes of the mountain toward her.

Startled out of her reverie, she realized that she was alone. She retraced her steps to find her friends — but the mist wrapped itself around her, and in no time she was utterly lost. Slowly and cautiously, she moved on through the mist, only realizing that she was going in the wrong direction when the thick, wiry heather through which she had originally climbed gave way to bare rock and crag. She stood still, afraid to move in case she should step over a cliff edge or fall into the deep cut of a mountain burn.

She heard footsteps behind her. She whirled around; a band of enormous ghostly forms was moving toward her. Fearful, she would have backed away — but a tricksy little breeze parted the mist for a moment, and she saw that the apparitions were deer. Most were hinds, with calves at foot; she found their presence comforting on the lonely mountain. They didn't seem to be afraid of her so she moved closer, thinking that they might lead her to safety. The deer moved slowly through the fog, grazing here and there, and so it was easy for the girl to keep up. A few steps at a time, they led her high up into the dark Cuillins, where eventually she found herself standing beside them by the mouth of a cave.

Thinking that she might wait there in safety until the mist dissolved, the girl slipped into the dark opening. But the cave, it seemed, was someone's home: inside, an old man and an old woman, each seated upon a wooden stool, gazed into a dark pool in the stone floor of the cave. The bright-eyed old woman courteously asked her name and how she had come to be there; the girl told her tale and begged shelter for the night, or at least until the mist should clear.

"Shelter for one night we cannot give," the old woman said, "but shelter for a year and a night you may have if you will help me in the dairy, for I grow old. The deer will take you back down the mountain when the time is done."

As she looked into the old woman's pale blue eyes, the girl found herself agreeing. So she spent many busy days caring for and milking the hinds and gathering sweet-scented herbs from the mountain peaks and pastures, which the old woman showed her how to find. There was thyme, meadowsweet, and wild mint; there was golden asphodel and bog myrtle. The old woman dried them and sprinkled them on the fire that she lit each day from dried heather; then she warmed the deer's milk and made crowdie cheese, flavored with the herbs. When she had made the crowdie, the old man fashioned from it shapes and figures of the things that they had seen on the pool's surface — for in it, all the world was mirrored. And he and his wife were the makers of the world's dreams.

Every evening, as the sun began to slip below the sea, the old man carried the pale dreams to the cave mouth and held them up to take on the colors of the sunset. The dreams that he held in his right hand were true dreams, and out of the twilight came eagles and falcons, larks and wrens to carry them throughout the world. But the dreams in his left hand were false phantoms, designed to mislead. Out of the dark cracks of the mountain came crows and ravens to spread their shadows around the world.

When the year and the night of the girl's service were ended, the old woman who had taught her so much about herbs and dreams came out of the cave and joined her on the mountainside. She spoke in a strange tongue to the leader of the herd of deer, a gentle hind with glowing, amber-colored eyes, who now was gray with age. She said farewell to the girl and told her that her service had been honest and true, and so she would find a reward waiting for her when she came to the seashore again.

The deer led her by a hidden but easy route down the mountain, and they came sooner than she had thought to the sea — but this was not the home shore that the girl knew. She started to walk along the beach to see if she could discover where she might be, but the deer wouldn't allow it; they gathered around her, enclosing her in a circle, and stood looking out to sea. A boat was sailing out of the sunset, and as it came closer, the girl saw that it was made of skins and in it was a fair young man with a golden torque around his neck. He landed his coracle on the sand and came to her, hands outstretched — and she was struck with a sudden sense of recognition and a strange yearning. He called her "the fair one of dreams" and told her that he had dreamed of her many times over the past year, back home in the halls of his father, the king. Last night, he said, in another dream he had been shown the way to find her, and so he had followed the dream paths and had come to ask her to marry him.

Delighted, the girl agreed, and they sailed away together across the sea. And when she became queen of her husband's country, she remembered what the old woman had taught her during her time of service in the mountains, and she in turn taught their people the meaning of many dreams. From this, they grew wondrously wise.

But now, much is forgotten.

Stories about the Cailleach — the old woman who creates and shapes the land in the Gaelic tradition — are so prevalent in Scottish folklore that when we find an Otherworldly old woman high in the mountains, it's inevitable that we think of her. In many stories about the Cailleach she is represented as a solitary being, but occasionally it is also told that she had a husband — sometimes called simply "the Bodach" (*bodach* means "old man" in Gaelic) and sometimes identified as Manannán Mac Lir, an old god of the Gaelic-speaking countries who is associated with the sea. So this old, beautiful, but little-known tale from the Isle of Skye offers a Cailleach figure weaving her magic not alone but with her husband. The two elders work together to create and disperse the world's dreams, each contributing in their own way, masculine and feminine principles in perfect harmony.

In Scotland, the Cailleach has many faces and frequently has close connections with deer; most commonly, she is said to have had a herd of wild deer that she milked, and she would travel with them through the hills and mountains of the Highlands and Islands. One folklorist, J. G. McKay, suggested that such stories about the Cailleach might have reflected the remnants of an ancient tradition of deer goddesses, citing a plethora of Scottish stories about "colossal Old Women" who owned, herded, and milked deer.

In this story, the old woman in the cave has deep vision. Along with her husband, she perceives and understands everything that is happening in the world by looking into the pool in their cave. She uses this knowledge to create the substance — crowdie, the simplest and softest of cheeses — out of which the old man crafts the dreams of the world. The motif of the wise old woman in the cave is a common one in European myth and folklore. Many oracles in Greek myth are associated with caves, and spending time in them seemed to be a major requirement for prophetic dreams or visions — both in established mystery cults and for individual seers. There were also many caves dedicated to Gaea, the Greek goddess who represents the Earth, and the association of cave-related divination with the goddess of the Earth seems to be very ancient.

Perfectly embodying the mentor archetype, this old woman takes the lost young girl under her wing and teaches her the art of using herbs, milking the fairy deer, and making the soft cheese that is the fundamental substance of the world's dreams. As a consequence, the girl emerges from the old woman's tuition with the knowledge of how to interpret dreams: a skill that she finds valuable in her husband's country, and which in turn she passes on to its people, to the benefit of all.

This story reminds us that, as we grow older, we should always take time to nurture our dreams and use them to help us dream our elder selves into being. Through such practices, we too might become "wondrously wise." Many women find that their dreams become more vivid around the time of menopause and pay more attention to them. It's a practice worth cultivating; as Carl Jung said, "In each of us there is another whom we do not know. He speaks to us in dreams and tells

us how differently he sees us from the way we see ourselves."*
Although many of our dreams don't make sense to us in a
narrative context, nevertheless the characters who populate
them and the images that appear in them hold information
that might be helpful to us along our path. They also reflect
the wisdom of our inner self: the part of us that understands
what we need even when our conscious mind doesn't. As we
wade through the often-muddy waters of menopause in search
of the ways in which we might reimagine ourselves, dreams
can reveal the hidden insights that might help us to find a new
path.

---

*   C. G. Jung, *The Collected Works of C. G. Jung*, vol. 10, *Civilization in Transition*
     (2nd ed.). Translated by R. F. C. Hull. Princeton University Press (1970),
     para. 325.

Biddy Early

Biddy Early is the quintessential example of a kind of wise woman known in Irish as the *bean feasa* — which literally means "woman of knowledge." Biddy was perhaps the most famous wise woman in nineteenth-century Ireland, and her reputation was such that people traveled from great distances to County Clare to see her. Biddy is believed to have been born around 1798 and is said to have been a kind but forthright and strong-willed woman. She insisted on taking her mother's surname rather than her father's; she drank, smoked, played cards, refused to attend Mass, had no time for priests, and had a penchant (especially when she was older) for husbands very much younger than herself.

Biddy was said to see into the Otherworld by looking into a blue bottle that had been given to her by the fairies. The fairies, then, were responsible for Biddy's deep sight and her ability to foretell the future, to know exactly what her neighbors were up to and to discover where lost objects and animals could be found. Biddy would agree to help a sick person only if they couldn't be cured with traditional procedures. In that case, she would presume that the problem had a supernatural origin, and she would ask whether, for example, the individual might have disturbed the fairies on their preferred ground — by plowing across a fairy ring, or blocking a fairy path; or whether certain necessary prescriptions and rituals — such as saying "God bless" in the right places and at the right times — had failed to be observed.

The kind of wise woman known as the *bean feasa* occurs in other parts of Europe too, though in Ireland she's a particularly well-developed character. In Britain, for example, she might be known as a "fairy witch" or a "cunning woman." She's differentiated from other healers by the fact that her methods are symbolic rather than physical: her primary role was to act as mediator between the community and the Otherworld. She was called on to heal psychological disorders — emotional and psychosomatic — for which, in those days, no other treatment existed. She was also responsible for establishing a kind of balance between this world and the Otherworld, which in turn would foster balance within her community. So, for example, in those days, certain psychological issues were believed to result from "fairy abductions," in which the fairies would steal away a healthy person and leave behind a weak and ugly fairy "changeling." Restoring the abducted individual to something approximating normal function would also restore the balance between worlds. These ideas, of course, were typical of a society which believed that both individual and community well-being could be achieved only by maintaining harmonious relationships with Otherworld forces.

The Fool and the Wise Woman

ENGLAND

Once in these parts, and not so very long ago, there lived a fool who wanted to buy himself a pot of brains because he was always getting into trouble through his foolishness, and people laughed at him all the time. He asked around a bit and was told that he'd be able to get anything he wanted from the wise woman who lived on the top of the hill. She dealt in potions, herbs and spells, and all manner of magical things, and could tell your future into the bargain. So he told his mother about this and asked her if he could go to see the wise woman and buy himself a pot of brains.

"You should do just that," she said; "you're sorely in need of a few brains, my son, and if I should die, who'd take care of a poor fool like you? You're no more fit to look after yourself than a newborn baby! But mind your manners when you go and be sure to talk to her nicely: those wise folk are easily offended."

So off he went one evening after his tea and he found her inside her cottage, sitting by the fire and stirring a big cauldron. "Good evening, missis," he said. "It's a fine night."

"Aye." She went on stirring.

"It might rain," he said, as he shuffled from one foot to the other.

"Maybe," she said.

"But maybe it won't," he said, and looked out of the window.

"Perhaps," she said.

He twisted his hat. "Well," he said, "I can't think of anything else to say about the weather, but let me see…the crops are coming along well."

"Well," she said.

"And…and…the animals are fattening up."

"They are."

"And…and…Well. I reckon we'll tackle our business now, since we've finished all the polite stuff. So. Have you any brains to sell?"

"That depends," she said, "on whether you want a king's brains, or a soldier's brains, or a schoolmaster's brains. Because I don't keep those brains at all."

"Well, no," he said. "All I need is ordinary brains — fit for any fool — just the same as everyone else has around here."

"Aye, well then. I might manage that, if you can do something to help yourself get them."

"What kind of thing, missis?" he asked.

"Well," the wise woman said, "bring me the heart of the thing you like best of all, and I'll tell you where to get your pot of brains."

"But," he said, scratching his head, "how can I do that?"

"That's not for me to say. Find out for yourself, my lad, if you don't want to be a fool all your days! But you'll have to answer a riddle as well, so I can check you've brought the right thing with you. And now I've something else to see to," she said, "so good evening to you." And she picked up the cauldron and carried it away with her into the scullery.

Off went the fool back to his mother, and he told her what the wise woman had said. "I reckon I'll have to kill that pig," he said, "because I like bacon better than anything in the world."

"Then do it, my lad," said his mother. "It'll be a strange but a good thing for you, if you can buy yourself a pot of brains and be able to look after yourself."

So he killed his pig, wrapped its heart in paper, and the next day he went off again to the wise woman's cottage. There she sat inside it, reading an enormous book. "Good evening, missis," he said. "I've brought you the heart of the thing I like the best of all." And he put the package on the table.

"Aye, so?" She peered at him through her spectacles. "Tell me this then: What runs without feet?"

He rubbed his chin, and thought, and thought — but he couldn't figure it out.

"Get on your way!" she said. "You clearly haven't fetched me the right thing yet. I've no brains for you today." And she clapped her book shut and turned her back on him.

So off the fool went, back home to tell his mother. But as he got near to the house, some people came running out of it to tell him that his mother was dying. And when he went to her bedside, his mother just looked at him and smiled in contentment, as if to say that she could leave him with a quiet mind, since he had got enough brains now to look after himself — and then she died. He sat down at the kitchen table and the more he thought about it, the worse he felt. He remembered how she'd nursed him when he was tiny, and helped him with his lessons, and cooked his dinners, and mended his clothes, and put up with his foolishness; and he felt sorrier and sorrier and began to sob.

"Oh, Mother, Mother!" he cried, "who'll take care of me now? You shouldn't have left me alone, for I liked you better than everything!" And as he said that he thought of the wise woman's words. "Oh, no! Must I take my mother's heart to her? No! I can't do that," he muttered to himself. "What'll I do? What'll I do to get myself that pot of brains, now I'm all alone in the world?" So he thought and thought and thought — and admittedly that was difficult — and the next day he borrowed a sack, bundled his mother's body into it, and carried it on his shoulder up to the wise woman's cottage.

"Good evening, missus," he said. "I reckon I've fetched you the right thing this time!" — and he plumped the sack down in the doorway.

"Maybe," said the wise woman, "but tell me this, now: What's yellow and shining but isn't gold?"

And he scratched his head, and thought, and thought — but he couldn't find an answer.

"You just can't think of the right thing, my lad. I suspect you're a bigger fool than I thought!" And she shut the door in his face.

"See there, now!" he said, and sat down by the roadside to cry. "I've lost the only two things I cared for, and what else can I find to buy a pot of brains with?" And he howled till the tears ran all the way down his face and into his mouth. A few minutes later, along came a young woman who lived nearby, and she stopped and looked down at him.

"What's up with you, fool?" she asked.

"Oh, I've killed my pig and I've lost my mother, and, as you say, I'm nothing but a fool," he sobbed.

"That's terrible," she said. "And haven't you anybody to look after you now?"

"No," he said, "and I can't even buy my pot of brains, for there's nothing left that I like best."

"What are you talking about?" She sat down next to him, and he told her about the wise woman and the pig, and his mother and the riddles, and that he was all alone in the world now and that nobody cared.

"Well," she said, "I wouldn't mind marrying you myself."

"Could you do it?"

"Oh, aye!" she said. "Folks say that fools make good husbands, so I reckon I'll have you, if you're willing."

"Can you cook?" he asked.

"Aye, I can," she said.

"And scrub?" he asked.

"For sure," she said.

"And mend my clothes?" he asked.

"I can that," she said.

"Then I reckon you'll do as well as anybody," he said. "But what'll I do about this wise woman?"

"Oh, just wait a bit. Something might turn up, and anyway, it won't matter if you're a fool, so long as you have me to look after you."

"That's true," he said, and off they went together to the priest to arrange for the burial of his mother, and afterward to get married. And she kept his house so clean and neat, and cooked his dinner so fine, that one night he said to her: "Lass, I'm thinking I like you best of everything after all."

"That's good to hear," she said. "So what now?"

"Well, have I got to kill you, do you think, and take your heart up to the wise woman for that pot of brains?"

"Heavens, no!" she cried, looking scared. "I won't have that. But see here — you didn't cut out your mother's heart, did you?"

"No, but if I had, maybe I'd have got my pot of brains," he said.

"No, no. Just as you did with your mother, take me to the wise woman as I am, heart and all, and I'll help you answer the riddles as well."

"Can you?" he asked, doubtfully. "I reckon they're far too hard for women to answer."

"Well," she said, "let's see about that. Tell me the first of them."

"What runs without feet?" he said.

"Why, water, of course!"

"So it does!" he said. "Well, then. What's yellow and shining but isn't gold?"

"Why, the sun!"

"My goodness, so it is!" he cried. "Come on, we'll go up to the wise woman right away!" And off they went.

As they came up the path, they found her sitting at the door, twining straws.

"Good evening, missus," he said.

"Good evening, fool."

"I reckon I've fetched you the right thing at last."

The wise woman wiped her spectacles. "Can you tell me what has first no legs, and then two legs, and ends with four legs?"

And the fool tugged at his earlobe and thought and thought, but he couldn't answer.

His wife whispered in his ear: "It's a tadpole."

Perhaps it is! he thought, and then he said, "That might well be a tadpole, missus."

The wise woman nodded. "That's right. And now I see you've got your pot of brains already."

"Have I? Where are they?" he asked, looking all around him and feeling in his pockets.

"In your wife's head," she replied. "The only cure for a fool is a good wife to look after him, and that you've got, so good evening to you!" And with that she nodded to them and took herself away into the house.

So they went home together, and he never wanted to buy a pot of brains again, for his wife had more than enough for both of them.

This funny and lighthearted story offers us a wise woman who doesn't need to rely on magic: all she needs in this situation is an understanding of human psychology. In this, she's reminiscent of Granny Weatherwax, the old witch who lights up the pages of several of Terry Pratchett's contemporary Discworld novels. She might be a witch, but the tools of Granny's trade are practical tasks and hard work; in spite of her considerable power, she rarely uses magic in any obvious or ostentatious form. Instead, she prefers to rely on what she calls "headology": a singular and wonderfully commonsensical variety of folk psychology. It was a delight to find her soulmate inhabiting an old English fairy tale.

As we saw with the character of Biddy Early a few pages ago, it wasn't unusual for a wise woman in the traditions of these islands to act as a kind of community psychologist. Like the *bean feasa*, the wise woman in this story sees deeply, and understands exactly what this vulnerable man really needs in order to thrive. Like Granny Weatherwax, she might come across as sharp-tongued, but she is kind to him, nevertheless.

Although it's very dated in its treatment of gender roles and the notion of a wife who must "look after" her husband (you could be forgiven for wondering what exactly he brought to the marriage — but he did, after all, provide her with a home, and he treated her kindly enough, which isn't always a given...), this story is worthy of inclusion anyway, because it clearly presents the two women in the story — the young and the old — as strong, independent characters with the wisdom and insight to see deep into the heart of a situation and know what must be done to resolve it. And to resolve it with kindness and compassion, not just for their own sake, but to help others to flourish too.

The Pythia

In the Temple of Apollo at Delphi in Greece during the Classical period, it was necessary for a woman to be over the age of fifty before she could take on the important role of oracle and be known as the Pythia. The Pythia would ritually enter into a state of trance, during which she uttered sounds or words that were revealed to her by the god Apollo. Similarly, in early Greek legends and literature, a prophetess known as Sibyl was represented as a woman of considerable old age who uttered predictions while in an ecstatic trance.

Elder-woman seeresses were common throughout Europe; during the Roman era they played a role in leading rebellions against Roman rule, as well as occasionally acting as envoys to Rome. Greek historian and geographer Strabo wrote of one Germanic tribe whose military expeditions were attended by priestesses who were also seers: "These were gray-haired, clad in white, with flaxen cloaks fastened on with clasps, girt with girdles of bronze, and bare-footed."

Like other Classical oracles, the Pythia wasn't a straightforward fortune teller. Her role was to offer advice about a particular situation: how a much-desired goal might be achieved, or a difficult situation averted. Many of her responses seemed to be purposely ambiguous — Apollo himself was known as

236

Apollo Loxias, "the ambiguous one" — but according to the Greek historian Plutarch, her ambiguity would have had another important function: to protect the Pythia from the wrath of the powerful people who came to consult her, if things didn't go according to plan.

The Pythia was particularly useful at moments of indecision, when it was difficult to make a choice. After she had offered her oracular advice, the priests who acted as her intermediaries would send it back to the community for continued deliberation. The initial visit to the oracle, then, was intended to prepare people to make their own decisions and to find a path forward if there was no consensus. This process allowed the oracle to use her wisdom to provide people with a way to make sense of the situations they found themselves in.

There Was an Old Woman
Lived Under the Hill

ENGLAND

There was an old woman lived under the hill,
And if she's not gone she lives there still.
Baked apples she sold, and cranberry pies,
And she's the old woman that never told lies.

The Sleeping Beauty in the Wood

FRANCE

Once upon a time in a faraway land, there lived a king and queen who had everything they might wish for in life — except for a child. And how they grieved over this lack. They made pilgrimages, took holy and healing waters, consulted every herb-wife and healer of repute, and did everything else that could be done — but without success. As her childbearing years passed, the queen despaired of ever conceiving, until one day, miraculously, she felt the faintest butterfly flutter low in her belly. Over the next weeks, it grew into a wondrous little wriggle. A child had quickened, and soon enough, a royal daughter was born.

A few weeks after her birth, the king and queen dispatched invitations to the child's christening. All the venerable fairies of the land — seven in all — were invited to be godmothers to the little princess, and each one, drawing on her many decades of experience, gave much thought to the gift she might bestow upon the child, so that she might flourish and thrive.

After the christening, a great banquet was held in the palace, in honor of the fairies. Their table was laid with the finest white cloth and laid out in magnificent style, and before each of them was placed a gold casket containing a gold spoon, knife, and fork, set with diamonds and rubies. But just after the guests had taken their seats, a great gust of wind blew open the huge doors of the hall; it ushered in a bluster of autumn leaves and a foreboding chill. A stooped old fairy dressed in dark robes appeared in the doorway. As the bright chatter in the hall hushed, she stood there silently, assessing the situation; then slowly she made her way down the long row of tables. Guests whispered, "It's her!" and "I thought she was long dead!" — because this old fairy hadn't been seen for over fifty years. She had hidden herself away in her faraway tower at the edge of the kingdom, till eventually she was all but forgotten.

The king hastily ordered that another place should be laid at the fairies' table — but there was no golden casket for her, because only seven sets had been made. She sat with the other fairies, but nothing would appease her: she was determined to believe that she had been intentionally slighted. She glared at the other guests and muttered threats. The fairy godmother who sat closest to her overheard her words and understood that no good could possibly come of any blessing the old fairy might choose to bestow on the infant princess. She slipped away from the table as the feast drew to a close, hiding herself behind one of the fine tapestries that adorned the hall, so that she might be overlooked when it was time to bestow gifts upon the child. Perhaps, she thought to herself, she could do something to counteract any evil that the old one might do.

Heralds in high galleries above the hall trumpeted a fanfare and, one by one, each fairy godmother made her graceful way to the cradle and announced her blessing for the princess. The first touched her forefinger to the infant's brow and decreed that she should be the most beautiful person in the world, inside and out; the next pronounced that she should be clever and kind, the third that she should be full of grace, the fourth that she should be a fine dancer, the fifth that she should sing like a nightingale, the sixth that she should have a love of music and great skill at making it too. Then the old fairy made her way to the cradle, her face contorted with spite. She pressed a gnarled finger to the sleeping princess's forehead and declared that, before her sixteenth birthday, she would prick her finger on a spindle and die.

A shocked shudder ran through the company, but then the seventh fairy slipped out from behind the tapestry and made her way across the hall to stand by the cradle. She touched the baby's fine silken hair, then declared in a loud, clear voice: "Take comfort, Your Majesties: I say that your daughter shall not die. Though my power can't undo my kinswoman's magic, I can at least amend it. When she pricks her finger before her sixteenth birthday, she will fall into a deep, long sleep: a sleep that will last for a hundred years. At the end of that time, a king's son will come to awaken her."

Within hours, the king's scribes had made hundreds of copies of a royal decree that forbade anyone in the kingdom, on pain of death, to use a spinning wheel or to keep a spindle in the house. Men-at-arms knocked on every door and took away spindles and wheels for burning on great pyres that blazed for many days. Eventually, the king was satisfied that there wasn't a single spindle left in any home, barn, or workshop in the land. He and the queen slept soundly once more — or at least, as much as any new parents have ever slept, before or since — and settled into the routines of royal family life with their precious little daughter.

Years passed and, indeed, the princess flourished; she displayed all the gifts that the fairies had bestowed upon her, and more. One day in her sixteenth year, while the king and queen were out hunting, she decided to occupy herself by exploring the more remote parts of the vast palace. Eventually, she came to an old door at the very top of a tower. It opened to reveal a gloomy chamber where, in the light from one small window, an old woman sat with her distaff, spinning. This old woman, who hardly saw a soul, had no idea that this was forbidden; and the princess, who had never been told about the curse in case knowledge of it should blight her childhood, watched her, transfixed.

"What are you doing?" she asked the old woman.

"Why, I'm spinning, of course," the old woman said, not knowing who the girl was.

"Spinning? How do you do it? Please could I try?" The spinner obliged and offered her the spindle. Perhaps it was because she was too eager, or because it was so strange to her — or perhaps because an old fairy had once ordained it — but no sooner did the princess take the spindle than she pricked her finger. As a drop of bright-red blood welled up from the wound, she fainted and fell to the floor.

The old woman cried out for help, and servants soon came running. They splashed water on the princess's beautiful face, patted her hands, rubbed her temples with reviving balm — but nothing would rouse her. By this time the king and queen had returned to the palace, and the commotion drew them up to the top of the tower. As soon as the king saw his daughter and the spindle beside her, the old fairy's prophecy came immediately into his mind. He ordered her to be carried to her chamber and placed in her richly draped bed to sleep in peace till the hour of her awakening should come. And there she lay, utterly still and silent, except for the gentle rise and fall of her breath.

On that very day, the seventh fairy was in the kingdom of Mataquin, twelve thousand leagues away. A dwarf — who wore a pair of magic boots that enabled him to cross seven leagues with each step — brought her news of what had happened to the princess. She set off at once in her fiery chariot, which was pulled by a pair of dragons, and in no time at all she arrived at the palace.

The once-bustling fortress was now a somber and subdued place. The fairy godmother found the king and queen at the sleeping princess's bedside and approved of everything they'd done. But she realized now that when the princess woke, it would be to a palace that was empty or filled with strangers, because everyone she had once known would be dead. She decided then that everyone around the princess should also sleep and so wake along with her in a hundred years' time. The fairy set off through the palace and passed from room to room, and as she touched them gently with her wand, ladies-in-waiting and officers, governesses and royal advisers, chambermaids and guards, washerwomen and errand boys, fell asleep at once.

Then she walked out to the stables and cast her enchantment over horses and their grooms, over great guard dogs and hunting hounds. Even the peacocks and hens pecking around the palace courtyard fell asleep, as did the fire in the great hall. She brought the princess's little lapdog back to the palace when her work was done and set him down next to the sleeping maiden on her great bed. And finally, she wove intricate spells so that everyone should wake up just at the same moment as the princess when the time came.

The king and queen kissed their daughter, tears spilling over and onto her beloved face; then they left the castle, so that they could continue their work of protecting and ruling the kingdom. Within a quarter of an hour of their departure, the fairy godmother had conjured a vast, thick wood of great trees, and dense, interlacing thorn thickets around the palace walls; neither man nor beast could penetrate it, and only the very tops of the highest towers could be seen. In this way, the fairy ensured that the princess would sleep peacefully for a hundred years, safely away from prying eyes and dangers of any kind.

The years passed, and for all those within the sleeping palace, they passed in vivid, never-ending dreams. The king and queen grew old and died, and because they had no heir other than the sleeping princess, the throne passed to another family. Each generation gave way to the next, and the story of the sleeping princess became just that: a story, a fantasy, a legend.

The present king's son went hunting one morning at the edge of the great wood. He caught a glimpse of the old palace turrets above the tree canopy and asked his attendants what they might be. They recounted the various tales they'd been told as children. One of them believed it to be a haunted castle, another claimed that it was the den of witches, and a third said that it was the lair of a child-eating ogre. Finally, an old huntsman said to him: "Your Highness, more than fifty years ago I heard my father say that a beautiful princess once fell asleep inside that castle, caught in a spell that could not be broken for a hundred years. And even then, only if a king's son should awaken her."

Now, that was a story that the young prince liked — and he felt sure that he was the very prince mentioned in the old huntsman's tale. Impelled by a desire both for love and for glory, he spurred his horse on toward the castle and the deep, dark wood. The prince's horse had hardly taken ten strides into the forest before the tall trees and thorn thickets ahead of them began to draw aside. A clear pathway soon formed ahead of him; it stretched all the way to the palace, which now he saw lay right in the heart of the enchanted wood. He urged his horse forward and the trees and brambles closed behind them, separating him from his companions — but, bravely, he continued down the path and soon arrived in the forecourt of the magnificent old palace.

The stillness of the place filled him at first with fear: so many men and women lay about as if they were dead. Soon, though, he noticed that their noses and cheeks were pink, and their chests still rose and fell. Everyone, it seemed, had fallen asleep in the middle of whatever it was they were doing. Serving dishes were scattered across the cobbles next to a kitchen maid; the blacksmith was slumped over his anvil, hammer on the floor, just out of reach of his open hand. Grooms slept over fodder buckets, and one fine horse slept upright, fully saddled and bridled.

The prince pushed open the door to the great hall and stepped over slumbering servants and snoring courtiers as he made his way toward a grand marble staircase. He climbed the stairs and passed through many finely furnished chambers before arriving finally on the threshold of a particularly grand apartment, clad all over with gold. There was a richly hung bed in the center of the room, and upon the bed lay a very beautiful young woman. Her golden hair was spread across the pillow and a little dog was sound asleep at her feet. He drew nearer, gazing down at the sleeping beauty; her skin was smooth and pale as wax, her soft cheeks were the hue of ripe summer peaches, and her lips looked as sweet as wild strawberries. He trembled with tenderness and fell to his knees beside her — and just as he did so, the enchantment slipped away and the princess's lashes fluttered. She opened her dazzling blue eyes and smiled at him as if she had known him all her life. "It's you," she whispered. "You've been a long time coming."

They fell into a delighted conversation that soon was interrupted by the little dog, who yawned and stretched, then yapped and licked at them both in joy. All about the palace, the bonds of enchantment were dissolving as its inhabitants slowly awoke. Later that evening, after a modest feast in honor of the late king and queen and dear, departed friends, the court chaplain was summoned to the little chapel in the east wing of the palace. The princess, dressed in her finest — if rather dated — gown, and the prince, scrubbed clean from his extraordinary hunting adventure, met at the altar. They were married, and in time they came to rule the kingdom together and to have a daughter of their own. We can't know for certain, but I rather suspect that the seventh fairy godmother would have been guest of honor at the christening of the new princess too.

Stories that include characters who are specifically called fairy godmothers are quite rare, but they've become so familiar to us because of the popularity of the French literary fairy tales in which they originally came to life. Nevertheless, women who are precursors of the later, star-spangled fairy godmothers, and who fulfill some of the same functions, appear in the oral folk tradition by different names: the henwife (who we met in the earlier story of "Fair, Brown, and Trembling") is the most common of those. The fairy godmother is usually a woman in midlife, and so embodies a wisdom and knowledge of the world that she's able to activate for the benefit of those around her. She can create marvels from the mundane and can see the potential that others possess and cultivate it — so encouraging them not only to believe in themselves but also to help themselves. Without their fairy godmothers to show them the way, the Cinderellas under their care would never be able to leave home and grow into confident young women, and the Sleeping Beauties would all be doomed to die young.

The reason for including this most familiar of stories here is the foresight and perspicacity of the seventh fairy. Many tales around Europe contain variants of the "sleeping beauty" motif, but Charles Perrault's 1696 version focuses a little more attention on the actions of this resourceful fairy godmother. She has the quick wit to spot trouble arising, and also the confidence to act on her perception. More than simply anticipating and acting, though, the seventh godmother sees right into the heart of the web of magic spun by the angry, forgotten fairy. She instinctively knows what can be saved and what cannot. She knows that undoing the spell that has been cast is impossible, but she also understands the nature and consequences of the spell, and so identifies a way to change its shape — transforming a seemingly irreparable situation into one that offers hope.

We of course are not fairies, and few of us will ever change the course of history, but if we can find ways to take up the mantle of that seventh wise godmother — through small acts of discernment and careful tweaks to the action — each of us can play a part in changing the world for the better. From "Cinderella" to "Sleeping Beauty," if fairy godmother stories teach us anything, it's that we always have the power to transform the lives of even the most unlikely children and to subvert even the most impossible curses. The fairy godmother teaches us never to give up on anyone or anything — and that, if we only cultivate the insight and imagination, we will always be alive to possibility and to hope.

Among the many bright threads of wisdom woven through this much-loved story is one that reminds us of the value of story itself. There is an old saying: "As long as someone tells your story, you are never truly forgotten." It's the longevity of the princess's story, the continuing memory of her, that pushes the prince toward his fate and finally produces the "happily ever after." It's the reason why these old stories endure, and the reason why they're important still today.

Wisdom for the World

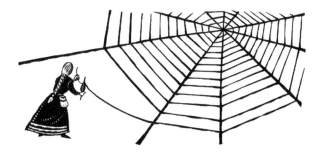

"Gifts for the Young" offered up stories of older women who act as guides and teachers for the young, but most Indigenous cultures also recognize and deeply value the many other gifts and unique kinds of wisdom that older women offer to the community, and to the wider world they live in. In contrast, in the West today we don't much talk about what it might be to be an elder — but we do have a very clear notion of what it is to be "elderly." The words seem to mean quite different things. The *Cambridge English Dictionary* online tells us that "elderly" is simply "a polite word for 'old.'" On Thesaurus.com, the word is associated with synonyms such as "hoary," "no spring chicken," "on the last legs," "declining," and "over the hill."

In contrast, being an elder implies having gravitas: "a leader or senior figure in a tribe or other group," says Lexico, another online thesaurus; the *Cambridge English Dictionary* tells us it's "an older person, especially one with a respected position in society."

Women are particularly likely to fall foul of sociocultural prejudices against older people. Although new cultural conversations about menopause and aging are beginning slowly to shift the discourse, it's still the case that in the second half of life we can be trivialized, marginalized, or actively ridiculed; in contrast to children, the culture would really rather we were neither heard *nor* seen. As a consequence, it's difficult to find inspiring role models to show us how we might become elder rather than becoming elderly — especially when, in the West today, to be old is rarely to be thought of as indispensable or even as particularly accomplished.

It's also the case that, as we get older, our confidence can sometimes ebb more than it flows — especially at the onset of menopause, when so many profound physical and psychological changes begin to kick in. These changes cause us to lose sight of who we are, because who we are is changing, and so it can be difficult even to imagine what the accomplishments and potentials of this time of life might be. But if contemporary Western culture offers no inspiring roles with which elder women can identify, we can change this situation simply by claiming the space for ourselves: by telling our own stories. Traditional folk tales present to us elder women whose contributions to the community and the wider world are considerable, and who are valued and respected for their wisdom. If we spend time with them, we can begin to reimagine new ways of being gifted elder women in this ever more challenging world.

The Spinners of Blessings

IRISH TRAVELLER

Long, long ago, a great community of old women traveled and worked in these lands. They wore their gray hair neatly braided down their backs, and long black dresses that were striped at the hem with red, yellow, and white. Sometimes there were other stripes of different colors too — one for each of their children. They carried small, beaded pouches at their hip, decorated with medals, tokens, and buttons. Each afternoon, the old women would roam the land, gathering up beets and other roots, herbs, flax, and the fallen bark of crab apple trees, and placing them in the finely woven willow baskets that they carried on their backs. Every now and again, they would pause next to a thorny thicket or bramblebush to tease away wisps and drifts of snagged fleece.

Each day at sunset, the old women returned together to their camp. They would spend the evenings working hard together, dyeing the wool they'd gathered that day in an enormous cast-iron pot that bubbled over a great, roaring fire. Into the cauldron it would go: white wool or brown, gray wool or cream, tan wool or black — but the yarn that came out of that pot was always colored a rich blood-red. All night long, the women would spin the newly dyed fleece, then weave charms and prayers into the woolen cords they were making so that each of the children of the world might receive one and be blessed. They sang as they worked: songs of hope and joy. The old women didn't sleep until dawn, and they woke each day as the sun reached its zenith, ready to roam and gather again till sunset. On and on, day after day, they continued this necessary work.

Years, centuries, and eons passed, and more and more children began to be born into the world. The old women struggled to keep up. They worked as hard as they could, but there was no way they could possibly create enough red cords for each newborn child. One evening, as they took turns to stir the dye pot, the old women agreed on a solution: together, they would weave one single red cord, long enough to encircle the world, so that no child would be left without a blessing.

It was mighty work, and the old women forgot to take time to eat or rest. Their fingers grew dark from feeding wood, turf, and coal to the great fire that roared beneath the dye pot, and from the dust of the ashes. Each day they gathered, dyed, and spun, weaving their prayers and blessings into the seemingly endless cord. The camp grew ever more silent as they focused all their attention on the work. It was hot, hard toil, this constant dyeing and spinning next to the fire. Rivulets of sweat ran down their faces, dripping onto the wool, rinsing the dye from the cord — and little by little, the cord began to turn as gray as the old women's braided hair. As time passed, the cord grew ever more silken and gossamer-thin — but it was still just as strong as the old women who wove it.

And still those old women worked on. The women too grew thin and bony, fine in stature, and though their hearts were as strong and warm as ever, they began to shrink. Some of the women worked one or two of their fingers away, and the remaining fingers became slender and long as they themselves grew smaller and smaller. Others kept their gathering baskets tied tightly to their backs, and they didn't take them off at all as they focused all their attention on gathering, dyeing, spinning, and weaving the cords. Eventually, they began to fade, and became creatures less of this world and more of the Otherworld. And after a time, they looked like little more than bundles of fine, deft, twitching fingers with gathering baskets on their backs, bearing the now-faded stripes and shadings that had once embellished their dresses and their beaded pouches.

These old spinning women were the first spiders. And still they continue their tireless work each night, spinning gossamer-thin cords and protective blessings in webs that cover so much of our world, bringing protection and healing to all its people.

Women who spin and weave are ubiquitous in European myth and folklore, but unlike some other world traditions, few of them appear as spiders. Greek mythology offers us the story of Ariadne, still in the first flush of youth and beauty, who was turned into a spider for her audacity in challenging the goddess Athena to a weaving competition — but this beautiful tale from the Irish Traveller tradition seems to be unique in offering older women who are specifically associated with spiders. That's surprising, because there are clear resonances between the two. The threads woven by spiders are thinner than human hair and look as if they ought to be impossibly fragile — but a spider's thread is formed of protein molecules that are very tightly bound together, and so it has greater tensile strength than many types of steel. In just the same way, very old women might look impossibly frail, but they too have a steely strength born from years of hard work and endurance.

Sometimes, as can be seen in other sections of this book, the old spinning and weaving women of European myth and folklore weave the world into being; sometimes, they weave the trajectory of human lives into being. In this richly mythic story, they spin cords for the blessing and protection of children, always in service to their community and to the world. These old women have a responsibility, and they know it and don't shirk from it. They have a gift to offer the world that is indispensable, and that gift is the reason for their existence.

Some of the oldest spiritual traditions of Europe suggest that each of us is born with such a singular and necessary gift, and that the opportunity to offer this gift to the world is the reason why we're born into it. In Ancient Greece, Plato referred to it as an individual's "genius," but today it is often referred to as a "calling." In his bestselling book *The Soul's Code: In Search of Character and Calling*, psychologist James Hillman states: "Each person enters the world called." Each of us, in other words, comes to a particular place, at a particular time, for a simple purpose: to do or to be something that no one else could do or be. Not all of us will make great scientific breakthroughs or win the Nobel Peace Prize, but we might well be attentive listeners, organizers of community gatherings, fixers of broken things, inspiring teachers, problem-solvers, gardeners. More often than not, it's precisely the qualities that feel ordinary to us, and that we overlook and undervalue, that might reflect the heart of our calling. They're our contribution to the flourishing web of life on this planet, and to the process of its ongoing becoming.

Carl Jung suggested that, in contrast to the more outer-focused first half of our lives, the primary purpose of the second half of our lives is finally to reveal and understand our calling, and to dedicate ourselves to the wholehearted expression of our "genius." In thinking about this, Jung drew heavily on the writings of Aristotle, who used the word "entelechy" to express the idea that there is a unique seed within the psyche of each living being. This simply means that each of us is a unique expression of what it is to be human. Each of us has the opportunity, as the onset of menopause hurls us out of the externally focused story we were living during the first half of our lives, to uncover our most authentic self in the course of the new narrative that will unfold. As we try to uncover the plots and themes of that new narrative, it might be useful to explore the following questions: What unique gift do I bring to this world, at this time? How do I facilitate its evolution? How do I serve my own community, and the children who are its future? The selfless, hardworking sacrifice of these old spinning women reminds us that we are alive in this world, and so responsible for its well-being, all the way up to the end.

Conwenna

ENGLAND

In a time when history was a gossamer weave of legend and chronicle, and bards still sang of royal lineages born of giants, a young warlord of Cornwall fought his way to becoming High King of all Britain. His name was Dyfnwal Moelmud, and with the support of his queen, Conwenna, he became a good, fair king and a renowned lawmaker. Conwenna complemented him perfectly: when the king pronounced judgments, she offered mercy; when he threatened battle, she suggested diplomacy.

Not long after they married, Conwenna gave birth to a son. They called him Belinus, and he grew into a strong, healthy child. A year later, to their great delight, another son was born; they named him Brennius, and like his brother he grew swiftly and robustly. Wherever Belinus went, Brennius followed; however high Belinus climbed, Brennius was determined to reach greater heights. Then, in the blink of an eye — or so it seemed to Conwenna — her sons were stubble-chinned warriors, begging her blessing as they left to join their father on campaign.

The years turned without much change in the kingdom, till one day King Dyfnwal sickened and died. His body was laid to rest in the ancient temple of Concord, which the Romans had dedicated to peace and harmony in the land. But no sooner had the funeral chants ended than the first hammer blows of discord began to resound through the chambers and passages of the royal court. Belinus and Brennius, now powerful battle commanders, began to forge alliances and to gather troops and weapons, each of them intent on claiming the throne of Britain. Like Romulus and Remus and Cain and Abel before them, ambition burned away the bonds of brotherhood, and battles were fought throughout the land — but without resolution.

Tired of the ongoing conflict, the old king's friends and comrades-in-arms intervened: they withheld their troops and forced the brothers to compromise. It was agreed that Belinus, as the older of Dyfnwal's sons, should become king of southern Britain, and that Brennius should be crowned king of the North — but Brennius would still be subject to the rule of his brother. For five years, the fragile peace held. Enough time to repair homes, replant fields, and replenish stores, but not remotely long enough to grieve husbands, fathers, and sons fallen in futile battles, or to weep for mothers and grandmothers slain while defending their homes.

Brennius then married the daughter of the king of Norway without consulting his brother, and it seemed inevitable that Belinus should consider this new, northern alliance to be a threat to his southern kingdom. So again, he raised a great army. They invaded Northumberland and the two opposing armies finally met there in the Forest of Calaterium. If previous battles had tested bards' abilities to fashion new phrases for such horrors, this one went further. It raged for days, and fifteen thousand men became carrion for crows. Eventually, Brennius and his few remaining men fled to Gaul, and Belinus was crowned king of all Britain. Much like his father, Belinus ruled wisely and justly, and the land and its people enjoyed peace again.

In Gaul, Brennius carved out a kingdom for himself between the River Rhône and the Alps. He became a powerful and successful king and amassed a great force of Gaulish warriors. He reveled in his success — but thwarted ambition is a bitter poison. One winter, with his warriors hearth-weary and battle-hungry, Brennius promised that the following spring, instead of raiding neighboring lands, they would march north and cross the sea to Britain. To cheers and stamping feet, he promised them plunder and land if they would help him to take his brother's crown.

So Brennius returned to Britain, and the brothers prepared to meet again — each vowing that this time it would be a fight to the death. When the morning of the great battle dawned, the armies poured out of their camps to gather on the field of combat. Then, just as Belinus and Brennius were each urging their mounts to the front of their armies to rouse them for the conflict to come, a lone figure ran suddenly toward Brennius and on into the space between the armies. It was Conwenna. She threw her arms around his neck and kissed him; then, to the shock of all the fighting men gathered there, the silver-haired queen stepped back, tore her dress at the neck, and uncovered her breasts in front of them all.

"My son," she said, "remember these breasts that nourished you and your brother, the womb which carried you both, and the great pain I endured when bringing each of you into this world. In memory of the pain that I suffered for you and the love I feel for you, I implore you to listen to me. Forgive your brother. You have no reason to fight him; he's done you no harm."

Brennius took a step back, appalled by his mother's intervention. "So you say, Mother," he said, "but my brother has taken everything. Half of Britain is rightfully mine!"

"And indeed it was — until you wed the king of Norway's

daughter and raised an army against your brother, for which he quite rightly banished you." She sighed, trying to rein in her frustration. "But hasn't it occurred to you that your banishment from this kingdom has been the making of you? What could more effectively have inspired you to become such a fine and powerful king? What sweeter revenge on your brother than to become his equal, rather than his vassal?" Conwenna shook her head, seeing the boy, so desperate to prove himself, in the bitter man who now stood before her. "You two are cut from the same cloth — styled differently perhaps, but each bearing the bright tints of honor, valor, and service that once ran in your father's blood, and the rich hues of dignity, mercy, and compassion that still flow in mine. Just like we were, you and your brother are two halves of a whole. You might yet find ways to be strengthened by each other." He raised his eyes to meet hers and she saw in them something close to despair. "My son, perhaps the greatest enemy you face on this field today is yourself."

In that moment, the fate of thousands of men — and of Britain herself — hung on the edge of a sword. And then it came: a barely perceptible nod from her son. He pulled off his helmet and let it fall to the dew-damp earth, then he walked across the field to the opposing army. Belinus, seeing that his brother approached peacefully, closed the final gap; they spoke together until at last, their reconciliation was sealed with an embrace.

Conwenna appears in just a few lines of Geoffrey of Monmouth's 1136 bestseller, *Historia Regum Britanniae*, or *The History of the Kings of Britain*. And yet, this bright, shooting star blazes across the page, an older woman stepping into her power on the field of battle. In this old story, Conwenna acts both as peacemaker and as truthteller. In challenging times — the war-torn times in which she lived, and those we're living through today — it's more important than ever to find our voice, to speak the truth that no one else can, or that no one else dares. And in doing this, Conwenna creates the conditions that allow peace to prevail.

Conwenna steps into the center of the battlefield, that bastion of male power and aggression, and bares her breasts: the breasts of a queen, but the breasts of an old woman too. She shows great courage in putting aside her pride and making herself vulnerable, and so becomes a talisman for every woman who has had to put themselves in a difficult or dangerous position in a time of crisis, and for all those who might someday need to.

Truthtellers in European myth and folklore tend to be older women. This is undoubtedly because the wisdom that — once we've skirted around the erupting volcanoes of menopause — allows us to carefully manage our inner fire as we grow older, also helps us to understand just when it is that the truth really needs to be told. And it doesn't, always. We don't need to "speak our truth" just for the sake of it. Truth needs to be spoken when it has the capacity to heal and transform, rather than being used just to break things. And so, to be a truthteller, you don't have to fasten yourself firmly to one side of a viciously divisive debate and then join in the shaming and shouting on increasingly polarized social media platforms. You can express the truth that you believe in with grace and empathy — and, above all, by living it in a way that does no harm.

In a world that still permits people to assert themselves and dominate others through conflict and war, we need our elder-women truthtellers more than ever. We need women who can speak for nature and for broken communities, to help create the conditions for positive change. But while we do for sure need truthtellers, we need them, like Conwenna, to embrace truth in a way that makes it possible for peace, not war, to break out as a consequence — and to bring dignity and vulnerability to the fractured places of our world.

An' Katty and the Well-Keepers

ENGLAND

In Cornwall, there used to be a tradition of elderly women serving as tenders of holy wells, offering the unique healing gifts of those wells to the community. The best known of these is an old woman called An' Katty (Aunt Katty), who lived during the nineteenth century and was the well-keeper at Madron Well. On the first three Wednesdays in May, women would bring their children to the well to be cured of skin diseases. According to William Bottrell, a local chronicler of folk traditions at the time,* An' Katty made a good income in May through her attendance at the well, when she would direct the "high country folks" in the proper ways to take the waters. First, Bottrell tells us, she had the child who had come to seek healing stripped naked, plunged three times against the sun, and then passed quickly nine times around the spring, going from east to west, or with the sun. The child was finally dressed, rolled up in something warm and laid to sleep near the water. If the child slept and plenty of bubbles rose in the well, it was a good sign. But no word was to be spoken while they were near the water, or it would spoil the spell, and a fragment torn from the

---

*   William Bottrell, *Traditions and Hearthside Stories of West Cornwall*, vol. 2. Beare and Son (1873).

child's clothes must be left near it for good luck, usually hung on a hawthorn that grew by the chapel wall.

An' Katty used also to instruct young girls how to "try for sweethearts." During summer evenings, girls would come to the well to drop into it pins, gravel, or any small thing that would sink. All each girl had to do was to think of the person who the objects represented, and as the pins or pebbles remained together or separated, such would be the couple's fate. An' Katty was never paid for this work with money, but with balls of yarn and other things she might want at the time.

An' Katty at Madron Well was one of a long tradition of well-priestesses in Cornwall; at Gulval, for example, the eighteenth-century chronicler William Hals wrote about the "credulous country people" who visited the village well for healing and divination.* The well, he said, was tended by an old woman who kept the site tidy and clean, and proclaimed the "virtues and divine qualities of those waters," which she offered to visitors in return for a fee. This tradition of elder-woman well-keepers can also be seen elsewhere throughout Britain.

---

*   William Hals, *History of Cornwall.* Andrew Brice, Truro & Exeter (1750).

The Buried Moon

ENGLAND

A long time ago, the marshes were full of dark Things. Shad-owy creatures and crawling horrors; scuttling, biting Things, and wet, slimy sucking Things. Bogles and dead Things. No-body knew much more about them than that. It wasn't so bad when the Moon was shining and lighting up the safe ways through the marsh; then the dark Things would sneak away back into the crevices and hollows, and the people of the land could walk through it unafraid, almost as safe as they were during the day. But when the Moon was dark and hidden in the night sky...well, then, it was a different story entirely, and the Things that dwelled in the darkness would come out and terrorize anyone who might happen to be passing by. Some-times those people would never be seen again; sometimes they returned mad to the village.

It happened one day that the Moon heard about this: about the darkness that filled the marsh during her absence, and the dark Things that held sway at that time. Being the good Moon that she is, she was sorry for the people of the land and wept for their trouble. And then she dried her tears and decided that she'd better see what she could do about it. So the Moon came down from the sky to the marsh to find out for herself what happened during the dark times. For the only marshes that she knew were those that were lit by her own beautiful light, with her face reflected in the pools and small lakes, with pale, wet rocks and shining chandeliers of dewdrops dripping from the gorse bushes in early morning mist.

At the end of the month, the Moon wrapped herself in an enormous black cloak with a big black hood to cover her shining white hair so that no one should know who she was. Down from the sky the great Moon stepped. She walked through the marsh, and everything was dark, dark — dark but for the faint glimmer of stars in the pools and the light that came from her own tiny white feet, peeping out of her enormous black cloak. All around her as she walked, the Moon saw the dark Things. Witches rode past on great black cats; the evil Eye glared at her from the darkest corners; will-o'-the-wisps danced here and there with their lanterns swinging on their backs. Dead people rose out of the water, with white twisted faces and hellfire in their empty eye sockets.

The Moon drew her cloak tighter around her and trembled a little to see such darkness, but on she went till the track ran out and she stepped, as light as a breeze, from tussock to tussock between the greedy, gurgling waterholes in the deep, dark heart of the marsh.

But just as she came near to an especially large pool, her foot slipped on a flat, wet rock and she began to tumble in. She grabbed at a gorse bush to steady herself, but oh, the spiky leaves shocked and pricked her, and she let go and in she fell, deep into the still, dark pool. She trembled in the cold, and all around her were shadows and shifting Things, creeping toward her. She grabbed at a long bramble stalk to try to pull herself out, but as soon as she touched it, it twined itself around her wrists and held her fast. The more she pulled, the tighter it held, and its thorns bit into her tender white skin.

As she stilled herself for a moment, wondering what she might do now, she heard a voice in the distance, calling out;

then she heard steps floundering along, squishing in the mud, and slipping on the slick tufts of rushes. Finally, through the darkness, she made out a pale face with bright, frightened eyes. It was a man, and he had strayed off the path and become lost. Spotting the light that flickered out from beneath the Moon's cloak as she tried to free herself, he struggled on toward the pool, thinking that the light might mean help and safety. And when the Moon saw that he was coming closer and closer to the deep hole, she fought and fought to free herself, fearing that he too would become trapped in the pool, and maybe even drown. So hard she fought that the black hood fell off her shining white hair, and the beautiful light that spilled out drove away the darkness and set the terrors of the night to flight.

Oh, the man cried with joy to see the light again, and to see the dark, shadowy Things slink back into the dark corners and crevices of the marsh, for they couldn't abide the light. And now finally he could see where he was, and where he needed to be, and so off he trod, back across the marsh again, finding his way home. He was in such a hurry to get away that he hardly thought to wonder at the source of the light, or to look down at the brave Moon, who was so glad to see him safely back on his path that she forgot to call out to him for help.

Again she struggled, thinking how fine it would be to be out of the marsh, pulling and fighting as if she were mad — but still the bramble held tight. She succeeded only in tipping the black hood over her face, so that her light was hidden and the darkness returned, and out again crawled the dark Things. With screeches and howls they crowded around the pool, mocking the Moon and snatching and poking at her, shrieking with rage and spite, swearing and snarling. They knew her for their old enemy: the one who drove them away into the dark corners and kept them from working their wills. And so miserable was the Moon that she crouched down further into the pool, cold and shivering and lost.

The dark Things fought and squabbled about what they should do with her, till a pale light began to rise in the east as dawn began to think about breaking. The dark Things saw that they were running out of time, and so they caught hold of the Moon and shoved her even deeper into the water, and two giant bogles went and found a huge heavy rock and rolled it on top of the pool, to keep her from rising again.

And there lay the Moon, buried in the marsh, with no hope of help.

The days passed and it was time for the new Moon's coming — but the Moon did not come. The nights remained dark, and all the evil Things continued to rule over the marsh, wilder and madder than ever before, and there was nowhere safe to travel. The boggarts crept and wailed around the houses and peeked in the windows and snatched at the door latches; everyone had to keep their lights on all night to prevent the dark Things from coming across their thresholds. And still the Moon did not come.

Eventually, the people of the land went to the Wise Woman who lived in the old mill, to ask her if she could help them find out where the Moon had gone. The old woman looked in her brew pot, and she looked into her mirror, and finally she looked into her book — but nothing could be seen there about the fate of the Moon. "I can't tell what has happened to her," the old woman told them. "Go carefully, children, and I'll think on it awhile, and maybe I'll be able to help you yet. If you hear anything at all, come and tell me. In any case, make sure to put a pinch of salt, a straw, and a button on your doorsills at night, so that no Horrors can come across your threshold." So the people went away, weeping and wailing for the loss of the Moon.

Nights passed in darkness, and passed and passed, until one evening, his memory jogged by a conversation he heard at the inn, the man who had strayed into the marsh began to wonder to himself whether the light that he had seen in the pool might not have been the Moon. But because he had been lost that night, he knew that he would not be able to find her again. So he told the men at the inn what he had seen in the marshes that night, and off they went together, back to the Wise Woman in the mill.

The old woman listened; she looked in her brew pot, and looked into her mirror, and finally she looked into her book — and then she nodded her head. "It's dark, children," she said to them, "it's still dark, and I can't really see much. But do as I tell you and you'll find out for yourselves what has happened to the Moon." She told them that they must go into the marsh just before nightfall, each one with a stone in his mouth and a hazel wand in his hand, and they mustn't speak a single word till they were safe home again. And she told them that they should walk into the middle of the marsh until they came across a coffin, a candle, and a cross. "Then you'll not be far from the Moon," she said. "Look around there, and maybe you'll find her after all."

Well, the people cried out, saying they were afraid to go into the darkness of the marshes, but the old woman called them a bunch of fools. "Do as I tell you, and don't be afraid," she told them. "And if you don't — well then, stay in your houses and do without the Moon for as long as you live."

So the next night, they left the safety of their hearths and off they all went together, the men of the village — each of them with a stone in his mouth and a hazel twig in his hand, and each of them terrified but not uttering a word. They traveled on through the growing dark, stumbling and fearful of the sighings and mutterings all around them and the cold wet fingers that reached for them…but they happened eventually upon a large stone, half in and half out of the water, looking for all the world like some strange old coffin. At the head of it was a bramblebush, stretching out its arms in a dark, grue-some cross, and around the stone-coffin a tiny light flickered, like a candle. It was just as the wise old woman had said. And so, using all their combined strength, the men heaved up the stone. Forever afterward, they were sure that just for a mo-ment they saw a strange and beautiful face shining up at them out of the blackness of the water — but all at once they were blinded by the light, which came so quick and so dazzling. They covered their eyes and shuddered at the wailing of the dark Things as they fled from the light. And the next thing they knew, there was the full Moon back in the sky, shining down at them, bright and beautiful and kind as ever, making the marsh and its paths as clear as day, and stealing into all the dark cor-ners to fill them with light.

This very old tale from the Lincolnshire fens can be under-stood as a story about the lost heart of the feminine, consigned to a grave in the dark, watery depths of the marshes. The dark Things try to destroy the power of the Moon, hating her light and wanting to cover it up. In some cultures, the moon is called Grandmother, but it's the Wise Woman in this story who is the primary focus of attention here: the old woman who is the first port of call for her "children," the men of the village, who understand that she knows and sees things that they cannot. The tools of this Wise Woman are simple enough: a teapot, a mirror, and a book. There are none of the complex rituals and contraptions of "high magic," practiced in the past mostly by men — and by men in the higher echelons of society. Like that of the henwife who we met in "Fair, Brown, and Trembling," this is a wisdom that is rooted in the domestic, in the daily life of the community.

A Wise Woman isn't just capable of seeing what is wrong in a situation: she knows how to fix things. She can perceive the web of life and discern its patterns and interconnectedness; as a consequence, she understands when the world is out of balance and knows what might be done to put it right again. So the Wise Woman in this story, using the information provided to her, divines what must have happened and how it might be possible to rescue the lost Moon. But she has no patience with those who are too afraid to do what is necessary, calling the men of the village a bunch of fools for their fear of the dark bog.

Only a farsighted Wise Woman could know the way to find and restore the buried Moon, and this one reminds us that, if we have courage, we might reclaim lost light in even the bleakest of places. In this sense, she encourages us to value our intuition, one of many qualities associated with the archetypal feminine that have become so undervalued in today's overly rationalistic world. Psychologists usually define intuition as an ability to "know" things without the need for conscious reasoning about them. We might more colloquially call it "gut feeling": a strange inner knowing that something is going to happen, an inexplicable feeling that won't go away and that is later explained by something that occurs. In whatever ways we might experience it, intuition is associated with direct access to unconscious knowledge; an intuitive person then, or a Wise Woman, makes use of knowledge that is usually unavailable to us.

For many women, menopause ushers in a time of increased intuition as we begin to slow down and pay more attention to what's happening around us. But in a world that no longer

values intuition as a legitimate way of knowing, it's all too easy
to drown out that inner voice in the scuffles and skirmishes of
daily life. Inner wisdom and intuition aren't available to us if
we can't sometimes be alone and still so that we might listen for
their whispers, and if we don't find the time to engage in regu-
lar reflection about our thoughts and experiences. If, over time,
we learn to listen to the different voices in our heads — the intuitive and the analytical — then we'll become more skilled at
rehearsing different approaches to a problem and evaluating
their relative success. We'll learn to trust ourselves, and so to
more readily tune in to the voice of our inner Wise Woman.

The Finwife

ORKNEY

Back in the days when it was still of use to wish for a thing, there was a good man who lived happily with his wife and children in Faracleat on Rousay. Giant seasons tower over those rolling northern islands spawned long ago by a still-sleeping ocean. Winters stubborn as a blacksmith's anvil, summer days so long and bright that the horizon fades into insignificance. Well, this man was a successful trader who made three voyages a year across the capricious North Sea from the Orkneys to Norway — but while returning home from one of them, his ship was caught in a vicious gale and driven onto rocks near the Shetland coast. The merchant and his crew struggled through the surging sea and made it to shore alive, but they lost everything. It was autumn and strong winds prowled the islands like hungry wolves, whipping up storms that made further travel impossible. There was nothing for the Orkney men to do but ask for shelter with the kind folk of Shetland and settle in for the winter ahead.

The merchant took lodgings with an old woman who lived on her own, just a little way inland from the sea. She was a curious character: eyes as fathomless as the ocean, set deep in a face sculpted by long years of wind and sea spray; her long hair escaped in silvery tendrils from a great whalebone pin.

She wasn't exactly easy on the eye, but she treated the merchant kindly and they rubbed along well enough. He carried in peat for the fire, and on finer days made makeshift repairs to the old woman's cottage; she shared her food and gave him a warm place to sleep at night.

The year grew old and gray, and storms continued to batter the little house. On Christmas Eve, the merchant sat staring into the fire with a heavy heart and a chest full of sighs; he was homesick for his wife and their three small children. He turned down the old woman's offer of food and could find little to say. She tried to cheer him up and urged him to eat a few spoonfuls of her mutton broth, but he could not. At last, he said, "I'm not very good company tonight. How could I be — tomorrow is Yuleday, and it's the first I've spent away from home since I was married. I miss my wife and my little bairns."

"Well," said the old woman, "that's no surprise. Of course you'd want to be with your own family at such a time. I'm sure you'd give the very best cow in your byre, if you could only be beside your wife when the cock crows in the morning."

"Aye! That I would, with all my heart," and a wistful smile reached his eyes as he imagined waking up warm and cozy in his own bed, next to his wife.

The old woman chuckled. "All's well that ends well," she said, taking up a stick and poking at the smoldering turfs on the fire. "Why don't you take yourself a drop of gin and go to bed, and if you tell me your dreams in the morning, I'll give you a silver coin as a Yuleday gift." So the merchant took a drink and went to bed; he pulled the blankets tight around him and slept soundly until morning.

Across the turbulent ocean in Faracleat, the merchant's wife lay in her too-big bed and thought about her husband. Was he still alive, and if so, where was he? It would be a sad Yule in the house that year, for sure. She rolled over and finally fell sleep, but she woke in the morning with a firm feeling that someone was in the bed beside her. As she came to her senses, she heard the low, incessant snoring of a man beneath the blankets. She turned over and walloped the intruder with her fist. "You ill-bred villain! How dare you come into an honest wife's bed. Get out, you great beast, or I'll tear you to rags!" She grabbed him by the throat and squeezed tight.

"Is that your voice, my own sweet Maggie?" the man croaked, and when she heard him speak, she let go her grip.

"Bless me! If it isn't my dearest husband," she said — and so it was. He had been transported from Shetland to Rousay by the old woman's magic — for she wasn't just any old woman but a Finwife.

As the merchant and his wife hugged each other, a thought occurred to him. "You might not be so glad to have me home when you know what it cost to bring me back," he told his wife.

They dressed and he led her to the byre — and, sure enough, their very best milk cow was gone. The wife cried out, "Oh no! She's taken Brenda — the best milker in the byre!"

Now this story must be true, because the merchant's neighbor, a man called Johnnie Flett, was in Shetland the following summer. He saw that very same cow, which he knew well, tethered outside the old Finwife's house. He told the story to his friends, who sailed all about and told the story at the various ports where they landed, and other merchants carried the story far and wide until it came to our ears…and now you've heard it too.

This story comes from the remote northern islands of Orkney — the heart of Finfolk lore. It was once believed that a

Finwife began her life as a mermaid but could shapeshift into human form and so live on land as well as in the sea. If a Finwife should marry a Finman — which she was bound to do, unless she could attract a human husband — she would grow progressively uglier for the rest of her life. She would often be made to go ashore and work as a healer or spinner, and to send all her silver home or risk a beating. Consequently, human husbands were very much preferred; sometimes Finwives might go to live with them on land. The Finfolk were once thought of as a race of sinister sorcerers, but by the time their folklore came to be recorded, the fear they'd once evoked was beginning to fade.

Reciprocity is a common theme in myth and folklore: if a fair trade takes place between two people, or between humans and inhabitants of the Otherworld, then some essential cosmic balance is preserved. But when someone takes more than their allotted share, takes something that is not theirs, declines to offer something in return for a gift, or refuses to pay what they owe, the equilibrium of the world is shattered and the consequences might be severe. And so, at the center of this story is the exchange (unspoken, but clearly understood) of the merchant's best cow for magical transportation back to his home. The other exchange — the Finwife's offer of a silver coin if the merchant will tell her his dreams in the morning — is intriguing, especially since it doesn't come to pass. Perhaps it tells us something about the value that dreams once had — or perhaps it's just the Finwife's idea of a joke, since she knows perfectly well that he won't be there to fulfill this particular bargain.

On the surface, this is a simple enough story about the need to express gratitude for gifts that are offered to you by giving something in return, but stories of reciprocity offer us deeper teachings about value, and especially about valuing ourselves as much as we value others. How many of us find ourselves constantly giving — to children, family, friends, co-workers, employers, or partners — without expecting (or receiving) anything in return, and without considering how this exhausts and disheartens us? Midlife is well past the time to start valuing ourselves, recognizing our own needs, and thinking of our time and energy as precious. This requires us to carefully consider how and when we offer ourselves, to refuse to be exploited, and to expect reciprocity — whether what we receive in return is something material, the gift of gratitude and appreciation...or even the simple telling of a tale.

The Hedley Kow

ENGLAND

Once there was an old woman who just about scraped a living by running errands for the farmers' wives round about the village where she lived. She didn't earn much from her hard work, but since she would be offered a plate of meat at one house and a cup of tea at another, somehow she managed to get by. She always looked cheerful, as if she hadn't a want or a care in the world.

One summer evening, as she was trotting away homeward after a day's work, she came upon a big black pot lying at the side of the road.

"Now that," she said to herself, "would be just the very thing for me. Or at least, it would if I had anything to put into it! But who on earth can have left it here?" She imagined that the person it belonged to mustn't be far off, but she couldn't see a single soul anywhere nearby.

"Maybe it has a hole in it," she said, thoughtfully. "Yes, indeed — that'll be why they've just left it lying here. But it would still be perfect on the windowsill, with a little plant in it. I'm thinking I'll just take it home, anyway." And she bent her stiff old back and lifted the lid. "Mercy me!" she cried, stumbling all the way back to the other side of the road. "If it isn't full to the brim with gold pieces!"

For a while she could do nothing but walk round and

around her treasure, admiring the shiny gold inside it, wondering at her good luck, and saying to herself about every two minutes, "Well, I'm sure I feel just as rich and grand as can be!" But after a while, she began to wonder how she might manage to carry the large, heavy pot home with her. The only solution she could come up with was to fasten one end of her shawl to it and drag it behind her.

"It'll be dark soon," she said to herself, "and no one will be able to see what I'm bringing home with me, so I'll have the whole night to myself to think about what to do with it. I could buy a grand house and live like a queen, and not do a stroke of work all day but just sit by the fire with a cup of tea. Or maybe I'll give it to the priest to keep for me, and just get a gold piece whenever I need it. Or maybe I'll just bury it in a hole at the bottom of the garden. Or maybe put a bit on the mantelpiece, between the china teapot and the wooden spoons — just as an ornament, you know. Ah! I feel so rich and grand, I don't even recognize myself!"

By this time, already rather tired from dragging such a heavy weight behind her, she stopped to rest for a minute, turning to make sure that the treasure was safe. But when she looked at it, she saw that it wasn't a pot of gold at all, but a great lump of shining silver.

She rubbed her eyes and stared at it again — but she couldn't make it look like anything but a great lump of silver. "I'd have sworn it was a pot of gold," she said, "but I reckon I must have been dreaming. Anyway, this is a change for the better; it'll be far less trouble to look after and not nearly so easily stolen. Those gold pieces would have been a terrible bother to keep safe. Aye, I'm well quit of them, and with this bonny lump of silver I'm still as rich and grand as can be!" And so she set off homeward again, cheerfully planning all the fine things she was going to do with her money. It wasn't very long, though, before she grew weary again and stopped to rest for a minute or two.

Once again she looked at her treasure, and cried out in astonishment. "Oh, my!" she said, "Now it's a lump of iron! Well, that beats everything, and it's so convenient! I can sell it as easily as can be, and I'll get plenty of penny pieces for it. Aye, and it's much handier than a load of gold and silver that would have kept me from sleeping at night, always thinking the neighbors were coming to rob me. And it's such a handy thing to have in a house; you never can tell what you might need it for, and it'll sell for a good sum, for sure. Rich? I'll be just rolling in money!"

And on she trotted again, chuckling to herself at her good fortune, till after a while she glanced over her shoulder — "only to make sure it was still there," as she said.

"Oh, my goodness!" she cried. "If it hasn't gone and turned itself into a great big stone this time! Now, how could it have known that I was so badly needing something to hold my door open with? Aye, if that isn't a wonderful transformation, indeed! Oh, it's a fine thing to have such good luck."

All in a hurry to see how the stone would look in its corner by her door, she trotted off down the hill and came to a halt beside her own little gate. When she had unlatched it, she unfastened her shawl from the stone, which this time seemed to be lying unchanged and quite peacefully on the path beside her. Although the sun was setting, there was still plenty of light and she could see the stone quite plainly — when, all of a sudden, it gave a jump and a squeal, and it grew as huge as a great horse. Then it threw down four lanky legs, shook out two long ears, flourished a tail, and went off kicking its feet into the air and laughing like a naughty, mocking little boy.

The old woman stared after it till it was out of sight. "Well!" she said. "I really am the luckiest person here! Fancy me seeing

the Hedley Kow all by myself, and making so free with it too!
I can tell you, I do feel that grand...." And she went into her
cottage, chuckling to herself, and sat down by the fire to pon-
der on all her good luck.

This old folk tale is centered on the village of Hedley on the
Hill in Northumberland. The Hedley Kow, known to generations of the village's inhabitants, was an archetypical Otherworldly trickster, a kind of elf or "bogle," which was renowned
for its mischievous, shapeshifting habits. It seemed to take delight in frightening people by creating chaos all around them,
before laughing and then leaving. This strange being usually
appeared in animal form, which is presumably why it became
known as the "Kow."

But of course, it's the old woman in this delightful little
story who most concerns us. There's nothing obviously "special" about her: she has no magical powers — indeed, she has
no particular powers of any kind. She's just an ordinary, impoverished old village woman. But when it comes to her perspective on life, she's exceptional. The wisdom she offers to the
world is contentment with her lot, and the gift that she displays
in this story is a rare one: equanimity in the face of rapidly
declining fortune. This is a woman who understands that what
she has, although it's little, is quite enough.

European folklore is abundant with cautionary tales of
people who are dissatisfied and greedy, such as the Brothers
Grimm story "The Fisherman and His Wife." A poor fisherman, who lives with his wife in a hovel by the sea, catches a fish
one day. The fish tells the fisherman that it can grant wishes
and begs to be set free; the kindly fisherman releases it. But
when his wife hears the story, she insists that he go back and

ask the fish to grant her wish for a bigger house. The fisherman reluctantly returns to the shore and summons the fish, who grants his wife's wish. However, the wife continually demands that her husband go back to the fish to ask for more and more. Eventually, the wife wants to command the sun, moon, and heavens, and sends her husband to the fish with the demand: "I want to become equal to God." Instead of granting this, the fish just tells the fisherman to go home, and when he does, he finds that he and his wife have returned to their original impoverished state.

"The Hedley Kow" shows us the flip side of such stories. Our cheerful old woman hasn't bought into the cultural dogma that tells us we must always be wanting more, must always be in pursuit of progress — and usually at the expense of the planet. She might, on the surface, seem to be a little foolish — but, actually, she's one of the wisest elder women in this book. If she were alive today, she'd no doubt have been crowned as a famous social media influencer or self-help guru and would be out in the world extolling the virtues of the simple life. Happily, she is captured here for posterity, unfeted and with her integrity perfectly intact, to show us that appreciating what you have and where you are in life and finding ways to be happy with the reality of your present situation, are the greatest gifts of all.

Death and Rebirth

In the oldest European mythic traditions, the archetypal energies of life and death almost always go together — and in com-
bination they are almost always associated with women. Death
and (re)birth are two sides of the ubiquitous Great Mother archetype (who is actually, in the cosmology of many European
countries, a Great Grandmother); they are different faces of
the same deity. Every life bears within it the seed of its own
death, this old cosmology tells us — but no end is ever less than
a new beginning: Death is always in the business of incubating
new life. And as archaeologist Marija Gimbutas suggested, the
Old Woman "acts on a cosmic plane: she balances the life energy of humans, animals, plants, and even of the moon." She

reminds us that "there is no life without death. Thus, she is essentially concerned with regeneration."* Archetypally, then, death is not an ending, but a great transformation.

We see this cycle of death and rebirth in some of the old Scottish stories of the Cailleach, the old woman who creates and shapes the land in Irish and Scottish Gaelic traditions. In one of those traditions, stories tell of her two aspects: the hard, stony blue-faced Cailleach, and Brigid, known sometimes as Bride. On the old festival day of Bealtaine (the first of May) the old woman of winter, the Cailleach, dies and is reborn as Bride. Bride turns winter scarcity into summer abundance, but as autumn approaches and the light begins to fade, she weakens. By the festival of Samhain (the first of November), it's the Cailleach who rules the season, and Bride who has died and now awaits rebirth. There are many stories about this battle for the seasons that takes place between Bride and the Cailleach, but they can clearly be seen as two aspects of life in balance, of the need for both darkness and light, for both summer and winter, for death and rebirth — the ever-renewing cyclical nature of the world. Similarly, the goddess Morana (or Marzanna) in Slavic tradition is associated with seasonal rites that relate to the death and rebirth of nature: her death at the end of winter leads to the rebirth of the spring goddess Kostroma (or Lada or Vesna, depending on the country).

The old women in this part of the book are associated with death in many different ways. They are Death personified, messengers and harbingers of death, and midwives of rebirth and transformation. They are compassionate, strong, or sometimes simply strange. They should be better known.

---

*   Marija Gimbutas, *The Language of the Goddess*. HarperCollins (1989).

The Bird Yustritsa

RUSSIA

This old song from Russia portrays Death as a female bird. She eats humans when their time has come to die — but she will not eat the rare creatures of the sea. In several medieval Russian books, Buyan is described as a mysterious island in the ocean, which appears and disappears with the tide. Three brothers — the North, West, and East Winds — live there, and also the Zoryas, a group of solar goddesses. The island of Buyan features prominently in many Russian myths and folk tales; Koschei the Deathless is said to keep his immortal soul hidden there.

In the ocean-sea,
On the island Buyan,
Sits the bird Yustritsa.
She boasts and brags
That she has seen all,
Has eaten much of all.
She has seen the tsar in Moscow,
The king in Lithuania,
The elder in his cell,
The babe in his cradle.
And she has not eaten that
Which is wanting in the sea.

The Little Old Woman with Five Cows

SIBERIA

One spring morning, an old woman woke up and went out to the field where her five cows were grazing. She had a strange urge to look for a particular plant, and she searched through the long grass till she spotted it in a corner of the field. She dug up a piece, taking care to keep its stems and roots intact, and then she carried it back to her cottage. She wrapped it in a soft blanket and placed it on her pillow, then she went out to call her cows to the shed for milking.

She was just settling herself on the milking stool when she heard a sudden tinkling, like the sound of a tambourine, followed by a sound such as her scissors would make if they had fallen onto the hearthstone. It startled her so much that she upset her pail. She ran back to the cottage to see what had happened, but she couldn't find anything that might have caused the noise; she checked on the plant that lay on her pillow and, finding it undisturbed, returned to her milking. But a few minutes later she heard the same sounds — the tambourine and falling scissors — and so she rushed back to the house again. Inside her bedchamber an ethereal young woman was sitting on her bed. Her translucent eyes were as blue as chalcedony, her lips were as red as garnets, and her skin was as pale as alabaster. Her body was visible through her thin dress; her bones were visible through her thin body; her veins, running this way and that, like quicksilver, were visible through her bones. The plant had transformed itself into this astonishingly beautiful maiden.

Soon afterward, the son of the king of the region decided to go hunting. He rode deep into the forest until he found himself in the place where the old woman lived with her cows. A gray squirrel was sitting in a tree near the cottage; he raised his bow, took aim, and loosed an arrow — but it was dim and the sun was already beginning to set. He missed, the squirrel scampered away, and the arrow arced up into the sky and fell right down into the old woman's chimney.

She hurried outside to see what was happening. "Old woman!" the prince called. "Would you go inside and fetch me that arrow?" But the old woman took no notice of him. His cheeks flushed with annoyance: he was the king's son, after all, and he wasn't used to being ignored. He slid down from his fine black stallion and marched into the old woman's cottage, but when he saw the extraordinary maiden sitting by the hearth, he stopped dead — and then he fainted and fell to the floor. A few moments later, he revived and stared up at the young woman with shining dark eyes; it was nothing less than love at first sight. Then, without so much as a word to her or to the old woman, he ran out of the house, mounted his horse, and galloped back to the palace.

The young prince leaped down from his horse and ran into the throne room. "Mother, Father!" he cried. "I've just met the most beautiful girl in the whole world. She lives in a cottage with an old woman who has five cows. I really must marry her. Won't you please send some men to bring her here?"

The king and queen, who loved their only son dearly and wanted nothing more than his happiness, instructed nine men to ride swiftly to the old woman's cottage. As soon as they set eyes on the strange young woman, each of those brave warriors

grew dizzy and fell to the floor. When they regained consciousness, they fled from the cottage, fearing they'd been the vic-
tim of some sorcerer's spell. But one of them remained and,
shaking his head and clearing his throat, managed to speak.
"Old woman," he said, "the king would like to have this young
woman as a bride for his son and heir. We've come to escort
her to the palace."

The old woman nodded. "I'll give her to the king," she
said, "if, for a wedding gift, the bridegroom will fill my fields
with fine cattle and horses."

The young man agreed to this on behalf of the king, and
instructed his eight companions, who were cowering still outside the cottage door, to fetch the animals. The maiden gazed
at him with her strange, translucent eyes and said, "I'll go
with you."

She found a beautiful white horse waiting outside. The
horse could speak like a human; he wore a fine silver halter
and a silver saddle laid on top of a silver cloth. Next to the
horse was a fine young man on a black stallion, who introduced himself as the king's son. He wrapped a richly embroidered cloak around her, set her on her horse, and they rode off
together in the direction of the palace.

After they'd traveled a little way, the young prince turned
to the maiden and said, "There's a fox trap in the deepest part
of this forest and while I'm here, I'm just going to go and check
on it. You carry on along this track; in a little while it will divide
into two roads. A sable skin hangs at the start of the road that
leads east, but on the road that leads west, you'll find the skin
of a great male bear, complete with paws and head, and with
white fur around his neck. You need to travel along the road
where the sable skin is hanging."

He rode away and the young woman continued along
the track until she came to the fork — but then she realized

that she had forgotten the directions he had given her. She decided to take the road west, where the bear skin hung, and soon afterward she came to a small iron hut. A devil's daughter sprang out of it, dressed in an iron garment that reached to her knees. She had only one twisted leg, and a single bent hand jutted out from beneath her breast. A single furious eye was set in the middle of her forehead, and as she ran toward the maiden, a hideously long tongue shot out of her mouth and hung down to her breast. She dragged the girl from her horse and threw her to the ground, then she tore away the skin from her face and placed it over her own. She took the girl's clothes and put them on, and then she mounted the white horse and rode away.

The prince, returned from his trapping duties, stood waiting for his bride outside the palace. As she rode in, nine young men came from one side to take the horse's halter, and eight maidens came from the other side to do the same. But although everyone who looked at the beautiful young woman felt that there was something strange about her, and felt oddly depressed and sorrowful, no one could quite put their finger on what was wrong.

A great wedding feast was held, though it lacked the expected joy; afterward, everyone returned to their usual routines. The old woman was walking out to the field to find her five cows, when she noticed that the magical plant was now growing strongly in the corner where she'd previously found it. She dug up another piece of it, careful again to keep its long stem and roots intact; she carried it back to her cottage, wrapped it in a soft blanket, and placed it on her pillow. Then she called her cows into the shed and settled down to the milking. Once again, she heard a delicate tinkling, like the ringing of a many-belled tambourine, followed by a sound like a pair of scissors falling onto the hearthstone. She hurried back to

the cottage and the maiden was sitting on her bed again, looking more lovely than ever.

"Mother," she said, "after the prince took me away from
here, he said that he had to go and check a fox trap deep in
the forest. Before he left, he told me which path I should take
through the woods — but I forgot what he said and soon found
myself at an iron house that was the home of a devil's daughter. She tore the skin from my face and put it over her own,
then she dressed herself in my clothes. She rode away on my
horse, after throwing away the rest of my skin and my bones.
A gray wolf came along, and he picked up my lungs and heart
in his teeth and carried them here to your fields. It seems it
wasn't my fate to die altogether, and so I grew here again as
a plant. But this devil's daughter has married the prince and
contaminated his flesh and blood. What shall I do?"

A few days later, the king went riding on the white horse
that was endowed with human speech. The horse knew that his
true mistress had revived and, now that he finally had his attention, he told the king everything that had happened. "That
devil's daughter killed my mistress, but now she's alive again. If
your son doesn't take this lovely girl as his wife, I'll complain to
the Creator, on his great white stone throne, next to the silver
lake with its floating blocks of gold, silver, and black ice. I'll
shatter your house and put out your fire forever. You'll be left
with nothing to live on, because a good man really shouldn't
welcome a devil's daughter into his family. So here's what you
need to do to prevent that from happening. First, have your
son tie his devil's-daughter bride to the legs of a wild horse and
chase it away. Then he must stand under a stream of rushing
water for thirty days, so that it might cleanse him. Let worms
and reptiles suck away his contaminated blood; afterward, take
him out of the water and expose him to the wind at the top
of a tree for thirty nights, so that his heart and liver, and his

contaminated flesh and blood, might be purified by the north and south winds. After all that, he can be reunited with his real bride."

The king wept for his son, but they galloped back to the palace, and he ran to his son's chambers. "My son," he said, "from where and from whom did you take this wife of yours?"

"Why, as I told you," the prince said, "she's the daughter of that little old woman with five cows."

"Which horse did your wife ride to come to the palace?" the king asked. "And do you know anything about her origins?"

"I brought her here on the white horse who speaks our language. As we were riding, she told me that she comes from the Third Heaven, where the Creator sits on his white stone throne. The Creator's brother fashioned, from a flock of migratory birds, seven young daughters who then took the form of cranes. They flew down to Earth and landed in a field where they could feast and dance. Then a teacher came down to them; she took the finest of the seven cranes aside and said to her: 'Your fate is to go out to the Middle World and learn there to love it and its people. You'll marry the son of the king, and wear a skin made of eight sables. You'll become human, and you'll carry and raise children.' Then she cut off the end of the crane's wings. 'Turn into mare's-tail grass and grow!' the teacher said. 'A little old woman with five cows will find the herb; she'll turn you back into your human form and give you in marriage to the prince.' All of this seemed a little strange to me as she told it," the prince said, "but I was so entranced by her that it didn't matter."

The king shook his head. "The white horse told me what happened to your real wife. You told her which way to take through the woods, but she forgot your directions and took the wrong path. She rode west, past the bear skin, came to an iron house, and a devil's daughter attacked her. It stole the skin from her face, and her clothes and jewelry, and used them to disguise her own hideous form. This is the creature you married, and I can see that she's drained the life and will from you. You need to get rid of her, and the white horse told me how it might be done."

The prince, weakened and ashamed, told one of his men to seize the false bride from her chamber; he dragged her out of the palace while she writhed and raged. He tied her to the legs of a wild bay stallion that was penned in the paddock; it bucked and kicked the devil's daughter to death. Worms and reptiles rose up out of the earth to drink her blood and eat the pieces of her dead body that lay strewn across the ground.

The king followed the horse's advice about what should be done with his son, and when his contaminated body and blood were finally cleansed, he was brought home to the palace. As soon as he felt strong enough, he rode into the forest and on to the old woman's cottage. This time, she came out, delighted, to greet him. "We've been waiting for you," she said, and she led him up a grass-strewn path to a little tent. Inside it was a bed covered in a white horse skin, complete with hooves, and a fine wedding feast, made from a cow and a horse that she had killed, was spread out on a low table.

The beautiful young woman approached the tent with tears in her eyes. "Why have you come here?" she said to the prince. "You sent me to the iron house where the daughter of an eight-legged devil lived, and you let my blood be spilled and my body be taken as food for wolves. After that, how can you possibly ask me again to be your wife? My heart is wounded and my mind is troubled. I won't be marrying you."

"Ah, my love!" the prince said. "I didn't send you there: I told you to take the road to the east, where the sable skin hangs. I didn't know what would happen to you. But I know

now that your teacher, the Creatress, chose you for me, and that's why you're alive again. We're destined for each other."

The old woman shook her head. "Why aren't you happy, now that you've returned to life, after death," she said to the young woman, "and why aren't you happy that you've been found again, after being so very lost?"

"You're right," she said. The prince joyfully closed the space between them, took her in his arms, and kissed her. After that, amid much laughter and delight, they exchanged wedding vows; nine ancestral spirits came from the Upper World and twelve ancestral spirits rose from the Underworld to witness their marriage.

The next morning, the white horse arrived at the house. The prince and his new bride said goodbye to the old woman, then the prince on his black stallion and the beautiful maiden on the white horse set off on this new journey of their lives together. As they traveled, they knew it was still spring by the soft rain that fell on them, then that it was summer by the warmth of the midday sun on their backs. All too soon, the chill morning fog that clung to their cloaks told them it was autumn, and finally, as fat white snowflakes danced around them and fell to the ground, they knew that winter had come.

The little old woman in this Siberian folk tale acts as an archetypical midwife of transformation and rebirth. In facilitating the Otherworldly maiden's Earthly existence, she also facilitates the fate that the Creatrix determined for the maiden, and in this way becomes the Creatrix's agent, down here in the "Middle World."

In all cosmologies, the concept of fate is complex and

difficult to fathom — though it's rarely as deterministic as we might often be led to believe. There is always room for error, and there is always room for growth. When we're young and full of spirit, we're likely to reject the idea that the trajectory of our life might be influenced or constrained by anything or anyone other than ourselves. We might be convinced that we know exactly where we're going, and what kind of life is right for us, and so we steer firmly along a path that we like to imagine is straight, and in a direction that we like to imagine we can control. But during the course of a long life, with its inevitable setbacks, changes of direction, and shattered hopes and dreams, most of us come to realize that we can't just will into being the life we're determined to have. Accepting this is a sign of maturity, and so is the understanding that, if we make space in our fields for whatever chooses, unbidden, to grow there, the life that eventually emerges might be richer than we could ever have imagined. This mysterious process has sometimes been called fate. If we're wise, we might decide to befriend fate, and so learn to discern its delicate nudges as we travel along a particular path. In opening ourselves to such possibilities, we become a conduit for the forces of life and creation — in whatever form we might imagine them to take.

This is the path taken by the old woman in this story, as she follows the prodding of her intuition and goes out to the field to look for a particular plant, so allowing the Otherworldly crane to incarnate in human form. The old woman sets in motion the next stage of the Creatrix's plans for the young woman, by facilitating her marriage to the prince. Later, after she has been killed by the eight-legged devil's daughter and returns to the field as a plant, the old woman is again the midwife of her rebirth into this world. She then intervenes in her fate for a third time, by arranging her reconciliation with, and eventual marriage to, the prince.

Our old woman also makes the most of the opportunity presented to her, and so receives cattle and horses as the bride price. What we're left with, though, is the potency of the two questions that the old woman asks the strange maiden: "Why aren't you happy, now that you've returned to life, after death?" and "Why aren't you happy that you've been found again, after being so very lost?" Perhaps we need to be old before we can formulate these deep questions. Perhaps we need to have learned to accept our own mortality before we can really appreciate the gifts and opportunities offered to us by life. Perhaps, in other words, we need to be able to look death in the face before we can truly live. And perhaps, as those of us who are fortunate enough to have reached our elder years know all too well, we need to have experienced being lost before we can fully appreciate what it is to be found. Ultimately, though, such questions don't have easy answers; perhaps the essence of the answer lies simply in considering the question, because the mystery of life and our place in it is something to sit with, not to solve.

The Sheela Na Gig

Scattered among medieval religious buildings, castles, holy wells, bridges, and town walls throughout Britain and Ireland are many stone carvings of naked women exposing their genitals, with their long-fingered hands pointing at or holding open huge, cavernous vulvas. They are standing, squatting, kneeling, or sitting, and they're known as Sheela na gigs.

The upper half of these carvings is redolent of death: the Sheela na gig's breasts are old and withered; she has skeletal ribs, a skull-like head, hollow eyes; and she is often bald. The lower half, in contrast, is ripe with sexuality and fertility, and reminds us of the act of giving birth squatting or standing. In this respect, they reflect the fact that, across Europe, the old Mother Goddesses had two faces: they were associated not just with fertility and with the giving and maintaining of life — but also, when the time comes, with death.

Scholars disagree about the origins of these figures. Some argue that their primary location — on churches — along with their grotesque features, suggests that their purpose was to characterize female lust as hideous, sinful, and corrupting. Others believe that the carvings reflect a pre-Christian religion, focused on fertility and the Mother Goddess. Some Sheela na gigs are different both in material and style from the structures they're attached to, and some are turned on their side, which suggests they might have been taken from earlier structures and incorporated into Christian buildings.

Godmother Death

MORAVIA

Once upon a time there was a very poor man whose wife gave birth to a baby boy who was their first child. Because the family was so poor, no one was willing to stand as godparent to the boy: there was a high risk that they might need one day to support the child financially. Finally, the despairing father said to himself: "Well, if no one that I know is willing to serve as godparent to my son, I'll take matters into my own hands. I'll just walk out into the street with the baby, and I'll ask the first person I meet to be his godparent."

So he wrapped his son up in a warm shawl and brought him out into the street; the first person he spotted was a handsome woman, walking toward him. It so happened that this woman was Death, but because she looked just like any other well-dressed woman you might meet in the street, he had no way of knowing this. He explained his situation and asked her if she would be godmother to his son. Death said that she would, took the baby in her arms, and carried him into the nearby church. And there, the little boy was christened.

When they left the church after the short service, the child's father suggested that the godmother accompany him to an inn: he wanted to offer her a drink to thank her for her generosity. But she just smiled and said to him, "Why don't you come with me to my home, instead."

He agreed and, still carrying the child, she led the way to her apartment. It was on the ground floor of a beautiful old building and was large and beautifully furnished. She took him through an intricately carved wooden door that opened off the hallway, and on through a maze of high, vaulted, and dimly lit corridors. It grew darker and more and more silent and, eventually, the father began to understand that they had passed into the Underworld. The darkness deepened and deepened and seemed about to grow absolute, but then, in the distance, he saw a warm orange glow. They walked on until the corridor ended and they came face-to-face with a high and wide stone wall, with solid wooden shelves that reached from the floor to the ceiling. All along the shelves, vast numbers of tapers were burning: some small ones, some large ones, and a good many average-sized ones.

The woman turned to her godchild's father. "Look," she said, "I am Death, and this is the place where the duration of everyone's life is determined."

The father scanned the lines of tapers until he saw a tiny taper, almost burned down, on a shelf very close to the ground. "Whose is this little taper?" he asked.

"That one is yours," she replied, sadly. "And whenever any taper burns right down, I must come for the person whose life it represents."

He looked at the baby in her arms and closed his eyes in pain. "Godmother Death, I beg you to give me more time with my son."

"I'm very much afraid that I can't do that." She turned away to light a long taper for her godson. Seizing his chance while she wasn't looking, the father picked up a fresh taper, lit it, and placed it next to his own tiny one, which was now on the verge of extinguishing itself.

When Death saw what he had done, she was angry. "You

ought not to have done that," she said. "But now you've given yourself more time, and nothing can be done about it. Well, we'd better get you home again to your wife."

When they arrived back in the high-ceilinged hallway of her apartment, she took a gift from a great golden chest and accompanied the child and his father back to their home. Death placed the boy in his mother's arms and asked her how she was, and whether she had any pain. There was something about this fine lady that made the mother want to confide her worries and her griefs to her, and they talked together quietly for a very long time. Then the father sent for some beer, and they drank and ate together.

Just as she was leaving, Death said to her godchild's father: "You're clearly so poor that no one else was willing to serve as godparent to your son, but don't worry: I have another gift for you. I will enter the houses of several well-off people to make them ill, and you will go to them and cure them. I'll tell you all the remedies you need — I know them all — and everybody will be more than happy to pay you very well. But you must agree to this one thing: when I stand at someone's feet, you can help them, but if you see me standing at someone's head, you may not."

And that is exactly what happened. The child's father went from patient to patient in all the houses where Death had caused illness, and he cured everyone. Soon he became known as a most distinguished physician. Once, a prince was dying, and even after he had breathed his last, such was the father's fame as a physician that they sent for him to see if there was anything he could do. He went to the palace and found that Death was standing at the foot of the prince's bed. He anointed him with salves and gave him herbal powders, and this treatment restored him to life and full health. Of course, they paid him handsomely for his care.

Another time, a count was on his deathbed, and once again they sent for the physician. But when he arrived, he saw that this time, Death was standing at the head of the bed. The physician turned away from Death's clear, bright eyes, and said: "It's a bad case, but we'll do our best." He summoned the servants and ordered them to turn the bed around so that the patient's feet would now be facing Death, and then he began to anoint him with salves and to administer powders. The count recovered at once and paid him with as much gold as he could carry away.

Later that day, Death came to see the physician. She said: "If this should ever occur to you again, don't even think of doing it. It's true that you've helped the count to recover, but it will only be for a very short while. I must still take him away, because his taper has burned down. It's his time."

The physician carried on in this way for some years, until he grew very old. He grew weary finally and asked Death to take him away with her. But she couldn't, because he had lit that long, new taper for himself; she was obliged now to wait until it burned out. One day, several years later, the physician went to the house of a certain patient to restore him to health; as he approached his carriage afterward, he found Death waiting for him and she accompanied him on the journey home. She tapped him with a green twig under his throat; he fell into her lap and drifted off into his last sleep. Death laid him out in the carriage and slipped away, leaving his family to find him dead there when he arrived back home.

Everyone in the town and the surrounding villages mourned for him. "The loss of that physician is a great one," they said to each other. "What a good doctor he was! He was so skillful; we'll never see the like of him again." His son — Death's godchild — survived him, but unfortunately he didn't have the same abilities as his father.

The son went to church one day and his godmother, Death, met him there. "My dear godson," she said to him, smiling. "How are you?"

"Not altogether good," he said. "As long as I have my father's savings to draw on, everything will be fine. But after that — I have no idea what will become of me."

"Well, my son," Death said, "don't worry. I'm your god-mother, after all. I helped your father to make his fortune and I'll give you a livelihood too. You shall go to a physician and become his pupil, though you'll soon grow to be more skillful than him. But you must behave yourself." She rubbed some salve over his ears and took him to the house of a renowned physician. The doctor didn't know that this fine lady was Death, or who it was that she had brought to him for instruc-tion. She reminded her godson to study diligently, asked the physician to instruct him well — and then she left.

One day, the physician and his pupil went together to gather herbs, and each of the herbs that the young man touched called out to him and explained the remedial virtue that it had. And so, the herbs that he selected were beneficial for every disease they treated. Finally, shaking his head, the physician said: "You really are very much cleverer than I am. I can diagnose whoever comes to me, but you're the one who knows the herbs to counter every illness. I think we should set up together in partnership — but I'll be your assistant, and I'll stay with you till the end of my life."

Death's godson was successful in his doctoring, and he lived well and happily till the taper that she had lit for him on the day of his christening burned out in its own good time. On that day, he fell asleep finally and peacefully in the generous arms of his godmother, Death.

"Godmother Death" is a Moravian variant of the German story "Godfather Death," which appears in the fairy tales of the Brothers Grimm; Death is perhaps represented as a godmother rather than a godfather in the Moravian story because "death" is a feminine word in all Slavonic dialects.

Although death is a common theme in myth and folklore, it is rarely personified — and when Death is personified, more often than not it is in male form. But there are some exceptions: in Sardinian folklore, for example, the Femmina Accabadora is a middle-aged woman dressed in black with a long shawl covering her head, who is known as the Lady of the Good Death. She would bring death to the terminally ill — as often as not, with the aid of an olive-wood mallet.

This beautiful story also offers us a fully embodied female Death who excels in many qualities that we think of as feminine: grace, empathy, compassion, tolerance, and generosity. There's something wonderfully earthy about her too: she brings death to the father by tapping him under the throat with a green twig, she prepares her godson for his new life by rubbing salve on his ears, and she knows all the remedies for illness. Even when she is tricked — twice — by the man whose son she agreed to become godmother to, Death is disappointed rather than enraged. Unlike the nasty, vengeful, withered, ice-cold-handed Godfather Death in the similar story from the Brothers Grimm, she does not kill her godchild's father when he disobeys her by trying to save a patient who was supposed to die. Instead, she warns him that he must never do that again, because the patient's time has come and he will die soon anyway. The father learns his lesson, and Death gently takes him away with her only when the long taper of his life has burned out.

Nevertheless, Death is what she is and what she is for, and she is of necessity implacable in carrying out her duty when it is time for someone to go with her. But her godson's father, and the godson himself, are both fortunate enough to make that journey only after a life well lived, and the death she brings them is compassionate: they die swiftly and peacefully in her arms.

Harbingers of Death

In British and Irish myth and folklore, old women are associated with the coming of death: they are its harbingers, or messengers. They include the solitary *bean sí* (anglicized to banshee) in Irish folklore, who wails, shrieks, or keens to announce the death of someone in a family with which she is associated. She's usually portrayed with long, unkempt hair, she wears a gray cloak over a green dress, and her eyes are red from continuous weeping.

Gwrach y Rhibyn from the Welsh tradition is a phantom or apparition in the guise of an old hag with long teeth, several yards of disheveled hair, lank, withered arms (occasionally with leathery wings), and a cadaverous appearance, who, like the *bean sí*, warns of an approaching death. She similarly appears at night and utters a bloodcurdling howl at the window of her targeted house; sometimes, she travels invisibly alongside an unsuspecting walker as they approach a stream or crossroads in the dark. She calls by name the person who is about to die.

In the Scottish Gaelic tradition, the Caoineag ("weeper") foretells death in her clan by wailing at night near a waterfall, stream or loch, or a glen or mountainside. The *bean nighe* is another Gaelic harbinger of death, known in English as the Washerwoman at the Ford; she haunts desolate streams and washes blood from the clothes of those who are about to die. Unlike the Irish and Welsh traditions, humans can approach the *bean nighe*. On the Isles of Mull and Tiree she was said to have unusually long breasts that could interfere with her washing; consequently, she would throw them over her shoulders to hang down her back, out of the way. If you should happen across her, folklore tells us, you should not turn away, but approach her silently from behind. You should take hold of one of the breasts that is dangling down her back, put it in your mouth, and claim to be her foster child. She will then answer any question you ask her. If she tells you that the clothes she is washing belong to an enemy of yours, you can allow the washing to continue; if, on the other hand, the clothes belong to you or to a friend, you might be able to stop her from finishing her washing and so avoid your fate.

Old Bone Mother

SIBERIA

A long time ago in the sleeping lands, there was a village of seven hundred tents. Seven hundred people lived in those tents and seven brothers ruled over them. The oldest of the seven brothers had a son who slept day and night. One night, that young man had a bad dream: everyone in the community had been killed and he alone was left alive. He told his father about the dream and said: "You will survive the slaughter, though, if you sacrifice fourteen reindeer right away."

"Don't be ridiculous," his father answered. "Why should I believe anything you tell me? You sleep all the time, and you know less than a dog does."

"If you say so, Father," said the son, and went back to sleep again. The next morning, he woke up to find that every single person in the village had been killed, along with all their reindeer and all the dogs. He took up a sword and cut the ropes of the empty tents, and they collapsed onto the snow. Then he walked away, but with no idea where he might find another village. He wandered across the snow-laden land for a full seven months and seven days, and eventually happened upon a place where there had once been a tent. He hadn't eaten during the months he'd been walking and now was ravenously hungry, so he was delighted when he found a nice big bone that had been chewed by dogs. He gnawed at the bone, and started digging

under the snow to see if he could find anything else to eat —
but all he found was an iron shovel. He picked it up and started
walking again.

He walked and walked; for a very long time he walked.
Then, one day, he saw someone in the distance, sitting in a
sleigh that was pulled by two reindeer. As the sleigh drew closer,
he saw that it was a beautiful, well-dressed young woman. The
young woman pulled the sleigh up in front of him and said,
"Where are you going, boy?"

"I'm looking for people and for food," he replied. "I need
to eat soon, or I'll surely die."

"You must have come from our old campsite. Did you
happen to find an iron shovel there?" she asked.

"I did."

"That's my shovel," she said. "I was heading back there to
look for it."

"I'll give you the shovel, if you promise to take me to a
place where there are people."

"I'll gladly take you to our home," the young woman said,
"and I'm sure we can feed you too."

So he gave her the shovel, climbed into the sleigh, and they
set off across the snow. "Where are you from?" she asked. "I
don't know you."

"Nobody in the world knows me anymore," he said. "I'm
an orphan. But once I lived in a village of seven hundred tents,
ruled by seven brothers."

"I've heard of these seven brothers," the young woman
said. "What happened to them?"

"They died. They all died together one night, along with
all their people, reindeer, and dogs."

"Do you happen to know who owns these two reindeer
who are pulling my sleigh?" she asked.

"I have to say, they look very much like my father's reindeer."

"Well," the young woman said, "then let me tell you how those reindeer came to be owned by me. Your father visited our village one time, and he courted me on your behalf. He gave me these two reindeer and the shovel as my bride price. He gave me a sword as well, but that was stolen."

"Hopefully I'll be able to find that sword for you."

"You're my man, then," she said. And so, when they arrived at her village, they began to live there in her tent as husband and wife.

After a while, the time came for the villagers to move their camp. They harnessed two reindeer to each of their sleighs, but a hard-faced man with a beard tied a couple of very old reindeer to the young man's sleigh and, as a consequence, he soon fell behind all the others. He tried to hurry the reindeer along, but to no avail. It was only when the entire procession stopped to rest for a while that he managed to catch up with everyone else.

When he arrived at the campfire, the bearded man asked, "Who's that behind you?"

"No one," he said. "I'm traveling alone." But he looked behind him anyway, and as soon as he did, the bearded man took a spear and struck him down. The travelers went on their way, but his wife stayed behind. Just as she had begun to weep for her husband, a one-legged, one-handed, and one-eyed old man appeared out of nowhere and walked up to her husband's body. He hit the corpse with the iron staff that he was carrying, and said, "What are you doing, lying there? It's time to get up! Get up and go back to your village; your father is alive again, along with the rest of your community." And then he disappeared.

All at once, the young man woke up and started talking to himself. "I've slept for a good long while, but who on earth was that old man who told me that my father is alive, and asked me to turn back?" He couldn't see anyone except his wife, so he imagined he'd dreamed the whole thing. He rose slowly to his feet, and they walked on till finally they caught up with the others; they set up their tent and fell asleep next to each other.

On the second morning, the camp was broken up again and they all set off in their sleighs. Having the same old reindeer attached to his sleigh, the young man fell behind again. They stopped after a while so that he could catch up, and when he arrived the bearded man asked, "What kind of people are they who are following you?"

"There's no one behind me," the young man said, but he felt obliged to look back — and just at that moment the bearded man stabbed him with his spear for a second time. He was left there on the ground, but this time, his wife went away with everyone else. "He didn't really die last time," she told herself. "He'll show up at our tent soon enough."

After everyone had left, the one-legged, one-handed, and one-eyed old man appeared again. He hit the dead man with his iron staff and said, "Yesterday I told you to go back home; what on earth were you doing there in your wife's tent? Turn back now, if you want to keep your head. Your father is alive again, and he has been alive for a long time now."

The dead man woke up and decided that he had been dreaming again. He walked along to the camp, found his tent, and settled down to sleep next to his wife.

On the third morning, exactly the same thing happened. After he had been struck down by the bearded man for a third time, the one-legged, one-handed, one-eyed old man appeared, hit the dead man with his iron staff, and said: "For the third time, I'm telling you to turn back! You've been killed twice before. I keep on waking you up again, but I won't be able to do it anymore."

Well, the young man rose to his feet, but of course he

didn't turn back — he walked on to the camp again and found his tent. This time, though, he didn't go inside; instead, he sat down on a nearby sleigh and began to think. It dawned on him that the bearded man really did mean to kill him, and he grew angry. He took all the bows and weapons out of all the sleighs in the camp and destroyed every last one of them. Then he found his wife's sleigh and took from it the iron shovel that he had given back to her. He used it to smash up all the tents, and when their occupants ran out of them, screaming, he attacked them with the shovel and killed them all. The only people he spared were his wife, her father, and her mother. He carefully searched through the corpses, but he couldn't find the bearded man. Finally, he came across a set of tracks in the snow: the man had escaped. So he started to follow the tracks, and walked for a long time until he caught up with his murderer.

They faced each other and began to fight. They fought there for the whole winter, beating each other again and again till finally, the snow was red with their blood and they both fell down at the same time and died. They lay there over the entire summer and rotted. Foxes and wolves came and ate their corpses; they devoured everything — except for the bones. Autumn arrived and the one-legged, one-handed, one-eyed old man arrived along with it. He shook his head and addressed the young man's bones. "How often did I tell you that you must turn back! Now, I have no power to help you — but perhaps there is someone who can." He gathered up all the bones — the tiniest pieces too; he piled them all into a bag, heaved the bag onto his back, and set off on his way.

After walking for a while, he came to an enormous stone. He struck the stone with his iron staff, and it rolled to one side to reveal a hole. The old man crawled inside, into a dark, gloomy place that was filled with the sounds of shrieking, whistling, and singing. Someone — or something — tried to wrestle the bag away from him, but he clung on to it and crept on. After a while, the darkness gave way to a faint glimmering of light. He saw that there were people all around him — but these people had neither skin nor clothing: they were nothing more than bare bones. The skeleton folk grinned at him, and he hurried past them toward the brightening light.

Soon, he came to a tent; he walked into it through an opening in its side. An old woman was sitting by a firepit, clad lightly in animal skins, tendrils of hair falling over her hunched shoulders, and a great necklace of bones that hung around her thin neck. On the other side of the firepit were two immo-bile monsters with enormous eyes stacked one above the other. The old man set the bag of bones on the ground by the old woman's feet and said: "Here's some firewood; why not throw it into the fire?"

"Good thing you brought some," the old woman said. "I had completely run out." So she lit a fire and threw the bones into it; eventually, they burned down to ashes. And after the one-legged, one-handed, one-eyed old man left, the old woman took the ashes, scattered them onto her bed, and lay down on them to sleep.

After three days, she rose from her bed and the young man was born again from the ashes of his bones. He muttered to himself: "What is this dark place where I've been sleeping?" There was no smoke hole in the tent, and although he wanted to get out, he couldn't find an opening. He poked all around the sides of the tent, but they were made of iron, and he could find no opening.

"How do I get out of here?" he asked the old woman, who was sitting by the fire. She stood up and tapped the iron wall with her foot: it parted. As he made for the opening, the young man suddenly noticed the two monsters by the fire and was so startled that he tripped over a rock and fell flat on his face. He heaved himself to his feet and asked the old woman, "What sort of monsters are these two? Are they human beings? Are they wild beasts?"

"They're not wild beasts, they're my parents," she said.

"Do they speak?" he asked. "Do they eat? What else do they do?"

"They don't speak," she said, "and they don't eat. In fact, they don't do anything at all."

"Have they always been like that?"

"Not at all. In their time they were excellent people, but then suddenly they turned to stone, and they've been stone ever since. They hear nothing, they see nothing, and they know nothing." Then she asked, "What do you want more than anything else in the world?"

"To know where my wife is living now," he said. "Then I would go to her."

The old woman grinned. "Live with me for a while. My reindeer will arrive soon, and they can take you safely away from here. But you're going to have to take me for your wife, or I'm afraid I'll have to turn you to stone."

The young man understood that it was the old woman who had turned the two people at the hearth to stone, and it was clear that the same fate would be his if he refused to take her for his wife. "Well then," he said, "I'll take you for my second wife." So they stayed together in the underground tent for three days until the reindeer arrived, pulling a sleigh. The young man and the old woman left the tent and climbed into the sleigh; she drove the reindeer through the Underworld. It was dark at first, and the skeleton people ran after them and tried to stab the young man with their spears — but they couldn't reach him.

At last, the ground before them began to rise and it began

to grow lighter — but suddenly, they came face-to-face with a wall made of rock. The old woman brought the reindeer to a halt. "Push away that stone that's blocking our way," she instructed her new husband. He tried to move the stone away from the opening, but it wouldn't budge, and so the old woman kicked it with her foot. It rolled away; they passed through the opening and out into the upper world, and rode on across the snow for a long, long time. Finally, they came to a tent. Inside it, the young man found his first wife, along with her mother and her father. He took both of his women and his first wife's parents with him and traveled back in the sleigh to his first home.

As he approached the place where his village had been, he saw that the seven hundred tents he had cut down were standing there again, along with many people, many reindeer, and many dogs. All of them were alive again.

The one-legged, one-handed, one-eyed old man was waiting just outside the village; he walked toward the sleigh with another person alongside him, and as they approached, the young man realized that this was the bearded man who had killed him three times. He jumped down from the sleigh and attacked his murderer; he was lucky this time and struck him down with a single blow. Then he lost control and, in his fury, killed the one-legged, one-handed, one-eyed old man too. He climbed back into the sleigh and drove it up to the village, but when he arrived he found that everyone was dead again, along with all their reindeer and all their dogs. Suddenly, the two women who had been his wives died too and fell out of the sleigh.

The young man was alone again; he turned north into the wind and began to walk away.

The ancient stories and sagas of the people of Siberia are magical and often bizarre; this one is no exception. As noted in an earlier tale, "Godmother Death," there are very few references in European folklore to Death taking a woman's form, but this story is especially fine because it presents this strange old woman, who lives in an Underworld filled with skeletons, as a bestower of rebirth after death.

In many parts of Europe, our ancestors once believed that the essence of a person was held in their bones. Archaeological and textual evidence supports this notion, and the veneration of bones as the source of spiritual potency is widespread throughout Europe; it seems to date back to the Mesolithic period. The idea passed down through many generations; it persists in European folklore and in several fairy tales that celebrate the power of bones. In "The Juniper Tree," for example, a well-known story collected by the Brothers Grimm, the bones of a murdered and cannibalized child are buried beneath a juniper tree. The spirit of the dead child, presumably lingering in the bones, rises up and flies out from the branches of the tree in the form of a bird; it sings a song that tells the story of what happened to him.

In this story, the character given the name of Old Bone Woman, just like Baba Yaga and other old women in Slavic folklore, is ambiguous. She wields the power of death as well as the power of rebirth; this can be seen in her ability to turn living things to stone. Nevertheless, the role she plays in this story is to take the dead and dismembered parts of the slain young man and conjure new life from them. She is able to achieve this even when the one-legged, one-handed, one-eyed old man (the typical description of a Siberian shaman) fails.

In European myth and folklore, death is not always final — any more than the dormant state of a winter-bound chrysalis is final. It's a process of transformation; the butterfly might yet emerge. Think of Sleeping Beauty in her hundred-years' sleep, or Snow White in her glass coffin: they appear to be dead, but ultimately, they're reborn. Because death is not always an ending: buried within it, potent and ready to germinate, are the strong, fertile seeds of new life.

Afterword

The compelling older women in this book deserve to be better known, and their stories deserve to be told — as antidotes to the constantly paraded, clichéd tales of the archetypal wicked witch, greedy old wife, or fumbling elderly fool. As well as shaping and changing those of us who find them — or those of us that they find — stories shape and change the world. Bringing a lost or forgotten story back into our world allows us to resuscitate the lost or forgotten archetypes that populate that tale, so they can then work their transformative magic on us. Like so many of the stories she inhabits, the Wise Woman archetype has been submerged for too long — but the more we tell stories about her, the more she'll live and grow. And the more time we spend with these stories and archetypes that reflect us and inform us, the more we'll live and grow.

One of the most practical ways that you, the reader, might help to rescue these stories from the vaults in which they've been so effectively buried, and ensure they live again to inspire new generations of women, is to share them with others. Learn to tell them, read them aloud to family and friends — in this way, we can all be story carriers.

Sharing such stories is like scattering seeds: some tales land on fertile soil and soon begin to grow; a few take a while to germinate; others never find the right conditions. One or two stories might have you in their thrall, while others trouble you, or you might find that a character unexpectedly begins to haunt the edgelands of your dreams. This is all to be welcomed, because an old notion suggests that stories choose us at least as much as we choose them. A story might return to you months or years from now and speak with an eloquence you couldn't have appreciated before. Or you might find one of the women in this book at your shoulder in a time of need, a moment that calls for courage or clarity to meet the vagaries of an increasingly uncertain world. In whichever way it happens for you, our fervent hope is that the stories in this book should inspire you to uncover and explore your own inner Wise Woman, and to find meaning and joy in the second half of your life.

Acknowledgments

Sharon

I'm enormously grateful to my agent Jane Graham Maw for her dedication to this project from the beginning, for finding the perfect publisher in Virago, and for many more things than words could reasonably express. A thousand thanks to Sarah Savitt for her support during the process of writing, to the wider Virago and Little, Brown team for their enthusiasm for and thoughtful work on *Wise Women,* and to the team at New World Library for their care with the American edition, and for publishing another book of mine.

Thank you to Oein DeBhairduin for permission to retell a story from his beautiful collection of Irish Traveller tales, *Why the Moon Travels* (Skein Press, 2020). I'm also grateful to Tom Muir for permission to retell "The Shetland Fin Wife," included in *The Mermaid Bride and Other Orkney Folk Tales* (The Orcadian, 1998). Many thanks are due to storyteller Henry Everett, who came to my book event in Devon and offered me several local stories featuring older women, including "The Tulip Pixies," which is included here under the title "Tending Eden." Thanks also to Dr. Gwilym Morus-Baird for his "Celtic Source" YouTube lectures about gigantic old women in the Welsh landscape: "A Welsh Cailleach?" and "Barclodiad y Gawres" ("The Giantess' Apronful"). Huge thanks to Marianne for tracking down and translating some of the content of two original Russian versions of "The Woman Who Became a Fox."

Above all, I'm grateful to the many hundreds of women who participated over the years in the Mythic Imagination Network and my *Hagitude* program, for their heartfelt commitment to exploring — and inhabiting — older women's myth and folklore with me; I'm grateful too to the many subscribers who are still delving deeply into this story work through Fairy Tale Salons on my Substack, "The Art of Enchantment," today. Thanks to New York story-witch Audrey di Mola for insights into "feeding the stories," and to all the others who've shared ideas during the years I've spent researching and working with the Wise Woman archetypes that made their way into this book.

As ever, love and thanks to David for always raging against the dying of the light, and my eternal adoration to the usual sister-hags for listening and keeping me sane in difficult times. You know who you are.

Angharad

A big thank-you to Sharon for inviting this collaboration, to Jane Graham Maw for guiding the book to a great home at Virago, and Sarah Savitt and the team there for their commitment to *Wise Women*.

Particular thanks to the storytellers of Cybermouth, and the legion of women who joined the *Hagitude* and *Cyfarwydd* programs, with whom I explored some of these stories. Their insights added a breadth of understanding to the medicine contained in these tales. Also to the team at the Vaughan Williams Memorial Library for diving deep into their archives for rhymes, ballads, and songs.

I owe a debt of gratitude to Steve Killick and Mike Parker for support and encouragement, to my parents for surrounding me with stories, to my daughter for demanding them of me as she grew, and to Mike for lovingly keeping the ship of life steady as I carved out time to write. Finally, this book would be nothing without the storytellers who kept these tales alive and those who set them in ink. I am deeply grateful to the lineage of story bearers who stand behind us.

Sources

The Woman Who Became a Fox: "The One-Eyed Man and the Woman-Vixen," *The Sun Maiden and the Crescent Moon: Siberian Folk Tales.* Collected and translated by James Riordan. Canongate Publishing (1989). Original versions of the story at https://mirckazok.ru/aleutskie-skazki /zheshchinalisitca and https://mirckazok.ru/aleutskie-skazki /odnoglazyi-chelovek-i-prevrashchenie-zhenshchiny-v-lisitcu.

Mother Mansrot: Jacob and Wilhelm Grimm, *Grimm's Fairy Tales.* Translated by Margaret Hunt. George Bell and Sons (1884).

Kate Dalrymple: Lyrics by William Watt (b. 1792).

The Magic Forest: Ivana Brlić-Mažuranić, "Stribor's Forest," *Croatian Tales of Long Ago.* Translated by F. S. Copeland. Frederick A. Stokes Co. (1922).

Ride a Cock-Horse to Banbury Cross: *Gammer Gurton's Garland: or, The Nursery Parnassus.* R. Christopher (1784).

The Giantess's Burden: John Jones, *The Folklore of Caernarfonshire.* Gwmni y Cyhoeddwyr Cymreig, Swyddfa Cymru (1908).

My Grandmother's Cottage: "Bwthyn fy Nain." Translated by Angharad Wynne. Hear it sung at https://www.peoplescollection .wales/items/506416.

Tending Eden: V. Day Sharman, *Folk Tales of Devon.* Thomas Nelson & Sons (1952).

Old Woman Song: Collected by G. B. Gardiner and J. F. Guyer (1908). Entry GG/1/20/1310, George Gardiner Manuscript Collection, Vaughan Williams Memorial Library.

The Nixy: *The Yellow Fairy Book.* Edited by Andrew Lang. Longmans, Green & Co. (1889).

There Was an Old Woman Toss'd Up in a Basket: Percy B. Green, *A History of Nursery Rhymes.* Greening & Co. (1899).

Kissing the Hag: "The Story of Eochaidh Muighmedóin's Sons," *Silva Gadelica (I–XXXI): A Collection of Tales in Irish with Extracts Illustrating Persons and Places.* Edited and translated by Standish H. O'Grady. Williams and Norgate (1892).

Old Woman, Old Woman, Shall We Go A-Shearing: *The Nursery Rhyme Book.* Edited by Andrew Lang and illustrated by L. Leslie Brooke. Frederick Warne (1897).

The Old Woman and Her Cat: *Dame Dearlove's Ditties for the Nursery.* John Harris and Son (1819).

The True History of Little Golden Hood: *The Yellow Fairy Book.* Edited by Andrew Lang. Longmans, Green & Co. (1889).

The Goose Girl at the Well: Jacob and Wilhelm Grimm, *Grimm's Fairy Tales.* Translated by Margaret Hunt. George Bell and Sons (1884).

Vasilisa the Fair: Aleksandr Nikolaevich Afanasyev, *Russian Folk-Tales.* Translated by Leonard Arthur Magnus. Dutton (1916).

The Little Old Lady of Kidwelly: Traditional Welsh nursery rhyme (see http://welshnurseryrhymes.wales/Gartref?cerdd=20). Translated from the Welsh by Angharad Wynne. The "little old lady" in this nursery rhyme might have been Lady Hawise de Londres, who lived in Kidwelly Castle as a child in the thirteenth century. Local legend has it that she once disguised herself as a seller of sweetmeats and cakes in order to gain access to the castle, when later she returned to claim her rights as castellan.

Habetrot and the Spinning Sisters: Joseph Jacobs, *More English Fairy Tales.* David Nutt (1894).

Spinning Wheel Song: English translation of Manx traditional words by Mona Douglas. Stainer & Bell Ltd, London (1929). This spinning song would have been sung as a round. Trit Trot is a Habetrot-like character in Manx folklore.

Fair, Brown, and Trembling: Joseph Jacobs, *Celtic Fairy Tales.* G. P. Putnam's Sons (1892).

Mother Holle: Jacob and Wilhelm Grimm, *Grimm's Fairy Tales*. Translated by Margaret Hunt. George Bell and Sons (1884).

Old Mother Goose: *Childhood's Favorites and Fairy Stories: The Young Folks Treasury*, vol. 1. New York: University Society (1927).

The Groac'h of the Well: Joseph Frison, "La Groac'h de la Fontaine," *Revue des Traditions Populaires* 2 (1914), pp. 54–56. Translated by Sharon Blackie.

Beira, Queen of Winter: Donald A. Mackenzie, *Scottish Wonder Tales from Myth and Legend*. Frederick A. Stokes Co. (1917).

Berrey Dhone: W. Walter Gill, *A Second Manx Scrapbook*. Arrowsmith (1932).

Grandmother Snow: Irina Zheleznova, *The Northern Lights: Fairy Tales of the Peoples of the North*. Raduga Publishers (1989). See also http://freebooksforkids.net/kotura-lord-of-the-winds.html.

The Carlin of Beinn Bhreac: Alexander Carmichael, *Carmina Gadelica*. Norman Macleod (1900).

The Green Man of No Man's Land: Francis Hindes Groome, *Gypsy Folk-Tales*. Hurst and Blackett (1899).

What Are Old Women Made Of?: A verse in the traditional English rhyme "What Are Little Boys Made Of?" written by Robert Southey around 1820.

The Witch of Beinn a' Glò: William Scrope, *Days of Deer-Stalking in the Scottish Highlands*. Hamilton, Adams & Co. (1883).

Watching for the Milk-Stealer: J. C. Atkinson, *Forty Years in a Moorland Parish: Reminiscences and Researches in Danby in Cleveland*. Macmillan and Co. Ltd (1891).

The Farmer's Curst Wife: Ballad 278A in Francis James Child, *The English and Scottish Popular Ballads*. Houghton, Mifflin and Company (1882).

Big Kennedy and the Glaistig: Donald A. Mackenzie, "The Glaistig and the Black Lad: A Lochaber Legend from the Gaelic," *The Celtic Review*, vol. 5, no. 19 (January 1909), pp. 253–58.

Hop Tu Naa: W. Walter Gill, *A Second Manx Scrapbook*. Arrowsmith (1932).

The Water Horse of Varkasaig: Otta F. Swire, *Skye: The Island and Its Legends*. Oxford University Press (1952); Maclean Press (1999).

The Dream Makers: Otta F. Swire, *Skye: The Inner Hebrides and Their Legends*. Collins (1964).

The Fool and the Wise Woman: Joseph Jacobs, "A Pottle o' Brains," *More English Fairy Tales*. David Nutt (1894).

There Was an Old Woman Lived Under the Hill: Anonymous, *The Only True Mother Goose Melodies*. Munroe & Francis (c. 1833).

The Sleeping Beauty in the Wood: Charles Perrault, *The Tales of Mother Goose*. Translated by Charles Welsh. D. C. Heath & Co. (1901). Originally published in 1696.

The Spinners of Blessings: Oein DeBhairduin, *Why the Moon Travels*. Skein Press (2020).

Conwenna: Geoffrey of Monmouth, *Historia Regum Britanniae*. In *Six Old English Chronicles*. Edited by J. A. Giles. Henry G. Bohn (1848).

The Buried Moon: M. C. Balfour, "Legends of the Lincolnshire Cars, Part 1," *Folk-Lore*, vol. II. David Nutt (1891), pp. 156–64.

The Finwife: Tom Muir, "The Shetland Fin Wife," *The Mermaid Bride and Other Orkney Folk Tales*. The Orcadian (1998).

The Hedley Kow: Joseph Jacobs, *More English Fairy Tales*. David Nutt (1894).

The Bird Yustritsa: W. E. S. Ralston, *The Songs of the Russian People*. Ellis & Green (1872).

The Little Old Woman with Five Cows: *Siberian and Other Folk Tales: Primitive Literature of the Empire of the Tsars*. Collected and translated by C. Fillingham Coxwell. The C. W. Daniel Company (1925).

Godmother Death: *Sixty Folk-Tales from Exclusively Slavonic Sources*. Translated by A. H. Wratislaw. Houghton, Mifflin and Company (1890).

Old Bone Mother: Matthias Alexander Castrén, *Nordische Reisen und Forschungen*. Translated by Katrin Siek. Buchdruckerei der Kaiserlichen Akademie der Wissenschaften (1857).

About the Authors

Dr. Sharon Blackie is an award-winning writer, psychologist, and mythologist, and an internationally recognized teacher and lecturer. Her most recent book is *Hagitude: Reimagining the Second Half of Life*. Sharon's awards include the Roger Deakin Award from the Society of Authors (2022) and a Creative Scotland Writer's Award (2009). She is a Fellow of the Royal Society of Arts and has taught and lectured around the world.

Angharad Wynne is an acclaimed storyteller, writer, speaker, and expedition leader.